Anthony Summers is the award-winning author of seven bestselling non-fiction books. Originally a journalist, he covered events in the United States and the conflicts in Vietnam and the Middle East for the BBC's flagship current affairs programme *Panorama*. **Robbyn Swan**, his co-author and wife, has partnered Summers on two previous books – biographies of Richard Nixon and Frank Sinatra. They have been consultants on documentaries for the BBC, the History Channel and CNN.

D0499094

Praise for *The Eleventh Day*

'*The Eleventh Day* confronts what the West refused to face in the years that followed 9/11 . . .The motivation for the attacks was "ducked" even by the official 9/11 Report . . . "Commissioners who argued that al Qaeda was motivated by a religious ideology – and not by opposition to American policies – rejected mentioning the Israeli-Palestinian conflict" . . . In other words, we still haven't been told the truth about the crime which – we are supposed to believe – "changed the world forever"'
Robert Fisk, *Independent*

'Superb . . .There's the bungling of the security services . . . the creepy suppression of 28 pages of the U.S. Congress's Inquiry report into 9/11, believed to endanger Washington's very special relationship with Saudi Arabia. But most impressive is their description of how and why the official 9/11 Commission deliberately ducked the issue of what motivated the murderers. "All the evidence," the authors correctly say, "indicates that Palestine was the factor that united the conspirators"'
Peter Hitchens, *Daily Mail*

'Lucid and well-researched'
Evening Standard

'We are in Summers' and Swan's debt'
The Spectator

'Meticulous . . . comprehensive and fair . . . Anthony Summers and Robbyn Swan have produced an extraordinary synthesis of what is known about the 9/11 attacks'
John Farmer, 9/11 Commission senior counsel and former Attorney General of New Jersey

'Retells the events with unbridled drama ... A broad-shouldered look at the deceit, destruction, and disaster that followed ... What caused all this [Muslim distrust of the United States] – the ill-will and the deception – is outlined in *The Eleventh Day* ... The book also raises uncomfortable but unavoidable questions about Saudi financial support for al-Qaeda and sets out how the 9/11 Commission was, in turn, misled and chose to overlook important evidence ... September 11 isn't over'
Boston Globe

'The book's essential contribution to the annals of the attacks is its painstaking examination of questions the 9/11 Commission finessed ... Did Saudi princes, charities or the military fund bin Laden and his hijackers, help them after they reached the U.S., and withhold intelligence that might have thwarted the attack?'
The Wall Street Journal

'*The Eleventh Day* is a game-changer. It is the new definitive timeline for 9/11, a superb and detailed extension of the work of the 9/11 Commission and Congress' Joint Inquiry. Anthony Summers' and Robbyn Swan's research and reporting is peerless in its depth, breadth and accuracy. Together, this experienced team has cleared the air of suspect research and speculation, an invaluable service to future researchers and historians'
Miles Kara, Professional Staff, Congress' Joint Inquiry and 9/11 Commission

'The definitive book on 9/11. *The Eleventh Day* is ... a house of answers regarding those pesky and unsolved questions surrounding September 11, 2001. Thanks to Summers and Swan we now know the deadly plot should have been thwarted. Did the American government fail the American people? Tragically and sadly, the answer is: yes'
Jean Sasson, author of *Growing Up bin Laden*

THE ELEVENTH DAY

THE ULTIMATE ACCOUNT OF 9/11

Anthony Summers
and **Robbyn Swan**

CORGI BOOKS

TRANSWORLD PUBLISHERS
61–63 Uxbridge Road, London W5 5SA
A Random House Group Company
www.transworldbooks.co.uk

THE ELEVENTH DAY
A CORGI BOOK: 9780552156189

First published in Great Britain
in 2011 by Doubleday
an imprint of Transworld Publishers
Corgi edition published 2012

Addresses for Random House Group Ltd companies outside the UK
can be found at: www.randomhouse.co.uk
The Random House Group Ltd Reg. No. 954009

The Random House Group Limited supports The Forest Stewardship
Council (FSC®), the leading international forest-certification organization.
Our books carrying the FSC label are printed on FSC®-certified paper. FSC
is the only forest-certification scheme endorsed by the leading environmental
organizations, including Greenpeace. Our paper-procurement
policy can be found at www.randomhouse.co.uk/environment

Typeset in 11/14pt Janson by Falcon Oast Graphic Art Ltd.
Printed and bound by CPI Group (UK) Ltd, Croydon, CR0 4YY.

2 4 6 8 10 9 7 5 3

"I don't believe for a minute that we got everything right. We wrote a first draft of history."

—LEE HAMILTON, vice chairman, 9/11 Commission

CONTENTS

AUTHORS' NOTE

OVER THE YEARS, THE EVENT TO WHICH THE WORLD gave the brief name "9/11" has burgeoned into a universe of facts and factoids. Our approach to the writing of this book was to build a chronology, which eventually ran to well over a thousand pages, to gather information from a multitude of sources, including published material in both paper and electronic form, and to conduct interviews of our own. We read as deeply as possible the many thousands of pages of staff reports, original memoranda, and other 9/11 Commission records that began to be released as of 2009.

Additional information on numerous points can be found in the Notes and Sources section at the back of the book. These are linked to the text by page number.

For ease of reading, we have adopted a single standard for Arabic names that are rendered differently in different texts. The name "bin Laden," for example, can be found elsewhere as "bin Ladin" or even "ben Ladin," and the organization associated with him as "al-Qaeda," or "al Qida"—and more. We have stuck to "bin Laden" and "al Qaeda."

The full rendering of many Arab persons' names is lengthy, and we have in many cases shortened them. After a full first mention, for example, "Khalid al

Mihdhar" becomes just "Mihdhar." We render "Ramzi bin al-Shibh," as have many other texts, simply as "Bin-alshibh." Though perhaps not strictly correct, or satisfactory to the purist, this makes for smoother reading.

Our aim has been to make readable sense out of a kaleidoscopic story, to offer rational explanation where there has been confusion or unnecessary controversy, and to serve history as well as possible.

A.S.   R.S.
May 2011

THE ELEVENTH DAY

PREFACE

TEN YEARS ON, MEMORY AND LOSS. WHERE TWO wonders of the modern world once soared high over the city, two great cascades feed reflecting pools of shimmering water. The abyss into which it flows is now a hallowed place of remembrance. Pilgrims about to descend to the underworld, the underworld of what once was the World Trade Center, will pass a ribbon of names etched into parapets of bronze.

They identify those killed in New York City on September 11, 2001: the 206 passengers and crew aboard the three planes that were used as missiles that day; the forty who died when a fourth airliner fell from the sky in Pennsylvania; the 2,605 office workers and visitors and would-be rescuers known to have died in and around the Trade Center; and the 125 men and women who died at the Pentagon in Washington. Included, too, are the names of the six people killed eight years earlier, in 1993, in the first attempt to bring down the towers with a truck bomb.

The memorial names 2,982 men, women, and children as of the spring of 2011. The true tally of 9/11 fatalities, however, is incomplete. Some of those who labored in the rubble of the fallen towers have died since, agonizingly slowly, from respiratory disease contracted in the fire and poisoned dust of the place they called Ground Zero. Some nineteen thousand others are reported to be sick and receiving treatment. By one prediction, disease will eventually cripple and kill as many again—more perhaps—as died on the day of the attacks.

We do not know, shall never know, how many have died in the far-off wars that followed the onslaught launched that September day. Fighting men aside, the vast majority of the dead have been civilians: unknown thousands—conservatively, many tens of thousands—of men, women, and children killed in Afghanistan and in Iraq.

Of the three thousand who died on 9/11 itself, fewer than half have graves. Some bodies were consumed by fire, others reduced to minute fragments of mortality, morsels of burned bone, decaying flesh, a single tooth with a silver filling. To this day, forensic pathologists are confronted by a monstrous human jigsaw, one they know they will never complete.

Consider five of the names that are etched, lettered in bronze, above the curtain of water at the 9/11 memorial.

Jimmy Riches, a New York firefighter, died in the lobby of the North Tower. His father, James, himself a Fire Department battalion chief, recovered his son's mangled body months later.

Donald McIntyre, a Port Authority police officer, also died at the Trade Center. His handcuffs, recovered at the scene, were given by his widow to a colleague assigned to hunt down terrorists in Afghanistan.

No identifiable remains were ever found for Eddie Dillard, an American Airlines passenger who died at the Pentagon. His widow, by odd happenstance, had been American's base manager in Washington, D.C., when his plane took off that day.

Ronald Breitweiser, a money manager, died in the

South Tower of the Trade Center. Only his arms and hands were recovered, identified by fingerprints—and by his wedding ring, which his widow now wears.

Only part of a leg and one foot were found—six years later—to account for Karen Martin, chief flight attendant on the plane that plunged into the North Tower. Attendant Martin was probably the first person harmed by the hijackers on 9/11.

SOMETHING ELSE WAS lost that day, something precious that touches on the stories of all the thousands who have died. The Greek tragic dramatist Aeschylus, twenty-five centuries earlier, understood well what it was. "In war," he wrote, "the first casualty is truth."

James Riches worked in the rubble for months, motivated in part by the hope of recovering his own son's dead body. He labored, like thousands of others, buoyed by the assurance of the Environmental Protection Agency, that the air in Lower Manhattan was safe to breathe. Today, no longer a fire chief, Riches Sr.'s health is irreparably damaged, his lung capacity reduced by 30 percent.

Like so many others, meanwhile, Riches wants vengeance against those who killed his son. The Saudi exile Osama bin Laden, said to have ordered the 9/11 attacks, became—in the West—a constant demon, a symbol of the dark forces of terror. President George W. Bush at first promised to get him "dead or alive," only to backtrack months later and say, "I don't know where bin Laden is . . . and really don't care. It's not that important."

In 2009, at the White House, Riches and others met Bush's successor, Barack Obama. "I pulled out Jimmy's bracelet and funeral mass card and gave them to him," the former fire chief said later. "I told him that I'm frustrated that I haven't seen justice for my son Jimmy . . . Please capture Osama bin Laden." Obama promised "swift and certain justice."

Police officer McIntyre's handcuffs, engraved "Mac," were later snapped on to the wrists of a fugitive named Abu Zubaydah—a native of Saudi Arabia like bin Laden. Imprisoned ever since, Zubaydah remains today the subject of serious controversy. For U.S. interrogators treated him with extreme brutality, using duress that has been defined by the International Committee of the Red Cross, and many others, as torture.

Eddie Dillard's widow, Rosemary, for all her grief, was one of a number of bereaved family members incensed by the ill treatment of prisoners and by plans to try them before military tribunals. "The secret and un-constitutional nature of these proceedings," they said, "deprives us of the right to know the full truth about what happened on 9/11."

Ronald Breitweiser's widow, Kristen, for her part, has been one of the most articulate of those whose lives were devastated. She testified to a joint House-Senate inquiry and fought for a further, full, independent investigation. When that aspiration was realized—in the shape of the National Commission on Terrorist Attacks Upon the United States—Breitweiser excoriated its failings. She believes that much is still hidden, and wants convincing explanations. The CIA, she points out, identified two of the hijackers as terrorists more than eighteen months before 9/11, learned they had visas to enter the United States, yet kept the information from U.S. law enforcement. Why?

Though the final chapter of the congressional report into 9/11 is said to discuss Saudi financial links to the hijackers, all but one page of the chapter was kept secret on the orders of President Bush. Why? At a 2009 meeting with bereaved families, Breitweiser says, President Obama said he was willing to declassify the suppressed material. As of this writing, two years later, the chapter remains classified. Why?

Though less than complete, and though it left some questions open, the Final Report of the National Commission—known as the 9/11 Commission Report—was overwhelmingly well received by an uncritical media. It went to the top of *The New York Times* best-seller list, and was nominated for a National Book Award. The CIA obstructed the Commission's work, as its chairmen—former New Jersey governor Thomas Kean and former congressman Lee Hamilton—later acknowledged. Senator Bob Kerrey, who served on the Commission, shared their concerns. Alleging a Bush White House cover-up, Senator Max Cleland had resigned from the Commission early on. It was, he said, a "national scandal." The final Report was in fact not final, Hamilton said, merely "a first draft of history."

A 2006 *New York Times*/CBS poll found that only 16 percent of those responding thought Bush administration members had told the truth about 9/11. Fifty-three percent of responders thought they were "mostly telling the truth but hiding something." Twenty-eight percent thought Bush's people were "mostly lying." A year later, a Scripps Howard poll found that 32 percent thought it "very likely" that the government had chosen to ignore specific warnings of the 9/11 attacks. A further 30 percent thought that "somewhat likely." A Zogby poll found that 51 percent of Americans wanted a congressional investigation of President Bush's and Vice President Dick Cheney's performance in the context of the attacks.

In 2008, a poll conducted by the Program on International Policy Attitudes—at the University of

Maryland—asked questions of sixteen thousand people in seventeen countries. Only 46 percent of those responding thought al Qaeda had been responsible for the attacks. Fifteen percent thought the U.S. government was itself responsible for the attacks, as a ploy to justify an invasion of Iraq. A large number of Americans, meanwhile, have thought Iraq was behind the attacks— a notion encouraged by the Bush administration but unsupported by the evidence. As late as 2010, though, an Angus Reid poll indicated that one in four Americans still thought 9/11 was "a fabrication designed to facilitate the campaign against terrorism." This all reflects an epidemic of doubt and disbelief. It has been spread in part, to be sure, by conspiracy theorists—the "9/11 truth" movement, as it has become known—preaching to the gullible through the phenomenal influence and reach of the Internet. Less well known is the prevalence of doubt in people one would expect less likely to challenge official orthodoxy.

Those who have expressed grave doubt or called for a new investigation have included five past or present U.S. senators, four members of the U.S. House of Representatives, a former governor, three state deputy or assistant attorneys general, members of state legislatures, numerous public officials and civil servants, diplomats, engineers, and twenty-six former Army, Navy, or Air Force officers. In 2010, two gubernatorial candidates in Texas, a Republican and a Democrat, both said they had questions as to whether the U.S. government had been involved in the 9/11 attacks.

Former CIA officers, FBI agents, and intelligence officials from other agencies have also spoken out. Twenty-five of them expressed their views in a letter to the Congress. Louis Freeh, who was FBI director until the summer of 2001, raised specific issues on

television and in a 2005 *Wall Street Journal* article.
Three sometime presidential contenders have
expressed concerns. Former Vice President Walter
Mondale said he favored a new investigation. "We've
never completed the investigation of 9/11," said General
Wesley Clark, former Supreme Allied Commander
Europe, "and whether the administration actually mis-
used the intelligence information it had." Former U.S.
senator Bob Graham, who had been cochair of
Congress's Joint Inquiry into 9/11, pointed the finger at
Saudi Arabia. The investigation, he said, found grounds
for "suspicion that the Saudi government and various
representatives of Saudi interests supported some of the
hijackers and might have supported all of them."
President Bush, he said, "engaged in a cover-up."

TEN YEARS ON, there is a lingering sense that the nation
and the world have been let down, deprived of the right
to know—deceived, even—on a matter of greater
universal concern than any event in living memory. It
need not have been that way.

The release in the past two years of some 300,000
pages of 9/11 Commission documents, a plethora of
other material, and new interviews make it possible to lay
some of the perceived mysteries to rest.

With access to the new information, we strive in this
book to blow away unnecessary controversy, to make up
for omissions in the record, and to throw light into the
shadows of deception. In a time of anxiety, to tell
the story as honestly as it can be told.

PART I

ATTACK

ONE

DID THE STORY BEGIN TWENTY YEARS AGO DURING
the Gulf War, when a great American army was
installed in Saudi Arabia, a land sacred to Muslims? Did
it begin in 1948, when the United States recognized the
declaration of a Jewish state to be known as Israel? Or on
the day in 1938 when Americans discovered in Saudi
Arabia one of the largest reserves of oil on the planet?
From then on, certainly, the West began an addictive
dance with danger, one that it dances to this day.

This is a story, moreover, rooted in a world and a
culture that few Westerners really know or can begin to
understand, yet played out in the heart of the United
States. Mystery and terror, a frightening mix. Yet there is
a simple point of entry, a routine event on an ordinary
American morning.

IN THE DAWN of September 11, 2001, in Massachusetts,
ninety-two people were getting up, breakfasting, heading
for Boston's Logan Airport. They were the passengers
and crew of American Airlines Flight 11, one of some
forty thousand planes scheduled to crisscross the country
that day.

To glance at some of the names on the passenger

manifest, to learn a little about them, is to glimpse the melting pot nature of the country. Philip Rosenzweig, an executive for Sun Microsystems; Thelma Cuccinello, a grandmother on her way to see a sister in California; Peter Gay, a vice president for Raytheon Electronic Systems, traveling with two colleagues; Laura Lee Morabito, U.S. sales manager for the Australian airline Qantas; photographer Berinthia Berenson, widow of the actor Anthony Perkins; David Angell, executive producer of the television series *Frasier*, accompanied by his wife, Lynn; Jeffrey Mladenik, an ordained minister and acting CEO of a trade publishing company; Lisa Gordenstein, an executive with a discount clothing company; Michael Theodoridis, on his way to a wedding with his wife, Rahma, who was six months pregnant; Walid Iskandar, a business strategy consultant for a British company, setting off to visit his parents; Alexander Filipov, a retired electrical engineer; Daniel Lewin, chief technology officer for Akamai Technologies in Cambridge, Massachusetts. Also on their way to the flight were five young men from the Middle East, an Egyptian and four Saudis.

The pilot who was to fly these people to California, John Ogonowski, flew twelve days a month and worked the rest of the time on his 150-acre farm. At fifty, he was a veteran of twenty-three years with American, married to a flight attendant. He had hoped to attend a farming event on the 11th, but the schedule proved unchangeable. At 5:00 that morning Ogonowski awoke, kissed his wife, peeked in at their three sleeping teenage daughters, and climbed into his pickup to drive to the airport. His copilot that day would be Tom McGuinness, a former Navy fighter pilot.

Flight 11, a "turn-around"—an airplane that had flown through the night from San Francisco—was parked at

Logan's Gate 32. Captain Ogonowski arrived to a scene of busy activity. The cleaners were working their way through the plane, the fuelers delivering 76,000 pounds of jet fuel. The nine flight attendants in their blue uniforms were gathering.

Karen Martin, in First Class, was in charge. At forty, she was renowned for her efficiency—"organized . . . on the stick to a fault." Her backup, Barbara "Bobbi" Arestegui, was diminutive—small enough, crews joked, to fit on the luggage rack. Several colleagues who had been scheduled to fly were not on board. One had called in sick, another had switched to a different flight—she wanted to accompany her father to a doctor's appointment. Two others, waiting on standby, were told they were not required.

The check-in process went normally. No one knew until later that, even before they reached the terminal, three of the Arab passengers had been involved in an odd incident. A driver next to them in the parking lot would remember how they had dawdled, leaving the door of their rental car open, "fiddling with their things." Irritated, he pushed at the offending door, shoved it against one of the Arabs, half expecting a shouting match. Instead, studiously avoiding a scene, the three Middle Easterners said not a word.

In the terminal, though, the check-in attendant found only passenger Filipov, the electrical engineer, to be acting out of the ordinary. He seemed nervous, paced up and down, seemed to know nothing of airport procedure. The attendant found it a little "suspicious." Otherwise, no one else's behavior caught her attention.

The copilot of the incoming flight, however, deplaning as the fresh crew took over, would remember a strange encounter. As first officer Lynn Howland left the airplane an Arab man stopped her to ask if she would be piloting the soon to depart Flight 11. When she said she would not, he turned away in an "extremely rude" way. Later, shown a picture of the Egyptian passenger on Flight 11, she at once identified him as the man who had approached her.

At check-in, a computer profiling system had selected three of the five young Arab passengers as potentially suspect. Their checked baggage was screened for explosives, the men themselves given special scrutiny by security. Like the carry-on bags of all passengers, theirs were X-rayed. Nothing was spotted.

All five young Arabs, one reportedly carrying a wooden crutch, then proceeded to the gate. One of them—the Egyptian, the agent thought—arrived "sweating bullets . . . his forehead was drenched." With no good reason to stop him, she handed the man his boarding card. He and a companion were the last to board, there to be greeted by senior attendant Karen Martin.

The Egyptian settled down in First Class in aisle Seat 8D, next to passengers David and Lynn Angell. One of the Saudis sat next to him. Two of the others sat further forward, near the cockpit, next to Laura Lee Morabito. Another sat directly behind Daniel Lewin.

The food was on board by now, the in-flight movies loaded. Her final checks completed, Karen Martin prepared to recite the airplane's safety features. Her colleague Madeline Sweeney, whom everyone knew as "Amy," had grabbed a few moments to call her husband. She wanted to say she was sorry not to have been able to see her five-year-old daughter off to kindergarten. Now, though, it was time to switch off all cell phones.

Flight 11 pushed back from the gate at 7:40 and by 8:00 it was soaring skyward. September 11 was a glorious morning for flying, with virtually no cloud or wind— "severe clear" in pilots' parlance.

The Air Traffic Control transcript of air-to-ground exchanges shows that Flight 11 flew routinely for thirteen minutes. "Departure. Good morning. American 11 heavy with you," Captain Ogonowski told Boston control. "Passing through, ah, 2,000 [feet] for 3,000." Boston alerted him to a small Cessna nearby, asking him to climb and turn right. Then, with a "So long," management of Flight 11 passed to other controllers.

The laconic back-and-forth continuing, Ogonowski climbed his plane toward its assigned altitude of 29,000 feet. Then, just after 8:13, Federal Aviation Administration controller Pete Zalewski, at Boston Center—one of the FAA's twenty-one Air Route Traffic Control Centers—told the pilots to turn twenty degrees to the right. "20 right. American 11," a pilot acknowledged, and the plane turned.

Sixteen seconds later, when Zalewski told them to climb, Flight 11 did not reply. The controller would try again and again for the next eleven minutes. "American one one . . . do you hear me? . . . American eleven, if you hear Boston Center, ident please . . ." Only static came back across the ether, with one exception—later to be logged as "a brief unknown sound (possibly a scream)."

At 8:18, unbeknownst at the time to the controllers, a telephone rang at an American Airlines office almost a thousand miles away, in the town of Cary, North Carolina. Vanessa Minter, an employee accustomed to dealing with calls about reservations, heard a woman's voice say, "I think we're being hijacked."

Flummoxed, failing to find the emergency button on her phone, Minter transferred the call to a colleague. He did press the button, automatically starting a recording, and brought in a supervisor named Nydia Gonzalez. Soon Gonzalez was passing on what she heard to American's security office in Texas.

The woman calling was a senior Flight 11 attendant, forty-five-year-old Betty "Bee" Ong. Using a seatback Airfone, Ong had dialed a number that crews knew well—they used it to help passengers with onward travel plans. She sounded "calm, professional, and poised," and we know exactly what she said for four and a half minutes, the standard duration of the recording system. The rest of the conversation—Ong talked for about twenty-eight minutes—is as remembered by the employees who dealt with the call:

> Ong: [I'm] number 3, in the back. The cockpit's not answering. Somebody's stabbed in business class and, ah, I think there's Mace that we can't breathe. I don't know. I think we're getting hijacked.

The seconds ticked by. Time was lost as the staff on the ground asked repetitive questions, mostly to confirm Ong's identity. Then:

> Ong: . . . Somebody is coming back from business . . . hold on for one second . . . Karen and Bobbi got stabbed. [This last sentence, the tape shows, was spoken by a fellow attendant close by.] . . . Our number 1 got stabbed . . . our galley flight attendant and our purser has been stabbed. And we can't get into the cockpit. The door won't open.

An airline employee on the ground made an unhelpful interjection. "Well, if they were shrewd they would keep the door closed . . . Would they not maintain a sterile cockpit?"

"Karen" was lead flight attendant Karen Martin, "Bobbi" her backup Barbara Arestegui. Martin, Ong said, lost consciousness, then came around and was being given oxygen. Arestegui appeared not to be seriously injured. The passenger in First Class Seat 9B, however, appeared to be dead.

The man in Seat 9B had perhaps tried to intervene and fight the hijackers. He was Daniel Lewin, an American-Israeli who had served in a crack Israeli commando unit. Lewin spoke Arabic, and may have understood before anyone else what the hijackers intended. Ong said the passenger in Seat 10B, directly to his rear, had stabbed Lewin to death. The man in 10B was one of the five young Arabs who had boarded that morning. The killer and another hijacker, Ong said, had gotten into the cockpit. The sound of "loud arguing" had been heard.

Four minutes into the call, Ong's colleague Amy Sweeney began trying to phone American Airlines back at the airport in Boston. At 8:32, using a borrowed calling card, she began speaking with duty manager Michael Woodward.

Sweeney, who also reported the stabbings, said the hijackers had "boxes connected with red and yellow wire"—a bomb, she thought. One, she said, spoke good English. So far, passengers in Coach seemed unaware of what was going on.

If the cockpit door had been locked, as required by FAA rules, how had the hijackers gotten in? All American flight attendants held keys, and that was almost certainly why the attendants in First Class—Martin and Arestegui—had been attacked.

There is no knowing exactly what happened when the hijackers erupted into the cockpit. "There was no warning to be more vigilant," Captain Ogonowski's wife, Peg, would later say. "These people come in behind him. He's sitting low, forward, strapped in—the same with his co-pilot. No warning . . ."

Ogonowski and copilot Tom McGuinness had been

trained not to respond to force with force. FAA policy was still geared to hijackings designed to take over airliners, not destroy them. It called for pilots to "refrain from trying to overpower or negotiate with hijackers, to land the aircraft as soon as possible, to communicate with authorities, and to try delaying tactics." According to an FAA security report, the agency did know that "suicide was an increasingly common tactic among terrorists in the Middle East." Its brief to its pilots, however, offered no guidance on how to deal with hijackers bent on suicide.

Attendant Ong had not sounded panicky as she reported from Flight 11. From time to time, though, she asked staff on the ground to "Please pray for us." There were moments, she said, when the plane was being flown erratically, "sideways." It was descending. The phone line had started to fade in and out. Her colleague Amy Sweeney said she could see they were now "over New York City."

Then Ong exclaimed, "Oh, God! . . .. Oh, God! . . ." and began to cry. Sweeney screamed and said, "Something is wrong. I don't think the captain is in control. We are in a rapid descent . . . We are all over the place . . . I see water! I see buildings! . . ." Next, a deep breath and, slowly, calmly, "Oh, my God! . . . We are flying low. We are flying very, very low. We are flying way too low." Seconds later, again, "Oh, my God, we are way too low . . ."

American Airlines' people on the ground could no longer hear either flight attendant. In Boston, duty manager Woodward got only "very, very loud static." In North Carolina, Gonzalez was saying, "Betty, talk to me. Betty, are you there, Betty? . . ."

And finally, "I think we may have lost her."

TWO

I T WAS JUST OVER HALF AN HOUR SINCE THE HIJACKERS had struck.

In an offuce in Lower Manhattan, high in the North Tower of the World Trade Center, a data processor glanced up from his computer. On the horizon to the north, a dot in the sky got his attention. Unusual to see a plane over there, he thought, and turned back to his work.

Moments later, from his perch on a structure on East 77th Street, a steelworker was startled by the sight and the roar of an airliner flying so low that—it seemed to him—it almost hit the antenna atop the Empire State Building. At Madison Avenue and 45th Street, construction workers stared in astonishment. In SoHo, twenty blocks north of the Trade Center, a composer seated in a restaurant window heard a jet thunder overhead. Pigeons, normally blasé, rose in alarm. A window-gazing student at Stuyvesant High—on the banks of the Hudson River—glimpsed the plane for a second and blurted a stunned, "Did you see that?"

A "freakish noise" sent author-photographer Lew Rubenfien rushing onto the roof of his apartment building.

It was the sound jet engines make on a runway when they have been powered all the way up for takeoff—though much more violent, somehow enraged. . . . The plane was moving far faster than you ever saw one go so low in the sky. . . . I began to shout telepathically, "Get away from the building, get away from the building." . . .The plane made a perfect bull's-eye, leaving a jagged tear . . . and then, just as it happens in dreams, everything stretched a long way out. . . . There could only have been a fraction of a second. . . . Then, at last, the building exploded. Hot and orange, the great gassy flower blew out.

It was 8:46 A.M.

The impact had been caught on film thanks to the snap reaction of French documentary maker Jules Naudet, filming nearby with a unit of the New York Fire Department. "I look up, and it's clearly an American Airlines jet," the Frenchman said later. "I turned the camera toward where it was going to go . . . I see it go in. I'm filming it." The image he shot, destined to become iconic, precisely matches Rubenfien's verbal description —orange burst at the core, great bloom of gray smoke or vapor to the left.

In the North Tower, the man who had seen the plane as a distant dot had not been looking when it came right at him. To Chuck Allen of Lava Trading, busy in his 83rd floor office, the memory instead would be of a "muffled, sucking, unbearably loud noise. Like the sound of two high-speed trains crossing in high proximity to each other."

Through the windows, still unbroken, he saw debris falling, paper floating. Liquid was running down the windowpanes. There was a grinding and squeaking in the walls and—Allen was vividly conscious of it—the entire building leaned to one side. Then, gradually, it righted itself.

On the 86th floor, the windows had shattered. James Gartenberg, a broker with Julian Studley real estate, reported by phone that the glass had blown "from the inside of the building out." And that: "The core of the building, the interior core part of the building, collapsed."

American Flight 11 had sliced into the tower between the 93rd and 99th floors. The liquid Allen saw on the windows was almost certainly jet fuel from the plane's wing tanks, a dribble of the ten thousand gallons said to have been on board.

Filmmaker Naudet, far below, stayed with the crew of firefighters as it switched from exercise mode to rapid response and rushed to the tower. Minutes later, in the downstairs lobby, he saw what exploding aviation fuel can do. Fireballs had shot down some of the many elevator shafts, detonating on several floors and then in the lobby. "The windows had all been blown out," Naudet said. "The marble had come off the walls. I saw two bodies burning on the floor. One was screaming, a woman's scream . . . I just didn't want to film that."

Some fourteen thousand people worked each day in the Trade Center towers. Its Twin Towers—North and South, each 110 stories high—loomed more than a fifth of a mile over Manhattan. They were the tallest buildings in the city of skyscrapers, symbols of America's financial power, the heart of a great complex that housed offices, a shopping mall, a hotel, and two subway stations. Vast numbers of workers had not yet been at work when Flight 11 hit. They had been milling around on the lower levels, buying newspapers, grabbing a coffee or a snack. It was primary election day in the city, moreover, and many had stopped to vote before going to the office. Some commuters had been delayed, too, by especially heavy traffic through the tunnels in Manhattan.

Innumerable lives were saved that morning by being late.

As filmmaker Naudet had seen, some were killed or terribly injured in the North Tower lobby. It was the 91st floor far above, though, just below the impact point, that became the frontier between certain death and possible, even probable, survival. Above, on levels 92 to 105, were the hundreds of international bankers, the bond traders, investment and insurance managers and their staffs, who regularly came in early to get a jump on the markets. Higher still, near the tower's summit, were the customers and staff of Windows on the World, the celebrated restaurant atop the Trade Center—and engineers who manned television and radio transmitters.

Of the 1,344 souls on those upper floors, none would survive. Some had died instantly, and hundreds had no way of escaping.

On the 92nd floor, which was intact for a while, debris blocked the stairways. At Carr Futures, John San Pio Resta; his wife, Silvia, seven months pregnant; and trader Damian Meehan were trapped. So, too, was Michael Richards, a sculptor who used studio space on the same floor—an anomaly in a building dedicated to commerce—provided by the Lower Manhattan Cultural Council.

Meehan had time to phone one of his brothers, to tell him the elevators were gone and that there was smoke. His last words were "We've got to go," as he headed for one of the blocked stairways. We know nothing of the last moments of the San Pio Restas and Michael Richards. Richards had last been seen at midnight, saying he planned to work till morning. Long preoccupied with the theme of aviation, his final work had been a bronze of himself amidst flames and meteors, pierced by airplanes.

The area immediately above the 92nd floor was a tomb. Fred Alger Management lost thirty-five people,

Marsh and McLennan, spread over several floors, 295. For Marsh analyst Patricia Massari, on the phone to her husband when the plane hit, there had been time only for "Oh, my God!" Then the phone went dead. The remains of one of her colleagues would be found five blocks away.

Cantor Fitzgerald, the bond trading company, had occupied floors 100 to 105. Six hundred fifty-eight people had been in their offices at the moment of impact. Michael Wittenstein had hung up in the middle of a call to a customer, then—courteous to a fault—phoned back to apologize. "I believe," he had time to say, "there was an explosion in the boiler room."

Andrew Rosenblum broke into a conversation with his wife to say there had been "a really loud bang," that he would call right back. When he did, on a cell phone, he said he and colleagues needed air. They had used a computer to smash a window, and his wife heard coughing, gasping for breath. Kenneth van Auken tried to call his wife but got the answering machine. "I love you," he said. Then again, "I love you very much. I hope I'll see you later."

All 658 people at Cantor Fitzgerald would soon be dead. One staffer's body would be found months later, intact, in his suit and tie, seated upright in the rubble.

From Windows on the World, they used to say, you could see for fifty miles on a clear day. That morning, a very clear one, the seventy-nine greeters, waiters, chefs, and kitchen staff had been busy. Regulars had been at breakfast meetings. In the ballroom, a conference sponsored by the British firm Risk Waters had been about to begin. Guests had been greeted, an audiovisual presentation prepared. Manager Howard Kane, on the phone to his wife, had—inexplicably to her—dropped the receiver at exactly 8:46. She wondered for a moment if her husband had had a heart attack. Then she heard a woman scream, "We're trapped." Another man picked up the phone to say there was a fire, that they needed the phone to call 911.

Death came slowly at Windows on the World. The story told by the cell phones showed that customers and staff hurried down a floor, to the 106th, to wait for help. Assistant general manager Christine Olender, who phoned downstairs for advice, was told to phone back in a couple of minutes. To help with the smoke, it was suggested, those trapped should hold wet towels to their faces—difficult, for the water supply had been severed. They got some water from the flower vases, a waiter told his wife.

"The situation is rapidly getting worse," Olender reported. "What are we going to do for air?" Stuart Lee, vice president of a software company, got off an email to his home office. "A debate is going on," he wrote, "as to whether we should break a window. Consensus is no for the time being." Then they did break the glass, and people flocked to the window openings.

Every person still alive on those upper floors, some thirteen hundred feet above the ground, was facing either intense heat or dense smoke rising from below. Some pinned their hopes of survival on the one way out they imagined open to them—the roof.

"Get everybody to the roof," former firefighter Bernie Heeran had told his son Charles, a trader for Cantor Fitzgerald, when he phoned for advice. "Go up. Don't try to go down." A colleague, Martin Wortley, told his brother he hoped to escape by helicopter. People had been taken to safety from the roof in the past. On September 11, two police helicopter pilots arrived over the North Tower within minutes—only to realize that any rescue attempt would be jeopardized by the billowing, impenetrable smoke.

Regulations in force at the Trade Center in 2001,

moreover, made it impossible even to reach the roof. The way was blocked by three sets of doors, two that could be opened only by authorized personnel with a swipe card, a third operable at normal times only by remote control by security officers far below. The system did not work on 9/11, for vital wires had been cut when the plane hit the tower. Those hoping to escape knew nothing of this.

Early on, one of the helicopter pilots sent a brief message. "Be advised," he radioed, "that we do have people confirmed falling out of the building at this time." In the lobby, a firefighter told filmmaker Naudet simply, "We got jumpers."

VIEWERS AROUND THE WORLD were by now watching events live on television. At the time, however, few in the United States saw the men and women of the Trade Center as they jumped to certain death. Most American editors ruled the pictures too shocking to be shown.

The jumping had begun almost at once. Alan Reiss, of the Port Authority, would remember seeing people falling from high windows within two minutes. Naudet thought "five, ten minutes" passed before he and those around him heard what sounded like explosions—the sound the bodies made as they struck the ground. "They disintegrated. Right in front of us, outside the lobby windows. There was completely nothing left of them. With each loud boom, every firefighter would shudder."

In the heat of an inferno, driven by unthinkable pain, jumping may for many have been more reflexive action than choice. For those with time to think, the choice between incineration and a leap into thin air may not have been difficult.

Firefighters had never seen anything on this scale, the sheer number of human beings falling, a man clutching a briefcase, another ripping off his burning shirt as he jumped, a woman holding down her skirt in a last attempt at modesty. Some fell in pairs holding hands, others in groups, three or four at a time. Some appeared to line up to jump, like paratroopers.

At least one jump seemed involuntary. Gazing through a long lens, photographer Richard Smiouskas was watching five or six people huddled together in a narrow window when one figure suddenly fell forward and away. It looked as though he had been shoved.

"As the debris got closer to the ground," firefighter Kevin McCabe said, "you started seeing arms and legs. You couldn't believe what you were watching . . . [then] it was like cannon balls hitting the ground. Boom. I remember one person actually hitting a piece of structural steel over a glass canopy . . . I remember turning my face away . . . you'd just hear the pounding . . . tremendously loud, like taking a bag of concrete and throwing it into a closed courtyard. A loud echo . . . Boom. Boom . . ."

To Derek Brogan, McCabe's companion, it "looked like it was raining bodies." The bodies spelled danger. "We started to get hit," said Lieutenant Steve Turilli. "You would get hit by an arm or a leg and it felt like a metal pole was hitting you. It was like a war zone."

Cascading humanity.

JUST FORTY-NINE MINUTES had passed since the hijacking aboard Flight 11 had begun, seventeen since the great airplane roared over Manhattan to bring mayhem and murder to the North Tower. Now, in the sky high above the carnage, a police helicopter pilot spotted something astounding. "Christ!" he shouted into the microphone. "There's a second plane crashing . . ."

THREE

"WE HAVE *SOME PLANES*."
      More than three quarters of an hour earlier, as air traffic controller Pete Zalewski tried to get a response from the hijacked Flight 11, he had suddenly heard an unfamiliar voice on the frequency—a man's voice, with an Arabic accent. Zalewski had trouble making out the words, but moments later a second, clearer transmission persuaded him and colleagues that a hijack was under way. The hijacker, they would conclude, had been trying to address the passengers and—unfamiliar with the equipment—inadvertently transmitted to ground control instead.

A quality assurance specialist then pulled the tape, listened very carefully, and figured out what the Arabic voice had said on the initial, indistinct transmission. "We have some planes. Just stay quiet and you'll be okay. We are returning to the airport."

This was a giveaway that—had the U.S. military been able to intervene in time—could have wrecked the operation. The hijackers had seized not two but *four* airplanes. What remained unknown, until even later, was that there may have been plans to seize even more.

NATIONAL TRANSPORTATION SAFETY BOARD
Vehicle Recorders Division
Washington, D.C. 20594

December 21, 2001

Air Traffic Control Recording

```
1224:38  AAL-11  we have some planes. just stay quiet and you'll be okay we are
                 returning to the airport. [BOS 1204-1233 Sector 46R]
1224:46  46R     and uh who's trying to call me here? [BOS 1204-1233 Sector 46R]
1224:53  46R     American eleven are you trying to call? [BOS 1204-1233 Sector
                 46R]
1224:56  AAL-11  nobody move. everything will be okay. if you try to make any
                 moves, you'll endanger yourself and the airplane. just stay
                 quiet. [BOS 1204-1233 Sector 46R]
1233:59  AAL-11  nobody move please we are going back to the airport don't try
                 to make any stupid moves. [BOS 1204-1233 Sector 46R]
```

As America's Flight 11 had been boarding, United Airlines Flight 175—also departing from Boston—had been readying for takeoff. Copilot Michael Horrocks, a former Marine, called his wife about then, joking that he was flying that day with "some guy with a funny Italian name." Flight 175's captain was Victor Saracini, a veteran like Flight 11's Ogonowski. The team of flight attendants included Kathryn Laborie and Alfred Marchand—a former police officer—in First Class; Robert Fangman in Business; and Amy King and Michael Tarrou—a couple thinking of getting married—in Coach.

Their fifty-six passengers were the usual mix: a computer expert, a scout for the Los Angeles Kings hockey team, a commercials producer, a senior marketer for a software company, a systems consultant for the Defense Department. There were also foreigners: three Germans, an Israeli, a British man, and an Irish woman—and five young Arabs, three Saudis and two Emiratis.

All the Arabs had booked seats in First or Business Class.

As they had in the case of Flight 11, ground staff were to recall odd details about the passengers from the Middle East. Two Arabs bungled the boarding process—one of them boarded using his companion's boarding card, and a new one had to be printed. One man asked twice in poor English if he could purchase a ticket, when he already had one. Two waiting passengers, possibly the same man and a companion, behaved strangely at the gate ticket counter. They stood in line, only to walk away on reaching the counter, line up again, and walk away again. In all, they went through the process three times. They seemed nervous, "looked down at the ground as if they were attempting to avoid eye contact." Nevertheless, they both eventually boarded successfully.

Captain Saracini took United Flight 175 into the air before 8:15 and climbed steadily to 31,000 feet. Twenty-three minutes into the flight, a controller looking for the missing Flight 11 asked him and his copilot to see if they could spot it. They did, and were told to stay out of its way. Three minutes later, as 175 entered New York airspace, Saracini came on the air to report to controller Dave Bottiglia:

SARACINI: We figured we'd wait to go to you[r] Center. Ah, we heard a suspicious transmission on our departure out of Boston, ah . . . sound[ed] like someone keyed the mike and, ah, said, ah, "Everyone, stay in your seats."
BOTTIGLIA: Oh, okay. I'll pass that along . . .

Saracini had probably decided to wait a while before reporting the suspect transmission from Flight 11 because—surmising that it indicated a hijack—he wanted to avoid being overheard. United passengers using headsets could listen in on the cockpit chatter simply by listening to Channel 9—it was a form of entertainment. It is possible that on Saracini's plane, unbeknownst to him, some of those listening in were the men planning to hijack the aircraft.

Whether or not they overheard the cockpit chatter, hijackers struck Flight 175 within five minutes of the captain's report about the sinister transmission. At 8:47 the transponder code—the signal that identifies an aircraft—changed twice in the space of a minute. Four minutes later, when ground control asked the pilots to readjust the transponder, there was no response. In the same minute, the airplane deviated from its assigned altitude, climbed, and then—near Allentown, Pennsylvania—began a turn to the southeast. Pilots Saracini and Horrocks were silent now.

Others on board found a way to communicate. Five minutes after the change of course, the phone rang at Starfix, a United facility in California assigned to handle crew calls about minor maintenance problems. The mechanic who took the call, Marc Policastro, found himself talking to a male flight attendant aboard Flight 175, probably Robert Fangman. He said the flight had been hijacked, the pilots killed.

On another phone, a passenger named Peter Hanson got through to his parents' home in Connecticut. He described the hijack, speaking in low tones as his father made notes. "I think they've taken over the cockpit," Hanson said. "An attendant has been stabbed. Someone else up front may have been killed. The plane is making strange moves."

On the ground at New York Center, the silence from 175 by now had controller Dave Bottiglia thoroughly alarmed. He alerted an air traffic manager, Mike McCormick. The turn Flight 175 had been making became a U-turn, until the plane was pointed directly at

New York City. "We might," Bottiglia heard McCormick say, "have multiple hijacks."

At 8:58, another phone began ringing. Passenger Brian Sweeney, the Defense Department consultant on the plane, was trying to reach his wife, Julie, in Massachusetts. She was a teacher, already at school, so he left a voice message. "Hey Jules, it's Brian. I'm on a plane and it's hijacked, and it doesn't look good. I just wanted to let you know that I love you, and I hope to see you again. If I don't, please have fun in life. Please be happy. Please live your life. That's an order."

Sweeney, a former Navy lieutenant who had taught at the Top Gun Fighter Weapons School, did get through to his mother, Louise—with a very different sort of message. He and other passengers, he said, were thinking of storming the cockpit. "I might have to hang up quickly, we're going to try to do something about this."

Peter Hanson, meanwhile, managed another call to tell his father, who again made notes: "It's getting bad, Dad . . . They seem to have knives and Mace. They said they have a bomb. It's getting very bad on the plane. Passengers are throwing up . . . The plane is making jerky movements . . . I think we are going down . . . Don't worry, Dad. If it happens, it'll be very fast."

Hanson Sr. had heard a woman's scream in the background. His son said, "My God! My God! . . ." Then the call ended.

It was 9:02. Ground controllers north of New York were gradually catching up with the reality. Boston Center told New England Region that the tape of the Flight 11 hijacker showed that he had spoken of "planes, as in plural." Also: "It sounds like—we're talking to New York—that there's another one aimed at the World Trade Center."

Even as they talked, controllers at New York Center

were watching the radar blip that was Flight 175. "He's not going to land," one man exclaimed, leaping to his feet. "He's going in . . ."

THE BOEING 767 roared in from New Jersey, looking for a moment as though it might collide with the Statue of Liberty. It rocked from side to side, then the nose pointed down. Fire marshal Steven Mosiello, already at the Trade Center, heard rather than saw it as it came ever "closer . . . louder and louder." The *Irish Times*'s America correspondent, Conor O'Clery, watching the scene at the Trade Center through binoculars, saw the plane "skim" across the Hudson River.

On the 81st floor of the South Tower, Fuji Bank official Stanley Praimnath was at his desk, talking on the phone. Praimnath would recall how, in mid-sentence, for no apparent reason, "I just raised my head and looked to the Statue of Liberty. And what I see is a big plane coming towards me . . . I am looking at an airplane coming, eye level, eye contact, toward me—giant gray airplane . . . with a red stripe . . . I am still seeing the letter U on its tail, and the plane is bearing down on me. I dropped the phone and I screamed and I dove under my desk."

Three floors up, on the 84th, Brian Clark of Euro Brokers had been consoling a woman colleague distraught at the sight of people jumping from the North Tower. He escorted her to the door of the ladies' room, on the far side of the building, when: "*Whomf!* It wasn't a huge explosion. It was something muffled, no flames, no smoke, but the room fell apart . . . For seven to ten seconds there was this enormous sway in the building . . . I thought it was over."

It was 9:03. United Flight 175 had struck the South Tower between the 77th and 85th floors, at an angle.

Clark's chivalrous action in helping a distressed colleague had saved his own life. It had taken him to the side of the building furthest from the point of impact. Praimnath found himself, still under his desk, covered in debris, peering out at what looked like part of the airplane's wing. He began shouting for help and was soon extricated by Clark, who had headed down a passable stairwell. The two were to make the long descent to the ground and safety.

Many others who had been working in their part of the tower had died instantly. Those who survived the initial impact and headed up, rather than down, would not survive.

Fifty minutes had elapsed since the terror began.

For those fighting for their lives in the towers, those rushing to the rescue, those charged with orchestrating the air traffic still in the sky, and those responsible for the defense of the United States, all was now confusion and chaos—against a drumbeat of breaking news, the biggest, most stunning news in the lifetimes of almost everyone it reached.

FOUR

CNN HAD THE BREAK. ON THE HEELS OF A REPORT about maternity wear, Carol Lin cut into a commercial within two minutes of the first strike.

"This just in. You are looking at obviously a very disturbing live shot ... We have unconfirmed reports this morning that a plane has crashed into one of the towers of the World Trade Center ... Clearly something relatively devastating happening this morning there on the south end of the island of Manhattan."

On *Good Morning America*, ABC's Diane Sawyer and Charles Gibson had been smiling through a serving of breakfast-time fluff. Then, four minutes after CNN, they launched into nonstop blanket coverage. Like all the other networks, ABC was confronting a major national story armed with a minimum of facts.

"Was it in any sense deliberate?" asked Sawyer, now serious-faced. "Was it an accident? ... We simply don't know." Behind the cameras, assuming pilot error, one ABC staffer made a reference he was to regret—to "stupidity." On the radio, someone said the pilot must have been drunk.

The early news flashes triggered differing reactions at the highest levels of government. At the National Security Agency outside Washington, where America spies on worldwide phone and email communications, director Michael Hayden glanced at CNN's live shots of the burning North Tower. He thought, "Big fire for a small plane," and went back to his meeting.

Breakfasting with a friend at the St. Regis Hotel, CIA director George Tenet responded very differently. His instant reaction, he would recall, was that this was a terrorist attack. "It was obvious that I had to leave immediately. . . . I climbed back into my car and, with lights flashing, began racing back to headquarters."

Earlier that morning, at a meeting at the Pentagon, Defense Secretary Donald Rumsfeld had made a prediction. In the coming months, he said, there would be an event "sufficiently shocking that it would remind people again how important it is to have a strong, healthy Defense Department." He has not said what he thought when passed a note with news of the crash at the Trade Center, but he left for his office.

Richard Clarke, the long-serving national coordinator for security and counterterrorism, assumed the worst, summoned senior security officials to a videoconference, and headed for the White House.

Vice President Dick Cheney and National Security Adviser Condoleezza Rice were already at the White House. Rice merely thought, "What an odd accident!" Cheney, told of the crash while going over speeches with an aide, began watching the TV coverage.

The President, George W. Bush, was absent from the capital and would be all day, a circumstance that was to do his image no good in the hours that followed. When the first plane hit, he was in Sarasota, Florida, on his way to visit an elementary school—part of a drive for child literacy. White House photographer Eric Draper was in a limousine with press secretary Ari Fleischer and Mike Morell, a senior CIA official, when Fleischer's cell phone rang.

"I heard him say, 'Oh, my God! I don't believe it,'" Draper recalled. "'A plane just hit the World Trade Center.'" Fleischer then turned to Morell to ask if he knew anything about a "small plane" hitting one of the towers. Morell, who phoned CIA Operations, was told that the plane was in fact a large one.

Most likely, the President first learned of the crash as the motorcade arrived at Emma E. Booker Elementary. Navy captain Deborah Loewer, director of the White House Situation Room, ran over with the news as, at about the same moment, chief of staff Andy Card asked Bush to take a call from Condoleezza Rice in Washington. Rice knew less, apparently, than the CIA.

"The first report I heard," Bush would recall, "was a light airplane, twin-engine airplane. . . . And my first reaction was, as an old pilot, 'How could the guy have gotten so off course to hit the towers?' . . . I thought it was pilot error . . . that some foolish soul had gotten lost and made a terrible mistake." He told school principal Gwendolyn Tose-Rigell, "We're going to go on and do the reading thing," and they went off to meet a class of second graders.

A THOUSAND MILES to the north, the first fire chief to reach the North Tower had called in three alarms in quick succession. Even before the second plane hit, a thousand first responders had been deployed. They included men who were off duty, who dropped everything on hearing of the crash and rushed to the scene. One man thought idly that the job would last "twenty-four hours easy—that's a few hundred dollars, no problem." In fact, he was joining what was to be the largest rescue operation in the history of New York City—focused principally on saving lives. Senior firemen rapidly concluded that it would not be possible to put out the fire in the North Tower.

Instructions to evacuate the North Tower had been announced over the public address system within a minute of the crash. The system had been knocked out of action, though, so no one heard the announcement. In the South Tower, where the system did still work, the disembodied voice at first advised, "There is no need to evacuate . . . If you are in the midst of evacuation, return to your office." The instruction changed at 9:02, when occupants were told they could leave after all. Some four thousand people, two thirds of those reckoned to have been in the South Tower, had by that time chosen to leave anyway.

Then at 9:03, Flight 175 hit the South Tower. For the networks, broadcasting live, the task of reporting became incalculably complex—and totally impromptu. This from the ABC *Good Morning America* transcript:

> SAWYER: Oh, my God! Oh, my God!
> GIBSON: That looks like a second plane has just hit . .
> SAWYER: Terrible! . . . We will see that scene again, just to make sure we saw what we thought we saw.
> GIBSON: We're going to give you a replay . . . That looks like a good-sized plane, came in and hit the World Trade Center from the other side . . . it would seem like there is a concerted attack . . .
> SAWYER: We watch powerless . . .

On Channel 5's *Good Day New York*, the anchorman Jim Ryan took a flyer and got it right. "I think," he said, "we have a terrorist act of proportions we cannot begin to imagine at this point."

At the NSA, director Hayden said, "One plane's an accident. Two planes is an attack," and ordered that top priority be given to intercepts originating in the Middle East.

At the Defense Department, assistant secretary for public affairs Torie Clarke, accompanied by colleague Larry Di Rita, hurried to Secretary Rumsfeld's office with the news. He said he would take his daily intelligence briefing, then meet them at the Executive Support Center where military operations are co-ordinated during emergencies. They left Rumsfeld standing at the lectern in his office—he liked to work standing up—one eye on the television.

Word of the second strike was slow to reach CIA director Tenet, still in his car racing back to head-quarters. "With all hell breaking loose," he remembered, "it was hard to get calls through on the secure phone. . . . I was in a communications blackout between the St. Regis and Langley, the longest twelve minutes of my life. It wasn't until I arrived at headquarters that I learned that, as we were tearing up the George Washington Parkway at something like eighty miles an hour, a second plane had hit."

Counterterrorism coordinator Richard Clarke learned of the second attack as he drove up to the White House. He was told Condoleezza Rice wanted him "fast," and found her with the Vice President. "The Secret Service," Rice said, "wants us to go to the bomb shelter." Cheney, famous for his imperturbability, was looking a little shaken. He "began to gather up his papers," Clarke recalled. "In his outer office the normal Secret Service presence was two agents. As I left, I counted eight, ready to move [Cheney] to the PEOC, the Presidential Emergency Operations Center, a bunker in the East Wing."

Clarke, for his part, headed for the West Wing, to pre-pare for the videoconference of counterterrorism and other senior officials he would soon chair. He asked, "Where's POTUS?"—White House shorthand for the President— and learned Bush was at the school in Florida.

"Get ready to read all the words on this page without making a mistake. Look at the letter at the end everyone, with the sound it makes. Get ready!"

As the second plane hit the Trade Center, George Bush had been listening intently to teacher Kay Daniels and her class of second graders. The teacher was going into a routine the children knew well, using a phonics-based system designed to promote reading skills. She intoned, "Boys and girls! Sound this word out, get ready!" "Kite!" chorused the children, then "kit!" then "seal" and "steal," and so on, as Ms. Daniels beat time. Then, "Boys and girls, pick your reader up from under your seat. Open your book up to Lesson 60, on page 153." The children and the President picked up the readers.

In a nearby room, members of Bush's staff had been watching the news coverage from New York—the Marine assigned to carry the President's phone had asked for the television to be turned on. One of those watching as Flight 175 hit was Captain Deborah Loewer, the woman who had run to tell the President about the initial crash. "It took me about thirty seconds," she recalled, "to realize this was terrorism."

Loewer spoke rapidly to chief of staff Andy Card, and—we calculate within about ninety seconds—Card was in the classroom and whispering in the President's ear. By one account he said, "A second plane hit the second tower. America is under attack." As likely, given Loewer's role as Situation Room director, is a version that had Card telling Bush, "Captain Loewer says it's terrorism."

*

IN NEW YORK at about that time, high in the South Tower, Brian Clark of Euro Brokers was pausing to pull Stanley Praimnath out of a wrecked wall, glimpsing fires raging through cracks in walls.

Operators at the Fire Department were logging a stream of emergency calls:

> 9:04 MC [male caller] CAGGIANO . . . STS [states] PEOPLE TRAPPED ON THE 104 FLR . . . IN BACK ROOM . . . STS 35–40 PEOPLE

> 9:04 MC—STS 103 FLR—CAN'T GET OUT—FIRE ON FLR— PEOPLE GETTING SICK

IN THE CLASSROOM in Florida, Bush's expression changed. Told of the second strike, the President pursed his lips, gazing back at his chief of staff as he moved away. ABC's Ann Compton, watching him, thought "his eyes got wide." Teacher Daniels thought he seemed distracted. Natalia Jones-Pinkney, one of the pupils, thought he "looked like he was going to cry." "His face just started to turn red," said Tyler Radkey, another student. "I thought, personally, he had to go to the bathroom."

In the adjacent room, the Marine carrying Bush's phone turned to the local sheriff and said, "Can you get everybody ready? We're out of here." Not so—not yet, for the President did not move.

"On the count of three," teacher Daniels said, "everyone should be on page 153 . . ." The children obeyed, and so did Bush. "Fingers under the title," came the order. "Get ready!" The children chorused the title of a story: "The Pet Goat . . ."

For long and unforgettable minutes, the President of the United States sat dutifully as the second graders read:

The girl had a pet goat. She liked to go running with her pet goat. She played with her goat in her house. She played with her goat in her yard. But the goat did something that made the girl's dad mad. The goat ate things. He ate cans and he ate cakes. He ate cakes and he ate cats. One day her dad said, "That goat must go. He ate too many things."

On the other side of the room, press secretary Ari Fleischer had held up a handwritten sign for Bush's attention. It read, in large black letters, "DON'T SAY ANYTHING YET."

IN THE NORTH TOWER, realtor James Gartenberg and secretary Patricia Puma had by now realized they were stuck in their office. "A fire door has trapped us," Gartenberg told a WABC reporter who reached him on the phone. "Debris has fallen around us. I'm with one other person . . . on the 86th floor, facing the East River . . . I want to tell anybody that has a family member that may be in the building that the situation is under control at the moment . . . So please, all family members take it easy."

It was a brave statement, but neither Gartenberg nor Puma would survive.

The flood of calls to the Fire Department continued:

09:07 CALL FLR 103—ROOM 130—APPROX 30 PEOPLE—LOTS OF SMOKE—FC [female caller] IS PREGNANT

09:08: FC SCREAMING

09:08: FC STS FIRE DEPARTMENT NEEDED TO PUT OUT FIRE

09:09: MC STS 2WTC—PEOPLE ARE JUMPING OUT THE SIDE OF A LARGE HOLE—POSS NO ONE CATCHING THEM

09:09: ON FLR 104—MC STS HIS WIFE IS ON THE 91 FL—STS STAIRS ARE ALL BLOCKED—STS WORRIED ABOUT HIS WIFE

In Florida, the children chorused on:

The goat stayed . . . the girl made him stop eating cans and cakes and cats and cakes. But one day a car robber went into the girl's house. He saw a big red car in the house and said, "I will steal that car." He ran to the car and started to open the door. The girl and the goat were playing in the back yard. They did not see the car robber. More to come.

The President, seemingly all attention, asked, "What does that mean—'More to come'?" It meant, a child told him brightly, that there would be "More later on."

MORE WAS IN FACT already happening. Since 8:56, well before Bush began listening to the second graders, FAA ground controllers had begun worrying about a third airliner. American Flight 77, bound for Los Angeles out of Washington's Dulles Airport, had failed to respond to routine messages, and deviated from its assigned course. Its transponder was turned off and it could not be seen on radar. The controller of the moment, in Indianapolis, knew nothing of the events in New York. He thought the plane had experienced serious technical failure and was "gone."

Soon after 9:00, as the second hijacked airplane crashed into the South Tower, controllers began circulating information that Flight 175 was missing, perhaps crashed. Air Force Search and Rescue and the police were alerted, American Airlines notified. Some at American, meanwhile, thought for a while that it was Flight 77—not United's 175—that had crashed into the Trade Center's South Tower. "Whose plane is whose?": the gist of one conversation between an American manager and his counterpart at United summarizes the general confusion.

United dispatcher Ed Ballinger, responsible for sixteen of the airline's transcontinental flights, had learned that a Flight 175 attendant had called reporting a hijacking. He composed a cautious message to 175 that read, "How's the ride? Anything Dispatch can do for you?" It was too late. By the time the message went out, at 9:03, the crew and passengers on board the plane were beyond help. In the same minute, Flight 175 struck the South Tower.

Four minutes after that, Boston area Air Traffic Control advised all commercial airplane pilots in its sector to secure their cockpits. Boston also recommended that the FAA's Command Center issue a nationwide warning, but the Command Center failed to do so. At 9:19 at United, however, dispatcher Ballinger acted on his own initiative and began sending messages to all "his" flights. They read: "Beware any cockpit intrusion. Two a/c [aircraft] hit World Trade Center."

By 9:05, aware now of the Flight 11 hijacker's transmission about having "planes," FAA's New York Center issued orders forbidding any aircraft to leave, arrive at, or travel through, their airspace until further notice. "We have several situations going on here," a New York Center manager told the Command Center. "We have other aircraft that may have a similar situation going on here." With 4,546 airplanes under their control in the United States that morning, the managers were facing into a situation covered by no training manual.

CONTROLLERS REMAINED totally ignorant of the true status of American 77, the third plane in trouble— though not for want of trying on the part of one of its crew. At 9:12, flight attendant Renee May—assigned to First Class on this latest missing aircraft—got through by phone to her mother in Las Vegas. She spoke just long enough to say six hijackers had taken control, and that passengers and crew were being moved to the back of the plane. She asked her mother to call American Airlines and raise the alarm. Then she got out, "I love you, Mom," before the call was disconnected.

May's mother got through to American in Washington, waited while she was put on hold, then relayed her daughter's message. With staff already distracted by news of events in New York, some wondered whether Flight 77 had hit the World Trade Center. The import of May's call became lost in the general confusion.

In the West Wing of the White House, the video-conference of senior officials was yet to get under way. After the second strike, meanwhile, Vice President Cheney had picked up a phone and said, "I need to talk to the President . . . The Cabinet is going to need direction."

AT THE SCHOOL in Florida, the President's reading session with the children finally came to an end. "Hoo!" he exclaimed. "These are great readers . . . *Very* impressive! Thank you all so very much for showing me your reading skills . . . Thanks for having us."

Why had Bush continued to sit in the classroom—for more than five minutes—after being told of the second strike on the Trade Center? Why, many were to wonder, had he not responded instantly— even with a single terse presidential instruction—when Card told him the second crash indicated a terrorist attack?

Two months later, the President would offer a sort of explanation. He had gone on listening to the school-children, he said, because he was "very aware of the cameras. I'm trying to absorb that knowledge. I have nobody to talk to ... and I realize I'm the commander-in-chief and the country has just come under attack."

Once out of the classroom, Bush joined aides watching the TV news, saw the Trade Center burning, and talked on the phone with Cheney and Rice. He decided to make a brief statement, then fly back to Washington.

Unknown to the President, though, as he mulled what to tell the national audience, crisis was spiraling into calamity.

FIVE

SIX TIMES, MAYBE MORE, THE PHONE HAD RUNG THAT morning in the office at the Justice Department of Theodore Olson, the solicitor general. The caller was his wife, Barbara, and she finally got through some time after 9:15. Mrs. Olson, a prominent attorney who often made television appearances, was no shrinking violet. Now, though, she sounded hysterical.

Olson knew his wife was flying to California that day. He had seen the television coverage of the Trade Center attacks, had thanked God there had not been time for his wife's flight to get to New York. Now Barbara was on the line—from American 77.

Her flight had been seized, she said, by men "with knives and box cutters." After an interruption—Mrs. Olson was cut off—she came back on the line and spoke with her husband for about ten minutes.

The pilot, she told him, had announced that the flight had been hijacked. Had Flight 77's legitimate pilot, Charles Burlingame, remained alive and told his passengers what was happening? Today, there is no way of knowing. Mrs. Olson, who by now sounded calmer, consulted with someone nearby and said she thought the plane was headed northeast. She could see houses below, so the plane must—she realized—have been flying fairly low. She and her husband talked of their feelings for each other, and Olson assured her that things were "going to come out okay." In his heart, he thought otherwise.

Nothing more would be heard from anyone aboard Flight 77. Ted Olson tried to reach the attorney general, John Ashcroft, only to find that he, too, was out of Washington and in the air. Olson spoke with the Department of Justice Command Center and provided his wife's flight number, but the effort went nowhere. With the minutes rushing by, the solicitor general of the United States proved no more effective than had flight attendant Renee May's mother, calling American Airlines to report her daughter's desperate call.

Flight 77 had been flying on undetected, for ground controllers worked on the assumption that it was still flying not east but west. Then at 9:32, controllers monitoring radar at Dulles Airport, outside Washington, spotted an unidentified airplane speeding toward the capital. Reagan National, the airport situated alongside the Potomac River in Washington itself, was notified. So were Secret Service agents, who were by now fretting both about the safety of the Vice President—still in his White House office—and of the President, still at that school in Florida.

ISOLATED FROM THE ONRUSH of events, but very aware of the catastrophe in New York, the President was launching into his thank-you remarks to the teachers and fifth-grade students—remarks rapidly reshaped to take account of the attacks and suggest that the nation's leader was at the helm:

> Ladies and gentlemen, this is a difficult moment for America. I unfortunately will be going back to Washington. . . . Today we have had a national tragedy.

Two airplanes have crashed into the World Trade Center in an apparent terrorist attack on our country. . . . I have ordered the full resources of the federal government to go to help the victims and their families and to conduct a full-scale investigation to hunt down and find those folks who've committed this act. Terrorism against our nation will not stand. Now, if you'll join me in a moment of silence. . . . May God bless the victims and their families and America.

Bush was gone from the school moments later. A Secret Service agent emerged at a run to tell local police officers, "We're under terrorist attack. We have to go now." The presidential motorcade sped off, heading for the Sarasota airport. Before it got there, however, events would torpedo the plan to return to Washington.

FROM THE TOWER at Reagan Airport in Washington, a supervisor had been talking urgently with the Secret Service's Operations Center at the White House. "We've got an aircraft coming at you," he said, "and not talking with us." It is less than four miles from the airport to the White House. Within three minutes, by 9:36, according to the Secret Service record, the agents who had been waiting in Cheney's outer office—submachine guns in hand—acted. "They came in," the Vice President remembered, "grabbed me and . . . you know, your feet touch the floor periodically. But they're bigger than I am, and they hoisted me up and moved me very rapidly down the hallway, down some stairs, through some doors, and down some more stairs into an underground facility under the White House." He was on his way to the Presidential Emergency Operations Center, a fortified bunker originally built for President Roosevelt in World War II, where he was to remain for many hours.

DULLES CONTROLLERS had reported that the suspect airplane was headed toward the restricted airspace around the White House, known as P-56. It was ten miles out, still pointed that way, when radar at Reagan National picked it up. Then it turned south. A National Guard cargo aircraft pilot, asked if he had it in sight, could see it clearly. It looked "like a 757 with a silver fuselage" descending, Colonel Steve O'Brien would recall.

Then, squinting through the haze, O'Brien saw the plane begin to turn back again toward the city. Suddenly, horrified controllers in the Reagan control tower no longer needed the reports of the National Guard pilot. There the airliner was, in plain sight and less than a mile away.

A fire engine captain and his crew on Interstate 395, en route to a training session, saw the plane in steep descent, banking right. A policeman on a motorcycle on Columbia Pike saw it, flying so low that its fuselage reflected the shapes of the buildings beneath. A Catholic priest, on his way to a graveside service at Arlington Cemetery, saw it—flying no more than twenty feet above the road, he said. Steve Anderson, an executive for *USA Today*, who saw it from his 19th floor office, couldn't believe his eyes.

"I heard an airplane, a very loud airplane, come from behind me," said Richard Benedetto, a reporter for the paper, "an American Airlines airplane. I could see it very clearly."

"I was close enough—about a hundred feet or so—that I could see the American Airlines logo on the tail," said Steve Riskus. "It was not completely level but . . . kind of like it was landing with no gear down . . . It knocked over a few light poles on its way."

"I looked out my driver's side window," said insurance company employee Penny Elgas, "and realized I was looking at the nose of an airplane . . . I saw the end of the wing closest to me and the underside closest to me . . . I remember recognizing it as an American Airlines plane . . . The plane seemed to be floating as if it were a paper glider."

AT THE PENTAGON, on the south bank of the Potomac, the news from New York had set some people thinking. "What do we have in place to protect from an airplane?" someone had asked Pentagon police chief John Jester. "Nothing," he replied. There were measures in place to counter a terrorist attack on the ground, but there was no antiaircraft system. Jester raised the "Protection Condition" to "Alpha," all he could do in the circumstances.

Controller Sean Boger, in the little tower beside the Pentagon heliport, wondered aloud why it was that no airplane had ever hit the Pentagon—even by accident. The vast complex was, after all, only a mile from Reagan National. Then, out of nowhere, Boger saw "the nose and the wing of an aircraft just like, coming right at us."

The plane hit just as Jester's deputy was passing on the "Alpha" alert order. Six hundred feet from the point of impact, Jester heard the noise, felt a shaking, but—so huge and so solidly built is the Pentagon—thought it was caused by "furniture on a pallet rolling over an expansion joint." Others heard the sound as a muffled "thwoom."

Flight 77, still with some 5,300 gallons of fuel in its tanks, had hurtled into the military nerve center of the United States at a speed later calculated to have been about 530 miles per hour. The plane struck the west side of the Pentagon just above ground level, going on in diagonally at an angle of about forty-two degrees.

To Penny Elgas, watching petrified in her car, the airliner seemed to "simply melt into the building. I saw a smoke ring surround the fuselage as it made contact with the wall."

"I saw the plane," another driver, Rebecca Gordon, said. "It was there ... Then it was gone ... it just vanished."

"I expected to see the tail sticking out," recalled Sheryl Alleger, a naval officer who saw the crash site afterward. "But—nothing. It was like the building swallowed the plane."

As the airplane pierced the structure, a great mass of flame blossomed above the Pentagon's roof. There were explosions. The carnage and destruction covered a ragged area of more than an acre of the vast complex.

A total of 189 people, 64 on the airliner and 125 military and civilian staff of the Defense Department, were killed—many instantaneously, more within minutes. Some of the Pentagon's dead would be found still seated at their desks and conference tables. Forty-nine people suffered injuries sufficient to warrant admission to hospitals.

Christine Morrison, a survivor, described vividly what happened to her. "From the back of the room there was a heatwave-like haze ... moving. Before I could register or complete that thought, this force hit the room, instantly turning the office into an inferno hell. Everything was falling, flying, and on fire, and there was no escaping it ... I felt the heat and I heard the sizzling of me ... Oxygen disappeared; my lungs felt like they were burning or collapsing. My mind was like sludge and thoughts took forever to form and longer to reach the brain, and even longer to make use of them ... Everyone lost his or her sense of direction."

Morrison would emerge into the daylight relatively unharmed. Juan Cruz Santiago was terribly injured. In the words of the official Defense Department history, he was "engulfed by fire. Most of his body was scorched with second, third, and fourth-degree burns ... Hospitalized for three months, Cruz underwent some thirty surgeries, including skin grafts to his face, right arm, hands, and legs. He was left with cruel damage to his face, eyes, and hands."

Louise Kurtz, who had been standing at a fax machine, was—in her words—"baked, totally ... I was like meat when you take it off the grill." She lost her ears and fingers, underwent multiple skin grafts, and spent three months in the hospital.

Astonishing escapes included Sheila Moody, in the accounts department, who had been seated near the outer wall of the building. Instead of calling out when she heard a rescuer close by—she was stifled by smoke and flames and unable to make a sound—she had been able only to clap her hands. A staff sergeant heard her and got her to safety. Thirty-four others in the department died.

April Gallop, in information management, had brought her two-month-old son to work with her because the babysitter was sick. After the plane hit, and waist-deep in debris, she was horrified to see that the infant's stroller was on fire—and empty. She found the baby, however, curled up in the wreckage and virtually unscathed, and both were rescued.

The crash site being the Pentagon, trained military men were on hand at once. Marines—doing "what we're supposed to do," as one of them put it—went into the wreckage time and again. They and the hundreds of fire-fighters who arrived would more than once have to retreat—once when it became clear that part of the building was going to collapse, again when it was feared that another hijacked plane was approaching. The fire-fiighting operation lasted thirty-six hours.

*

WHEN THE PLANE HIT, Defense Secretary Rumsfeld was still in his office with his CIA briefer. The room shook, even though his quarters were at the furthest point from the impact—in a building each side of which is longer than three football fields. Told that an airplane had crashed, Rumsfeld set off fast to investigate, bodyguards in his wake. They came eventually, a member of the escort recalled, to a place where "it was dark and there was a lot of smoke. Then we saw daylight through a door that was hanging open."

The defense secretary would remember emerging to see the building ablaze, "hundreds of pieces of metal all over the lawn," "people lying on the grass with clothes blown off and burns all over them." He examined a piece of wreckage, saw writing on it, and muttered: "American Airlines . . ." He helped push a gurney, was photographed doing so, then headed back inside.

Assistant secretary Torie Clarke, waiting in the Executive Support Center as instructed, remembered seeing Rumsfeld arrive at about 10:15, "suit jacket over his shoulders and his face and clothes smeared with ashes, dirt, and sweat." He was "quiet, deadly serious, completely cool."

WHILE DONALD RUMSFELD was on the move around the Pentagon, President Bush had been on the short limousine ride from Booker Elementary to the Sarasota airport. News of the Pentagon attack reached the party as they were en route, leading the President's Secret Service escort to advise against the planned return to Washington. Chief of staff Card agreed.

From the airport, on board Air Force One, Bush spoke with Cheney at the White House. "Sounds like we have a minor war going on here," he told the Vice President, according to an aide's notes. "I heard about the

Pentagon. We're at war ... somebody's going to pay."

The Secret Service wanted Air Force One off the ground fast. "They were taxiing before the door was closed," an officer recalled, "and the pilot shot off using only half the runway. There was so much torque that they actually tore the concrete."

Air Force colonel Mark Tillman, at the controls, took the plane up "like a rocket," a passenger remembered, "almost straight up." After flying northeast for a while, it turned west. Those recommending caution had won out. Instead of returning to Washington the President would simply fly on—destination, for the time being, undecided.

In the skies to the north, and even before the Pentagon was hit, the crisis had become yet more serious. Unknown to the President, unknown to anyone at the White House, and once again as predicted in the children's story at the Sarasota school, there was more to come.

SIX

AT HOME IN NEW JERSEY, A WOMAN NAMED MELODIE Homer had been worried by the television pictures from the World Trade Center. Her concern was for her husband, Leroy, copilot that morning on United 93, a Boeing 757 flying from Newark to San Francisco. Through a contact at the airline, Mrs. Homer sent him a text message sking if all was well.

That message was quickly followed by another. As Flight 93 cruised 35,000 feet over eastern Ohio, it received the warning dispatcher Ballinger was by now sending to all United aircraft: "Beware any cockpit intrusion—two a/c [aircraft] hit World Trade Center."

Captain Jason Dahl was evidently nonplussed. "Ed," he messaged back, "confirm latest mssg plz." It was 9:26, and clarification came swift and savage.

At 9:28, the sound of mayhem crackled over the radio from Flight 93. Cleveland control heard a shout of "Mayday!"; then, "Hey! Get out of here!"; and finally, sounds of physical struggle. Thirty-two seconds later, more fighting. Again, three times: "Get out of here! . . . Get out of here! . . . Get out of here!" And screaming.

Melodie Homer never would receive the reassuring reply for which she had hoped. Ballinger's warning had been in vain, and there would be no more legitimate transmissions from Flight 93.

Instead, at 9:32, came a stranger's voice, panting as though out of breath. It intoned: "Ladies and gentlemen. Here the captain. Please sit down. Keep remaining sitting. We have a bomb on board. So sit." Some investigators would surmise that lack of familiarity with the communications system led this hijack pilot—and, earlier, his accomplice on Flight 11—to transmit not to the passengers as intended, but to ground control.

Though the United pilots could no longer transmit, we know a good deal of what went on in the cockpit. Unlike voice recorders on board the three other hijacked flights, all either never found or irreparably damaged, Flight 93's Cockpit Voice Recorder survived. So did the Flight Data Recorder. Though often difficult to interpret, the voice recorder made for a unique partial record of the final thirty-one minutes aboard the plane.

The cockpit recording began four minutes into the hijack, as the hijacker "captain" tried to tell passengers to remain seated. The microphones picked up a clattering sound, followed by the voice of someone giving orders: "Don't move . . . Come on. Come . . . Shut up! . . . Don't move! . . . Stop!"

Then the sound of an airline seat moving, and more commands: "Sit, sit, sit down! . . . Sit down!" More of the same, and a voice repeating in Arabic, "That's it, that's it . . ." Then in English, loudly, "SHUT UP!" Someone other than the terrorists was alive in the cockpit, and evidently captive.

Though one cannot know for sure, the person being told to sit down and shut up was almost certainly one of the female flight attendants. Perhaps she was senior attendant Deborah Welsh, who spent much of her time in First Class. Or perhaps she was Wanda Green, who

was also assigned to the front of the airplane. Some
United attendants carried a key to the cockpit, and one
key was usually kept in the forward galley. By arrangement with Captain Dahl, reportedly, his attendants could
also gain access to the cockpit by means of a coded knock.
Welsh, aged forty-nine, was a veteran with a reputation
for being tough. She had once managed to shove a
drunken male passenger back into his seat. Green, the
same age as Welsh, doubled as a real estate agent and had
two grown children. One of these two attendants was
likely used to gain access to the cockpit.

The woman in the hijackers' hands did not keep quiet
or sit down. A minute into the series of orders to the
captive, a terrorist's voice is heard to intone in Arabic
the Basmala: "In the name of Allah, the Most
Merciful, the Most Compassionate." This is an
invocation used frequently by observant Muslims, often
before embarking on some action.

Next on the recording, the man exclaims: "Finish, no
more. NO MORE!" and "Stop, stop, stop, STOP!"
Repeatedly: "No! No, no, no, NO!" Time and time
again, frantically: "Lie down! . . . DOWN! . . . Down,
down, down . . . Come on, sit down, sit!"

For two minutes of this, the captive has not spoken.
Now, however, a female American voice is heard for the
first time. She begs, "Please, please, please . . ." Then,
again ordered to get down, she pleads, "Please, please,
don't hurt me . . . Oh, God!"

According to Deborah Welsh's husband, the attendant
had spoken of Muslim terrorists with scorn, thought
them cowards. If the captive in the cockpit was Welsh,
perhaps she now tried an acid response. After another
minute of being told to stay down, the female voice on
the recording asks, "Are you talking to me?" Her reward,
within moments, is violence.

Barely has the hijacker started in again on his mantra of "Down, down!" than the woman is heard pleading, "I don't want to die." She says it three times, her cries accompanied by words—or sounds—that are blanked out in the transcript as released. Then, the transcript notes, there is the "sound of a snap . . . a struggle that lasted for few seconds." Moments later, a voice in Arabic says, "Everything is fine. I finished." The woman's voice is not heard again.

Two minutes after the silencing of the attendant, the terrorist pilot tried again to make an announcement to the passengers. He asked that passengers remain seated, adding this time: "We are going back to the airport . . . we have our demands. So, please remain quiet."

About a minute later, at 9:40, a surviving flight attendant on board got through to Starfix, United's maintenance facility in California. This was Sandra Bradshaw, probably seated toward the rear of the plane in Coach. Those who handled the call thought she sounded "shockingly calm" as she told of hijackers, armed with knives, on the flight deck and in the cabin. Bradshaw said that a fellow flight attendant had been "attacked" and—as relayed to United Airlines Operations by a Starfix operator—that "knives were being held to the crew's throats."

It may be that Captain Dahl and copilot Homer were not killed at once. Well into the hijack, the voice recorder transcript shows that a "native English-speaking male" in the cockpit says—or perhaps groans—"Oh, man! . . ." A few minutes later a hijacker is heard saying in Arabic, ". . . talk to the pilot. Bring the pilot back."

A flight attendant—perhaps CeeCee Lyles, who also worked in Coach—at one point passed word that the hijackers had "taken the pilot and the copilot out" of the cockpit. They were "lying on the floor bleeding" in

First Class. It was not clear whether the pilots were dead or alive.

Did the hijackers try to get the pilots, already wounded, to help with the controls? Did they then move them to the forward passenger area and leave them lying there? There is no way to know.

FAR BELOW, ALL WAS CHAOS. At the very moment that the attendant in 93's cockpit had fallen ominously silent—all unknown to those wrestling with the crisis on the ground—Flight 77 had slammed into the Pentagon. On his first day of duty in the post, FAA national operations manager Ben Sliney and his senior colleagues had no way of knowing what new calamity might be imminent.

A Delta flight on its way from Boston to Las Vegas missed a radio call, triggering suspicion. Was this another hijack? Boston had been the point of departure for two of the planes already attacked. Then word reached the FAA Command Center that Flight 93 might have a bomb on board.

At 9:25, Sliney had ordered a nationwide "ground stop," prohibiting any further takeoffs by civilian aircraft. At 9:42, when the Command Center learned of the crash into the Pentagon, FAA officials together decided to issue a command unprecedented in U.S. aviation history. Sliney reportedly boomed, "Order everyone to land! . . . Regardless of destination. Let's get them on the ground."

There were at that moment some 4,540 commercial and civilian planes in the air or under American control. For the more than two hours that followed, controllers and pilots would work to empty the sky of aircraft. It was the one drastic action that might avert fresh disaster.

By 12:16, the FAA was able to inform government agencies that all commercial flights had landed or been diverted away from U.S. airspace.

*

BACK IN WASHINGTON, Clarke's videoconference had finally gotten under way at about 9:37. Extraordinarily, though, it would be an hour before the Defense Department fielded anyone involved in handling the situation. Secretary Rumsfeld himself was out of touch, as noted, having headed outside to view the carnage at the Pentagon.

Absent anyone with a real grasp of what was going on—let alone expertise in how to deal with it—the first matter discussed in the videoconference had been not the crisis itself but the safety of the President and Vice President. In case they were killed or incapacitated, contingency plans were in place for those next in line to the presidency to be taken to a secret underground shelter outside Washington. Speaker of the House Dennis Hastert and Senator Robert Byrd, president pro tempore of the Senate, third and fourth in line, would soon be rushed to the shelter.

All over the capital, people were now pouring out of office buildings. Thousands rushed to get out of the downtown area. The Secret Service ordered an evacuation of nonessential personnel from the White House, and departure—already under way—became headlong flight. Agents yelled at women to take off their high heels and run, and the sidewalks were soon littered with shoes.

Rumor took hold. "CNN says car bomb at the State Department. Fire on the Mall near the Capitol," read a note passed to Clarke. There was no fire on the Mall. Vietnam veteran Richard Armitage, the deputy secretary representing the Department of State on the video-conference, had a blunt response when asked about the "car bomb." "Does it fucking look," he asked, looming large on the monitor, "as if I've been bombed?"

*

To THE NORTH, in New York City, humor survived in the midst of suffering. A firerfighter in the North Tower—on the way up—noticed a fellow coming down toting an odd piece of salvage, a golf club. "Hey!" exclaimed the fireman, "I saw your ball a few flights down." There were bizarre sights, too. Officers moving from floor to floor found a few people still hard at work at their computers—blind to the peril.

As in Washington, rumors flew. "There's another plane in the air," a senior fireman hollered into his radio. "Everybody stay put . . . We don't know what's going on." A police sergeant told a firefighter, "They hit the White House. And we have another inbound coming at us now." "Yeah," a radio dispatcher confirmed, "another one inbound. Watch your back."

There was no third hijacked airplane heading to New York. Some in the North Tower, meanwhile, were still unaware that even one airplane had hit the building. "What happened?" enquired Keith Meerholz, who had escaped with minor burns. "A plane hit each tower," a fireman confided, "but don't tell anyone." He did not want evacuation to become panic.

For those still alive on the higher floors of the tower, the grim ordeal continued. They were stranded, unable to go down—because of blocked stairways and jammed elevators—or up, with the faint prospect of rescue by helicopter, because of the locked doors.

Down on the 27th floor, from which most workers would escape, a man in a wheelchair named Ed Beyea waited patiently with Abe Zemanowitz, a colleague who had stayed protectively at his side. So far below the point of impact, with emergency services on the scene, real danger perhaps seemed remote. Yet neither man would survive.

Outside, paramedic Carlos Lillo was crying as he

worked. His wife, Cecilia, worked on the tower's 64th floor, and he was frantically worried about her. Cecilia would get safely down and out of the building. Carlos, who lost touch with his comrades, died.

The dying had begun in a horrific way for the firefighters. "The Chief said, 'You're going into the lobby command post,'" Paul Conlon remembered. "He pointed to the entrance of Two World Trade Center [the South Tower] .. It was probably two hundred yards .. There were people jumping .. Dan Suhr said something like, 'Let's make this quick ..' We got about halfway there, and Dan gets hit by a jumper."

Daniel Suhr, aged thirty-seven, had been with an engine company from Brooklyn. "It was as if he exploded. It wasn't like you heard something falling and you could jump out of the way . . . We go to pick him up. He's a big guy . . . Someone picked up his helmet . . . One of the guys says, 'He still has a pulse.' . . . I called the Mayday . . . The guys were doing CPR. The ambulance came up pretty quickly."

Suhr, dead on arrival at St. Vincent's Hospital, was the first firefighter to die, first on a list that, it would soon become clear, was to be numbingly long.

Communications, crucial to any firefighting operation, failed dismally that day. "We didn't have a lot of information coming in," Chief Joe Pfeifer recalled of the Command Center in the North Tower lobby. According to the Fire Department's own investigation, the portable radios in use on 9/11 did not "work reliably in high-rise buildings without having their signals amplified or rebroadcast by a repeater system."

"We didn't receive any reports of what was seen from the helicopters," Pfeifer said. "It was impossible to know what was done on the upper floors, whether the stairwells were intact or not." "People watching on TV," Deputy

Chief Peter Hayden said, "had more knowledge of what was happening a hundred floors above us than we did in the lobby."

As their chiefs worked blind, men struggled up the North Tower weighed down by equipment. Company followed company on the strenuous ascent into the unknowable. Of those they had come to rescue, some 1,500 souls had already died or were going to die, those trapped above the impact zone and the injured, handicapped, severely obese, or the elderly, for whom movement was difficult. Of the roughly 7,500 civilians who had been in the North Tower before the attack, however, 6,000 would manage to leave the building by 10:00 A.M.

Of perhaps 7,000 people in the South Tower, some 6,000 are thought to have made their way to safety by 9:30. Of about a thousand who remained, 600 would die.

Brian Clark and Stanley Praimnath, the man Clark had pulled from the wreckage on the 81st floor of the South Tower, had continued to make their painful way down. Slithering at first over ceiling tiles and sheet rock, they sloshed through water, groped through smoke, hurried past fingers of flame. Then the way seemed clear for the long trudge down to safety. "Let's slow down," Clark said as they reached the mid-20s. "We've come this far. There's no point in breaking an ankle." There no longer seemed any need to rush.

High above, hope of escape had withered. Sean Rooney, an Aon insurance executive, had tried to reach the roof and been defeated by the locked doors. From the 105th floor, on the phone to his wife, Beverly, he said, "The smoke is very thick . . . the windows are getting hot." Some two hundred other people were trapped in a nearby conference room.

Below, too far below, firefighters were still climbing,

climbing. One group, that reached the 70th floor, found numerous victims with serious injuries. Chief Orio Palmer, who got to the 78th floor, reported that there were many "Code Ones"—firefighterspeak for dead. Palmer could see pockets of fire but, speaking as though there would be time to do the job, said he thought it should be possible to put them out.

Emergency operators had continued to log piteous calls:

09:32 105 FLR—PEOPLE TRAPPED—OPEN ROOF TO GAIN ACCESS

09:36 FC STS THEY ARE STUCK IN THE ELEVATORS . . . STS THEY ARE DYING

09:40 MC STS PEOPLE PASSING OUT

09:42 PEOPLE STILL JUMPING OFF THE TOWER

09:39 FC MELISSA STS FLOOR VERY HOT NO DOOR STS SHE'S GOING TO DIE . . . STILL ON PHONE . . . WANT TO CALL MOTHER

Emergency workers in the South Tower lobby were overwhelmed by the number of injured people who could go no further.

Outside, butchered corpses. "Some of them had no legs," said Roberto Abril, a paramedic, "some of them had no arms. There was a torso with one leg, with an EMS jacket on top. I guess somebody just wanted to cover it. We kept going back, but at one point it was useless because most of the people that could get out were already walking."

*

EARLY THAT MORNING, a handful of high-ranking firemen
had pondered the unthinkable. How long would the fires
burn on the upper floors, chief of safety Al Turi
wondered, before there were partial collapses? Three
hours, perhaps? He shared his concern with chief of
department Peter Ganci and other colleagues. "The
potential and the reality of a collapse," deputy division
chief Peter Hayden said, was discussed early on. "I think
we envisioned a gradual burning of the fire for a couple
of hours and then a very limited type of collapse—the top
fifteen or twenty floors all folding in."

Rick Rescorla, security chief for Morgan Stanley, saw
it coming from the start. "Everything above where that
plane hit is going to collapse," he forecast right after the
strike on the North Tower, "and it's going to take
the whole building with it." He ordered his staff to
evacuate at once, even though they were based in the
South Tower—at the time still undamaged.

When the top of the South Tower in turn became an
inferno, the same thought occurred to firefighter Richard
Carletti. "Tommy," he told a colleague as they stood
staring upward, "this building is in danger of collapse."

Only months earlier, Frank De Martini, construction
manager for the New York Port Authority, had dismissed
the notion of one of the towers collapsing. "I believe the
building probably could sustain multiple impacts of jet-
liners because this structure is like the mosquito netting
on your screen door," he said in an interview. "And the jet
plane is just a pencil puncturing the screen netting. It
really does nothing to the screen netting . . . The building was designed to have a fully loaded 707 crash into it."

An early design study had indeed suggested that the
Trade Center would survive were a Boeing 707, the
largest airliner of the day—"low on fuel and at landing

speeds"—to strike one of the towers. Now, the buildings had been hit by far larger, far more powerful, 767s heavily laden with fuel. On 9/11, De Martini became concerned early on, and asked that structural inspectors be summoned. He was himself to die that day.

By about 9:50, photographs analyzed much later would show, the South Tower's 83rd floor gave the appearance of drooping down over the floor below. Video footage showed a stream of molten metal cascading from a window opening near one corner. A minute later, a police helicopter pilot warned that there were "large pieces of debris hanging" from the South Tower. They looked as though they were about to fall.

Even earlier, at 9:37, a man on the 105th floor of the South Tower had called 911 with a frantic message. As regurgitated ten minutes later by a computer, it read in part:

STS FLOOR UNDERNEATH—COLLAPSE

In the welter of calls pouring in, that message went unread—or misread. The 911 caller had in fact been referring to floors beneath him, and he had used the past tense. The floors beneath him, "in the 90-something," had *already* collapsed.

That word, from many mouths, and from early on. Collapse.

SEVEN

FOUR HUNDRED MILES AWAY, OVER OHIO, THREE dozen other civilians remained in their airborne purgatory. From about 9:30, for some thirty minutes, fourteen passengers and crew members of United Flight 93 managed to telephone either loved ones or operators on the ground.

The first to do so long enough to have a significant conversation, public relations man Mark Bingham, got through to his aunt's home in California. "This is Mark," he began. "I want to let you guys know that I love you, in case I don't see you again." Then: "I'm on United Airlines, Flight 93. It's being hijacked."

Two other callers from the plane not only provided information but gleaned vital news from those they phoned—news that may have influenced their actions in the minutes that followed. Tom Burnett, chief operating officer for a medical devices firm, made a number of brief calls to his wife, Deena. Speaking quietly, he asked her to contact the authorities, and told her that a male passenger had been stabbed—later that he had died. A woman, perhaps a flight attendant, was being held at knife point, and the hijackers claimed they had a bomb.

Jeremy Glick, a salesman for an Internet services company, also managed to phone. In a long conversation with his wife, Lyz, Glick said the hijackers had "put on these red headbands. They said they had a bomb . . . they looked Iranian." The "bomb" was in a red box, he said. The couple told each other how much they loved each other. Glick said, "I don't want to die," and his wife assured him that he would not. She urged him to keep a picture of her and their eleven-week-old daughter in his head, to think good thoughts.

Burnett's wife, who had been watching the breaking news on television, told him that two planes had crashed into the World Trade Center. "My God," he responded, "it's a suicide mission." By the time he phoned a third time, after news of the crash into the Pentagon, she told him about that, too. Burnett seems to have been seated beside Glick, and apparently relayed all this information to him.

Were they to do nothing, the two men must have agreed, they were sure to die anyway when the hijackers crashed the plane. They resolved to fight for their lives. "A group of us," Burnett told his wife, "are getting ready to do something." "I'm going to take a vote," Glick said on his call. "There's three other guys as big as me and we're thinking of attacking the guy with the bomb."

So began the minutes of brave resistance, the clearly defined act of courage that has lived on in the national memory. Glick and others were equipped in more ways than one to confront the hijackers. He was six foot one and a former college judo champion. Burnett, at six foot two, had played quarterback for his high school football team. He admired strong leaders, had busts of Lincoln, Theodore Roosevelt, and Churchill in his office, liked Hemingway's books and Kipling's poetry. Mark Bingham was a huge man, six foot four and at thirty-one still playing rugby. A few years earlier, he had fended off a mugger who had a gun. His mother got the impression, as he talked from Flight 93, that her son was talking "confidentially" with a fellow passenger. She felt that "maybe someone had organized a plan."

At 9:42, a GTE-Verizon supervisor based near Chicago began handling a call from yet another power-fully built Flight 93 passenger. Todd Beamer, a star Oracle software salesman, was married with two sons, and his wife was expecting again. He first dialed his home number, but either failed to get through or thought better of it. Instead, explaining that he did not want to upset his pregnant wife, he asked phone supervisor Lisa Jefferson to pass on a loving message.

As they talked, Beamer suddenly exclaimed, "Shit! . . . Oh, my God, we're going down . . . Jesus help us." From the passengers around Beamer came prolonged shrieks of terror. Then he said, "No, wait. We're coming back up. I think we're okay now."

Today we have an explanation for those moments of panic. The Flight Data Recorder shows that, as Beamer and operator Jefferson talked on, the plane had gone into a rapid descent.

Shaken, Beamer asked Jefferson to say the Lord's Prayer with him. "Our Father, who art in heaven . . ." Across the airwaves, they prayed together. Then Beamer began to recite the Twenty-third Psalm. "The Lord is my shepherd; I shall not want . . . Yea, though I walk through the valley of the shadow of death . . ."

Just before Beamer and the operator had begun talk-ing, Cleveland control lost Flight 93's transponder, the signal that indicates an airplane's location and altitude. "We just lost the target on that aircraft," controller John Werth exclaimed, and began struggling to find it on radar. He was in contact, too, with an executive jet still in flight in the area, which reported sighting 93. At 9:55, the recovered flight recorder shows, the hijacker pilot dialed in a navigational aid relating to the plane's direction. He was heading, it indicated, for Washington, D.C.

For some six minutes, a female passenger named Marion Britton had been talking to a friend on one of the seatback phones. She said she thought the plane was turning and going to crash. There were sounds of screaming again, and the plane did turn. But there was no crash, not yet.

Jeremy Glick, still on the phone to his wife, Lyz, said, "I know I could take the guy with the bomb." Then, joking—he had mentioned that the hijackers had knives—"I still have my butter knife from breakfast."

Todd Beamer, continuing his conversation with GTE supervisor Jefferson, told her that he and a few others were getting together "to jump the guy with the bomb." Was he sure that was what he wanted to do? "Yes," came the response. "I'm going to have to go out on faith . . . I don't have much of a choice."

There was, it seems, more to the passengers' plan than merely overpowering the hijackers. If the legitimate pilots were out of action, that alone would have been pointless. Beamer, however, talked as if there was some-one on the plane who could act as pilot if they overpowered the hijackers. He gave Jefferson "the impression their plan would be to try to land it safely."

There was indeed a pilot among the passengers. Donald Greene, a senior executive of Safe Flight Instrument Corporation, was licensed to fly single-engine four-seaters or copilot a King Air twin-engine turboprop, and flew regularly. To fly and land a Boeing 757 like Flight 93, though, with its complex systems and massive power—40,200 pounds of thrust—would have been another matter. Could Greene have pulled off such a feat? The weather, a key factor for any pilot flying visually rather than on instruments, was perfect, with excellent visibility. It was possible, given time and painstaking instructions radioed from the ground, that a pilot with Greene's experience could do it. Those hoping to overpower the hijackers well knew, after all, that they had nothing to lose.

The plane was flying erratically again. Operator Jefferson heard the sounds of an "awful commotion": raised voices, more screams. Then: "Are you guys ready?" and Todd Beamer's voice saying, "Let's roll!"—a phrase that, in family life, he liked to use to get his children moving.

"OK," Jeremy Glick told Lyz, "I'm going to do it." His wife told him he was strong and brave, that she loved him. "OK," he said again. "I'm going to put the phone down. I'm going to leave it here and I'm going to come right back to it." Lyz handed the phone to her father, ran to the bathroom, and gagged.

For some minutes, passenger Elizabeth Wainio, a Discovery Channel store manager, had been on the line to her mother. She had been quiet, her breathing shallow—as if she were already letting go, her mother thought. Her deceased grandmothers were waiting for her, Wainio said. Then: "They're getting ready to break into the cockpit. I have to go. I love you. Goodbye."

Sandra Bradshaw, the flight attendant who had earlier phoned to alert the airline, now got through to her husband. She was in the galley, she said, boiling water for the passengers to throw on the hijackers. Then, "Everyone's running up to first class. I've got to go. Bye . . ."

CeeCee Lyles, Bradshaw's fellow crew member, also got through to her husband, told him rapidly about the hijacking, that she loved him. Then, "I think they're going to do it. Babe, they're forcing their way into the cockpit . . ."

The Cockpit Voice Recorder registered the moment the hijackers realized what was happening. At just before 9:58, a hijacker asks, "Is there something? . . . A fight?" There is a knock on the door, followed by sounds of fighting. Then, in Arabic, "Let's go, guys! Allah is Greatest. Allah is Greatest. Oh guys! Allah is Greatest . . . Oh Allah! Oh Allah! Oh the most Gracious!" Then, loudly, "Stay back!"

A male voice, a native-English-speaking voice that Tom Burnett's wife has recognized as that of her husband, is heard saying, "In the cockpit. In the cockpit."

Followed by a voice exclaiming, in Arabic, "They want to get in there. Hold, hold from the inside . . . Hold."

Then, from several English speakers in unison, "Hold the door . . ." And from a single English speaker, "Stop him," followed repeatedly by "Sit down! Sit down!" Then, again from an English speaker, "Let's get them . . ."

Flight 93, now down to five thousand feet, had begun rolling left and right. The pilot of a light aircraft, on a mapping assignment for the Pennsylvania Department of Agriculture, saw the airliner at about this moment. "The wings started to rock," he recalled. "The rocking stopped and started again. A violent rocking back and forth."

Jeremy Glick's father-in-law, listening intently on the phone his daughter had handed him, now heard screams in the background. On the Cockpit Voice Recorder, there is the sound of combat continuing. Then, in Arabic:

"There is nothing . . . Shall we finish it off?"

"No. Not yet."

"When they all come, we finish it off."

Then, from Tom Burnett: "I am injured."

The Flight Data Recorder indicates that the plane

pitched up and down, climbed to ten thousand feet, turned. Glick's father-in-law, phone clapped to his ear, heard more shrieks, muffled now, like those of people "riding on a roller coaster."

In Arabic, on the voice recorder, "Oh Allah! Oh Allah! Oh Gracious!"

In English, "In the cockpit. If we don't, we'll die!"

In Arabic, "Up down. Up down . . . Up down!"

From a distance, perhaps from Todd Beamer, "Roll it!"

Crashing sounds, then, in Arabic, "Allah is the greatest! Allah is the greatest! . . . Is that it? I mean, shall we pull it down?"

"Yes, put it in it, and pull it down."

"Cut off the oxygen! Cut off the oxygen! Cut off the oxygen! . . . Up down. Up, down . . . Up down."

More violent noises, for as long as a minute, then—apparently by a native English speaker: "Shut them off! . . . Go! . . . Go! . . . Move! . . . Move! . . . Turn it up."

In Arabic, "Down, down . . . Pull it down! Pull it down! DOWN!"

Apparently from an English speaker, "Down. Push, push, push, push, push . . . push."

In Arabic, "Hey! Hey! Give it to me. Give it to me . . . Give it to me. Give it to me . . . Give it to me . . . Give it to me . . . Give it to me . . . Give it to me."

Intermittent loud "air noise" on the cockpit recorder.

Moments later, in Arabic, "Allah is the greatest! Allah is the greatest! Allah is the greatest! Allah is the greatest!"

Sounds of further struggle, and a loud shout by a native English speaker, "No!!!"

Two seconds later, in Arabic, in a whisper now, "Allah is the greatest! Allah is the greatest! Allah is the greatest! Allah is the greatest!"

Jeremy Glick's father-in-law, still listening on the

United Airlines Flight #93 Cockpit Voice Recorder Transcript

Key:
Bolded text = English translation from Arabic

10:00:06	**There is nothing.**
10:00:07	**Is that it? Shall we finish it off?**
10:00:08	**No. Not yet.**
10:00:09	**When they all come, we finish it off.**
10:00:11	**There is nothing.**
10:00:13	Unintelligible.
10:00:14	*Ahh.*
10:00:15	*I'm injured.*
10:00:16	Unintelligible.
10:00:21	*Ahh.*
10:00:22	**Oh Allah. Oh Allah. Oh Gracious.**
10:00:25	*In the cockpit. If we don't, we'll die.*
10:00:29	**Up, down. Up, down, in the *cockpit*.**
10:00:33	**The *cockpit*.**
10:00:37	**Up, down. Saeed, up, down.**
10:00:42	*Roll it.*
10:00:55	Unintelligible.
10:00:59	**Allah is the Greatest. Allah is the Greatest.**
10:01:01	Unintelligible.
10:01:08	**Is that it? I mean, shall we pull it down?**
10:01:09	**Yes, put it in it, and pull it down.**
10:01:10	Unintelligible.
10:01:11	**Saeed.**
10:01:12	*. . . engine . . .*
10:01:13	Unintelligible.
10:01:16	**Cut off the oxygen.**

ground, heard high-pitched screams coming over the line Glick had left open when he left to join the rush to the cockpit. Then "wind sounds" followed by banging noises, as though the phone aboard the plane was repeatedly banging on a hard surface.

After that, silence on the phone. Silence on the Cockpit Voice Recorder. Then, in less than a second, the recording ended.

NEAR THE LITTLE TOWN of Shanksville, Pennsylvania, a man working in a scrapyard had seen an airliner, flying low but seemingly trying to climb, just clear a nearby ridge. The assistant chief of Shanksville's volunteer fire department had been talking on the phone with his sister, who said she could see a large airplane "nosediving, falling like a stone." A witness who saw it from his porch said it made a "sort of whistling" noise.

Half a mile away, another man saw the final plunge. It was "barely fifty feet above me," he said, "rocking from side to side. Then the nose suddenly dipped and it just crashed . . . There was this big fireball and then a huge cloud of smoke."

It was 10:03. Thirty-five minutes had passed since the hijackers struck, four minutes since the passengers counterattacked.

The grave of Flight 93 and the men and women it had carried was an open field bounded by woods on the site of a former strip mine.

"Where's the plane crash?" thought a state police lieutenant, one of the first to reach the scene. "All there was was a hole in the ground and a smoking debris pile." The crater was on fire, and the plane itself had seemingly vanished. On first inspection, there seemed to be few items on the surface more than a couple of feet long. The voice recorder, recovered days later, would be found buried twelve feet under the ground. There were no bodies, it appeared, only shreds of clothing hanging from the trees. For a while, a white cloud of "sparkly, shiny stuff like confetti" floated in the sky.

Three hundred miles away in the little town of Cranbury, New Jersey, Todd Beamer's wife, Lisa, saw the first pictures of the crash site on television and knew her husband was dead.

In Windham, New York, someone told Jeremy Glick's wife, Lyz, that there might be survivors. Then her father returned from the garden, where—at the request of the FBI—he had kept open the line on which Jeremy had called. He had waited, waited, for an hour and a half. Now, as he came back in, Lyz saw that her father was weeping.

Hundreds of miles apart, the two wives, now widows, sank to their knees in grief. Sudden, unforeseeable grief was invading homes across the country, across the world.

EIGHT

AT THE TRADE CENTER IN NEW YORK, UNSEEN BY the cameras, a lone fire chief was grappling with the possibility for which no one had planned. John Peruggia, of Medical Services, was at the mayor's Office of Emergency Management—in normal times, the city's crisis headquarters.

By an irony of history, though, the office was located in the Trade Center's Building 7. That was too close to the North Tower, and Building 7 had been evacuated within an hour of the initial strike. Peruggia was one of a handful of officials who remained. He was still there, standing in front of the building and giving instructions to a group of firefighters, when an engineer—he thought from the Building Department—made a stunning prediction.

Structural damage to the towers, the official told him, was "quite significant ... the building's stability was compromised ... the North Tower was in danger of a near imminent collapse."

This was a warning Peruggia knew he had to pass urgently to the very top, to chief of department Ganci, now at his command post opposite the North Tower. With the usual command and control system out of action, the only way to get word to him was the old-fashioned way—by runner. Peruggia's aide that day,

EMT Richard Zarrillo, set off on a hazardous five-hundred-yard journey.

AROUND THAT TIME, Brian Clark and Stanley Praimnath, on the final lap of their escape from the South Tower, reached the concourse at plaza level. "We stared, awestruck," Clark remembered. "What we looked at was, normally, a flowing fountain, vendors with their wagons . . . tourists . . . a beautiful 'people place.' Yet this area, several acres, was dead . . . a moonscape . . . it looked like it had been deserted for a hundred years."

No one was running or obviously panicking. Clark and his companion were told to proceed "down to the Victoria's Secret shop, turn right, and exit by the Sam Goody store." Then a policeman urged them to get moving and not look up. They ran a block or so, and turned to look back. "You know," Praimnath said, "I think those buildings could go down."

"No way," Clark replied. "Those are steel structures."

HIGH IN THE TOWER the two men had just escaped, an Aon Insurance vice president named Kevin Cosgrove was on the phone to a 911 operator.

COSGROVE: Lady, there's two of us in this office . . . 105.
Two Tower. We're not ready to die, but it's getting bad
. . . Smoke really bad . . .
FIRE DEPARTMENT OPERATOR (joining the call): We're
getting there. We're getting there.
COSGROVE: Doesn't feel like it, man. I got young kids . . .
I can barely breathe now. I can't see . . . We're young
men. We're not ready to die.
911 OPER ATOR: Okay, just try to hang in there.

On the same floor, Cosgrove's colleague Sean Rooney

was still on the line to his wife, Beverly. Neither of them now hoped for rescue. "I think," Beverly said, "that we need to say goodbye."

FAR BELOW, on the ground near the towers, EMT Zarrillo completed his dangerous run to get to Chief Ganci and began blurting out the warning from Chief Peruggia. "Listen . . . the message I was given was that the buildings are going to collapse. We need to get our people out."

"Who the fuck," Ganci had time to say, "told you that?"

At that moment, Zarrillo would recall, there was "this thunderous, rolling roar."

FIREFIGHTER RICHARD CARLETTI, peering up at the South Tower, had noted a sudden change. It "started to lean. The top thirty floors leaned over . . . I saw the western wall start to belly out." The columnist Pete Hamill saw the walls "bulge out," and heard "snapping sounds, pops, little explosions." The explosive noises—to some they seemed "real loud"—were followed by a sort of "groaning and grinding."

High in the tower itself, Aon's Kevin Cosgrove finally lost patience with the 911 operator. "Name's Cosgrove," he said. "I must have told you a dozen times already. C.O.S.G.R.O.V.E. My wife thinks I'm all right. I called and said I was leaving the building and that I was fine . . . There are three of us in here . . . Three of us . . . Two broken windows. Oh, God . . . OH . . .!" Against a background of huge noise, Cosgrove screamed. Then the line went dead.

Beverly Rooney, still on the phone to her husband, heard sounds she, too, recalled as sounding like an explosion, followed by a crack, followed by a roaring sound. "The floor fell out from under him," she thought. "It sounded like Niagara Falls. I knew without seeing that he was gone."

Rooney and Cosgrove and so many others were gone. Then, and in little more than the time it takes to read these words, the South Tower itself was gone.

"The entire structure just sank down on to itself with a colossal whoosh," reported the British journalist David Usborne, who had watched from the park in front of City Hall. "For a second, the smoke and dust cleared enough to reveal a stump of the core of the building . . . But the clouds closed in again and nothing more could be seen. All of us simply stood and gaped, hands to our faces."

IN THE STUDIO at ABC, Peter Jennings had been juggling the cascade of brutal news, his eye on one live monitor, then another. "It may be," he said, puzzled by the vast new plume of smoke that had appeared where the South Tower had been, "that something fell off the building." Jennings asked a colleague closer to the scene what had happened.

"The second building that was hit by the plane," Don Dahler told him, "has just completely collapsed. The entire building has just collapsed . . . It folded down on itself, and it's not there anymore." The famously un-flappable Jennings allowed himself an on-air "My God! My God!" Then, as if in the hope that he had misheard, "The whole side has collapsed?"

Dahler said it again. "The whole building has collapsed . . . There is panic on the streets. Thousands of people running . . . trying to get away."

It was 9:59 A.M. One of the tallest buildings in the world had collapsed in no more than twenty seconds. "From a structure," in the words of a witness, "to a wafer."

*

In the wake of the roar there was darkness—an all-enveloping, suffocating, blinding dust cloud—and cloaked in the cloud a mass of humanity, rushing pell-mell for refuge.

Fire chief Ganci and his senior aides, and Zarrillo, the EMT who had brought word of a possible collapse, rushed into the garages of adjacent buildings. "I took ten or fifteen rolling steps into the garage," Zarrillo recalled, "and hugged into a corner, an indentation, and I felt two or three guys get in behind me . . . The dust, the cloud, came rolling in."

Chief Peruggia, still outside Building 7, became aware of the cloud as he answered a woman reporter's question. "I grabbed the female, threw her through the revolving doors of Number 7 . . . Everything came crashing through the front . . . Next thing I remember I was covered in glass and some debris . . . I had shards of glass impaled in my head . . . I was able to get all this debris and rubble off me and cover my face with my coat so that I could breathe. It was very thick dust. You couldn't see."

When the building began to fall, EMT Jody Bell had been strapping a hysterical patient into a stair chair. "Everybody's like, 'Run for your lives!'" he remembered. "She's hyperventilating . . . It's like, a tidal wave of soot and ash coming in my direction. My life flashed before my eyes . . . I started to run—took about ten steps, and the lady started screaming, 'Don't leave me!' . . . I got ahold of myself. 'Wait, what the hell am I doing?' I turned back, got her out of the chair. I said, 'Ma'am, can you run?' She said, 'Yes.' She took off. I've never moved so fast . . . The dust was like snowfall. The cars are covered . . . I'm breathing in mouthfuls . . . The scene was totally blacked out."

Firefighter Timothy Brown had just left the South

Tower, where he had seen people—only their legs and feet visible through the door of a stranded elevator—being "smoked and cooked." On his way to fetch medics when the tower fell, he had ducked into the lobby of the Marriott, the eight-hundred-room hotel adjoining the Trade Center.

"Everything started blowing towards us that wasn't nailed down . . . I'm guessing that the wind at its height was around 70, 75 miles an hour . . . You couldn't see anybody . . . You couldn't hear anything. It was becoming our grave . . . I thought it lasted four minutes . . . You could hear an eerie silence at first, and then you could start to hear people starting to move around a little bit, people that were still alive."

Sixteen of some twenty firefighters who had been on a stairwell in the hotel were not alive. The collapsing tower had sliced the Marriott in two.

Spared thanks to their final dash, Brian Clark and Stanley Praimnath had sheltered outside a church. They "stared in awe, not realizing what was happening completely . . . You at least thought people had a chance—until that moment. Then this great tsunami of dust came over . . . I suppose it was a quarter of an inch of dust and ash, everywhere."

To Usborne, the British reporter, the dust was a "huge tidal wave, barrelling down the canyons of the financial district . . . The police went berserk, we went berserk, just running, running for our lives . . . we were in a scene from a Schwarzenegger film . . . thousands of Hollywood extras, mostly in suits for the office, with handbags and briefcases, just tearing through the streets of the city. Every few seconds we would snatch a look behind us."

Columnist Hamill remembered dust blossoming perhaps twenty-five stories high, leaving the street a pale gray wilderness peopled by "all the walking human beings, the police and the civilians, white people and black, men and women . . . an assembly of ghosts . . . Sheets of paper scattered everywhere, orders for stocks, waybills, purchase orders, the pulverized confetti of capitalism."

INSIDE THE NORTH TOWER, few were even aware of the collapse. "We felt it," one said. "Our tower went six feet to the right, six feet to the left . . . it felt like an earth-quake." "You just heard this noise that sounded like the subway train going by," said another, "multiplied by a thousand."

"It didn't register," recalled James Canham, a fire-fighter who was on the 11th floor. "There was the sound of the wind blowing through the elevator shafts . . . air pressure coming in . . . the entire floor enveloped in dust, smoke . . . Then I had gone right into the stairwell. There had to be twenty people piled up—I mean actually in a pile . . . I told them to grab the railing . . . to grab the belt loop of the person in front of them . . . If it was a woman . . . the bra strap. I told them, 'Hold the bra, with the other hand hold the railing, and make your way down.' Panicking and crying as they were, they were listening . . . on their way . . . coughing . . . disoriented."

On hearing by radio of the South Tower's collapse, police officer David Norman—on the 31st floor—could not comprehend what the operator told him. "To think that a building of one hundred and some stories had fallen was like, you know, not believable . . . He then explained that there was no South Tower, that it was absolutely gone."

A great burst of energy, generated by the fall of the South Tower, had translated into a blast of air and dust shooting into the North lobby and on up into the build-ing. For a while it was pitch black. Debris rained down, fatally for some—including the Fire Department chaplain, Mychal Judge. He died in the lobby, hit on the head by flying debris, as he returned from giving last rites to the dead and dying outside.

Fire chief Pfeifer, still running operations in the lobby, knew nothing at first of the collapse on the other side of the plaza. Thinking that something catastrophic was going on above him, though, he decided to pull his men out. Police commanders made the same decision, and an evacuation began.

The order did not reach battalion chief Richard Picciotto, on the 35th floor, but he took the decision on his own initiative. "All FDNY, get the fuck out!" he hollered on his bullhorn. And, over the radio, "We're evacuating, we're getting out, drop your tools, drop your masks, drop everything, get out, get out!"

Outside, meanwhile, Fire Department chief Ganci had sent his command group off in one direction while—with just one colleague—he headed back toward the North Tower. He went back, an aide explained simply, because he "knew that he had men in that building." Some of those men, on the 54th floor, defied the order to evacuate. Intent on continuing to help civilians, they radioed, "We're not fucking coming out."

On the higher floors, civilians and firemen alike now had no chance of survival. For those really high up, it had long been so. Tom McGinnis, a trader with Carr Futures on the 92nd floor, had been trapped behind jammed doors since Flight 11 hit. He and colleagues had long been ankle-deep in water from either burst pipes or the sprinkler system. Now they were forced to the windows to get air. The phones were still working, and McGinnis told his wife he was going to crouch down on the floor. Then the connection was broken.

*

"WHAT WE DIDN'T KNOW," Chief Pfeifer said later, "was that we were running out of time." In the dark and confusion of the lobby, he and other chiefs were for all intents and purposes operating blind. Fire-fighter Derek Brogan recalled the chaos that greeted him when he got there from above. "There was gas leaking all over the place. The marble was falling on top of us . . . You couldn't see anything."

Brogan stepped outside, to realize it was suddenly "raining" bodies. Fireman Robert Byrne found himself dodging jumpers and falling debris, weaving between corpses "littering the courtyard." "Everything was on fire . . . I took a peek up . . . aluminum was coming down . . . going through thick plate glass like a hot knife through butter."

Pilots in the helicopters, circling above, could see what was coming. As early as five minutes after the South Tower's collapse, a Police Department pilot reported thinking that the North Tower's top floors might collapse. Nine minutes on, another pilot said he thought the tower might not last long. Twenty minutes on, the pilot who had made the first report radioed that the tower was now "buckling and leaning."

In the absence of an effective liaison arrangement between the Police and Fire Departments, this crucial information was not passed on to the firefighters.

AT 10:28, not quite half an hour after the South Tower's slide to ruin, time did run out.

Fireman Carletti, now watching from the safety of a fire truck, saw the antenna atop the North Tower "do a little rock back and forth, and I could just hear the floors pancaking. I heard it for about thirty pancakes . . . boom, boom, boom, boom." As when the first tower had fallen, others spoke of "explosions," "pop, pop, pop" noises, a "thunderous, rumble sound."

Firefighter Dean Beltrami saw "the entire facade starting to buckle . . . Nobody said anything. We just turned and ran." EMT Jody Bell saw the tower "looking like it was going to tip, and there was a piece of the building coming down right on top of me . . . The building was hitting other buildings . . . This time it was worse . . . We were just running . . . I was damn near ready to jump in the river . . . The debris went well into the Hudson. It almost went to Jersey."

"I opened up my eyes," said EMS chief James Basile, "dust and dirt, debris . . . total darkness, I guess for about two, three minutes. I thought, 'I guess this is what it's like to be dead.' Then I heard a woman screaming."

"This beautiful sunny day now turned completely black," said Chief Pfeifer, who survived the fall of the tower. "We were unable to see a hand in front of our faces. And there was an eerie silence."

The 110-story North Tower had become a pile of flaming, noxious rubble—like its twin before it, in about twenty seconds.

THE SILENCE WAS BROKEN by the high-pitched tones of locator alarms, the devices that are triggered when a firefighter goes down and does not move. Three hundred forty-three men of the New York Fire Department would never move again.

The number of firefighters killed on 9/11 was almost a third of the total killed since the department's inception in 1865.

Chief Ganci had been killed near the North Tower, and his body was one of the first to be found. Chief Pfeifer's brother Kevin would be found dead in the rubble, his fireman's pick at his side. Firefighting runs in families in New York, and fathers and sons, brothers and in-laws, would search for fallen comrades and kin for months to come.

Thirty-seven Port Authority police officers, including their superintendent, Fred Morrone, had died. Five of their bodies were found grouped around that of a woman in a steel chair, a device used to carry the disabled. They had died, it seemed, trying to carry her to safety.

The New York Police Department lost twenty-two men—and one female officer. She had brought an injured person out of the South Tower, only to be killed when she went back in to help another.

"The number of casualties," New York mayor Rudolph Giuliani said, "will be more than any of us can bear." Government officials would at first suggest, in a serious overestimate, that as many as seven thousand people had been killed in the city. The death toll was nevertheless stunningly high.

The number of fatalities in New York was eventually to stand at 2,763. That figure included the people in or near the Twin Towers, the passengers, crew, and hijackers aboard the two flights that crashed into the complex, and firefighters, police, paramedics, and other emergency workers. The highest number of casualties was in the North Tower—1,466, the majority of them above the point of impact—followed by 624 in the South Tower, all but 6 of them above the point of impact. One hundred and fifty-seven people died aboard the two planes.

Rarely mentioned, if at all, is the fact that this was not exclusively an American catastrophe. Five hundred and eleven nationals, perhaps more, from more than two dozen other countries, died in New York. They included dozens of Hispanic immigrants, delivery men, cooks, and dishwashers, with no work permits. They are almost all nameless now, remembered on no memorial.

THE TRADE CENTER COMPLEX rapidly became known as Ground Zero, for good reason. Assault by airplane had transformed it in an hour and forty-two minutes from iconic landmark to sixteen-acre wilderness. "All that remained standing," wrote *Atlantic Monthly* correspondent William Langewiesche, "were a few skeletal fragments . . . vaguely gothic structures that reached like supplicating hands toward the sky. After the dust storms settled, people on the streets of Lower Manhattan were calm. They walked instead of running, talked without shouting, and tried to regain their sense of place and time. Hiroshima is said to have been similar in that detail."

The towers had thrown mighty shards of steel and rubble to the ground and—such was the force involved—beneath it to a depth of thirty feet. Vehicles on the surface were flattened, power and telephone systems crippled, subways and watercourses severely damaged. Even before the collapse, plummeting rubble devastated nearby buildings.

The lesser giants of the complex had been known by numbers. Trade Center 3—the Marriott Hotel—was now wreckage. Great chunks of debris had fallen on Trade Center 7, which collapsed into its own footprint in the late afternoon. Trade Center Buildings 4, 5, and 6 suffered serious damage and were later demolished. Eight more structures, including World Financial Center 2 and 3—American Express—the Winter Garden pavilion, Bankers Trust, a City University of New York building, and Verizon Communications, were damaged but not beyond repair. Tiny St. Nicholas Greek Orthodox Church, in the shadow of the South Tower, had been flattened.

The attackers had succeeded in stopping the engine room of America's economy, if only briefly. Damage to Verizon Communications, gored by Building 7's fall, crippled the electronics that connect the financial markets to the New York Stock Exchange. Exchange chairman Dick Grasso delayed opening the market, then closed it as the strikes escalated. It would not open again until the start of the following week.

Unlike the New York Stock Exchange, located at a relatively safe distance from the Trade Center, its cousin the American Stock Exchange was jolted by the second strike. The towers' collapse left its offices filled with debris and remaining staff—the chairman and the president included—trapped for hours, covered in soot and dust. Seeing the exchange afterward, a leader of commerce would recall loftily, was like "visiting a third world country."

Its communications cut, NASDAQ's corporate offices closed. The New York branch of the Federal Reserve Bank was evacuated, not without a moment of comedy. The building had never before been left unmanned, and no one present knew how to lock up.

Many key financial figures were far from the decision making on the morning of 9/11. The chairman of the Federal Reserve, Alan Greenspan, was in the air halfway across the Atlantic, returning with colleagues from a meeting in Switzerland, when U.S. airspace closed down. His airplane, like others in mid-flight, had to turn back. Frantic calls to the White House eventually got Greenspan back to Washington courtesy of the military, part of the way aboard a U.S. Air Force tanker.

The minders of the American economy wrestled for days with problems ranging from sustaining liquidity to averting the nightmare scenario—potential public panic if the cash at ATM machines ran out, which in turn might spark a run on the banks. New York City, meanwhile, faced the daunting costs that had been inflicted in less than two hours. Reporting a year later, New York's comptroller would calculate the economic cost to the city at between $83 and $95 billion.

ON 9/11, after the second collapse, there was at first a long, empty moment, a vacuum in time. Then the start of an epic, heartrending, recovery operation.

NINE

"AMBULANCES GOING THIS WAY, ESU TRUCKS flying down the street . . . Nobody had any idea what was going on. Where is the command post? Where is staging? We had no radio . . . You looked where you thought the buildings should be, and if they were there, you couldn't see them . . . disorientation . . . I had already seen my third skyline in forty minutes."

Fire Department lieutenant Michael Cahill, on the period after the second Trade Center collapse. A time of "absolute panic . . . absolute panic . . . Most of us were just too tired . . . out of it . . . disorganized . . . Stuff in our eyes, cuts, bruises, equipment lost. Half the people we came with were lost."

Off-duty firefighters, former firefighters, men who worked in construction or salvage, all rushed to Ground Zero to help. One of them, crane operator turned fireman Sam Melisi, was one of the first would-be rescuers to pioneer routes through, over, and under the rubble. He had all the expertise and experience one could wish for, but was forced time and again to retreat.

It dawned on Melisi that the "tremendous devastation" of the Oklahoma City bombing, which he had worked six years earlier, had been nothing compared to this. "Visualize fiftyfold or a hundredfold, no matter where you turned ... You can never quite prepare for something like this ... on this magnitude. We started searching ... We were hoping to find many live victims. But as time went on we realized there weren't going to be that many."

There were only a few. Twenty people were rescued after the collapses, all but one emerging in the first twenty-four hours. Two civilians, trapped at first in what had been a shopping mall beneath the plaza, managed to squeeze out through an opening. Next out were twelve firefighters, a civilian, and a Port Authority policeman—thanks to "the Miracle of Stairway B."

When the North Tower collapsed, Captain Jay Jonas and his crew had been four stories up the stairway, trying to help a woman who could walk no further. Swept away on an avalanche of rubble and steel, Jonas had thought, "This is how it ends." They ricocheted down to certain death, only to find themselves alive—the civilian included—still on or near the stairway.

The difference now was that they were in pitch darkness, at something like ground floor level, in what was rapidly to become known as "the pile." Jonas began hearing radio transmissions from firemen buried elsewhere: "Just tell my wife and kids that I love them." "Mayday. Mayday ... I'm trapped and I'm hurt bad." The messages gradually petered out, for the men were dying.

Jonas kept sending his own Maydays. "It was a waiting game," he remembered. "We were trapped in there for over three hours ... I heard one fireman on the radio saying, 'Where's the North Tower?' and I'm thinking to myself, 'We're in trouble if they don't even know where the North Tower is.' " Deep in the rubble, Jonas had no way of knowing the reality evident to everyone outside, that the tower had simply vanished.

He realized the truth only as the dust began to clear,

when a beam of sunlight penetrated the darkness. It was coming through a hole that was to prove the group's salvation. "I survived," Jonas thought as he emerged. "All my men survived. And we have this small victory that is within us, that we brought somebody else out with us . . . We had a nice void. We had a nice little pocket. There's got to be hundreds of them. There's got to be a lot of people getting out of here."

In fact only three others were to be rescued. Port Authority engineer Pasquale Buzzelli had plunged down, also on a stairway, from the 22nd floor. The fall reminded him for a moment of an amusement park ride. Then he was hit on the head, saw stars, and fell unconscious. Buzzelli came to three hours later, covered in dust and reclining on a cement slab fifteen feet above the ground, there to be rescued by firemen. His only physical damage, a crushed right foot.

Two Port Authority police officers, Jimmy McLoughlin and William Jimeno, were found not by professional rescue workers but by two former U.S. Marines. Determined to be in the front line, they donned military fatigues, talked their way into Ground Zero, and clambered around hollering: "United States Marines! If you can hear us, yell or tap." After an hour of shouting, a muffled cry came back. The pair summoned help, and rescuers had Jimeno on the surface by midnight. McLoughlin, who was seriously injured, was extracted early the following morning.

There would eventually be an army of rescuers from all over the country, professionals with technical skills, volunteers with a contribution to make—and some who were no help at all. Every city has its cranks, but none outdid the fellow who jumped overboard, early in the aftermath, from a ferry evacuating people to New Jersey. The man then began swimming—back in the direction of the Trade Center. "I thought," he said as he was hauled out, "I could swim over to New York to help people." Not everyone on board wanted him rescued. "Shoot him!" someone shouted. "He may be a terrorist!"

HOSPITALS IN MANHATTAN and beyond, expecting an "onslaught of patients," had rushed to activate their disaster plans. Off-duty personnel, including a busload of surgeons attending a medical conference, dropped what they were doing and offered their services to the Fire Department. The expected flood of injured, however, never materialized. With most of those brought to hospitals released by midnight, the surgeons wound up loading water supplies.

On September 11 and for long afterward they found not survivors, not the injured, only the dead. Cadavers sometimes, but more often mere scraps of humanity. Those who found them saw things they will never forget.

"A person's torso, just no legs, no head, no arms, nothing, just chest and stomach area . . . Then like fifteen feet away I found a head to go with the torso . . . we tagged it."

"People had I-beams [steel joists] through them, and things like that."

"A woman's severed hand. You could still see the engagement ring on her finger . . . The constant smell of burnt flesh."

"The body of a young woman . . . her child underneath . . . an arm they found, a woman's, and when they pried open her fingers they found inside the fist of a baby."

"You couldn't walk more than a few feet in some areas without encountering body parts."

The charnel house that was the Trade Center would over time yield up 21,744 separate human remains. Chief medical examiner Dr. Charles Hirsch, whose task it would be to collect and identify them, was based on First Avenue, only two miles from the Trade Center. He and aides had rushed to a nearby site early on 9/11, to prepare a temporary morgue, and several of them had been injured by flying debris. Those still able to work then initiated the necessary, macabre process that—as this book goes to press—continues still.

Remains were brought to Dr. Hirsch's headquarters as they were found. They were analyzed, borne to a white tent nearby. There, a prayer was spoken over them. Then they were stored in refrigerated trailers pending identification. The operation would eventually require the installation of sixteen trailers.

To Hirsch, it came as no surprise that there should be so few complete bodies and so many thousands of body fragments. "If reinforced concrete was rendered into dust," he said, "it wasn't much of a mystery as to what would happen to people."

More remains would be found as the years passed—some as late as 2009—atop the damaged Deutsche Bank building, in manholes, under a service road at Ground Zero. An assortment of remains, from a complete cadaver dressed in a suit to tiny bone fragments, was found at a landfill on Staten Island, destination of the half million tons of debris removed from the site. The landfill's name, the name it had had since the late 1940s, was Fresh Kills. It was revealed in 2012 that some remains of those killed at the Pentagon, reportedly too small or charred to be identified, were also sent to a landfill – following cremation.

Within ten months of 9/11, however, science and detective work would identify 1,229 of those killed. In the years since, 404 more victims have been identified. It has been an unparalleled forensic achievement. Even so, 1,119 men and women—41 percent of the total who died—remain unidentified. The families of more than a thousand people cannot bury their loved ones.

THERE IS ANOTHER REASON, though, that the true death toll will long remain elusive. Listen again to the voices of those who endured 9/11 on the streets and in the buildings of New York City.

"I see this fifty-, sixty-story dust rolling down the block." "The ambulances looked like they were covered with gray snow . . . so thick you couldn't see a sharp edge from a smooth edge." "People were just full of dust . . . looked like zombies."

"Nobody could breathe. Everything was stuck in their throats and their eyes, mouths, faces, and everything." "Everybody's coughing, breathing in mouthfuls of shit."

"Our face-pieces were on, because the probie [trainee firefighter] was having trouble with chest pains, having difficulty breathing." "My lungs were filling up with this stuff. I don't know what it was. I thought I was going to die." "The sergeant asked me, 'You think we could die from this stuff?' I'm like, 'Right now? No. But eventually? Yes.' "

Less than an hour after the second strike, a Fire Department operator had logged a phone call from a woman on Duane Street, near the Trade Center. At 9:59 the dispatcher noted:

FC—CONCERN ABOUT THE RESPIRATORY EFFECT OF THOSE PARTICLES

The person calling about the "particles" must have come across as a fusspot, her call a mere nuisance. Who had time to think, then, about the bits and pieces falling from the towers and wafting on the breeze? The material spewed out by the towers, however, did have

significance—a significance that increased greatly once
the towers had fallen and the walls of dust had roared up
the canyons of Lower Manhattan.

"Dust" covers many evils. 9/11's dust contained:
asbestos (tests after the attacks showed hazardous
asbestos levels at sites up to seven blocks from Ground
Zero), lead, glass fibers, dioxin, PCBs, and PAHs
(potentially carcinogenic chemical compounds) and
toxins from perhaps fifty thousand vaporized computers.

New York firefighters had reason, historically, to fear
such pollutants. "We lost quite a few firemen back in the
seventies in a telephone building fire," remembered
Salvatore Torcivia. "They were exposed to PCBs when all
the transformers in that building burned and they didn't
have the proper equipment to protect themselves.
Numerous guys died the first year from cancer. Over the
next five to twenty years, all the guys from that job died.
The majority went within the first ten years."

Torcivia worked at Ground Zero every day for two
weeks. "There's gonna be a lot of people sick from this,"
he forecast later,

and not just firemen. I wasn't wearing a mask the whole
time . . . They issued us these paper masks used for
painting, but they don't stop anything . . . From day one,
everyone was complaining of the cough and the sore
throats . . . The second day or third day I was getting
told by private test groups at the site that the con-
taminants in the air were off the charts. They were so
high they couldn't register them. But we were also being
told by the city and the state that everything was within
the range where it's not gonna harm anyone. That just
wasn't so.

The firefighter coughed as he talked, a cough that

seemed to come from deep inside his chest. He had begun having problems within a month of 9/11.

> Going on the normal runs, we noticed that a lot of us were getting winded more easily . . . On regular walk-ups, where I never had a problem before, I thought I was gonna have a heart attack. I couldn't catch my breath . . . I went to the Fire Department surgeon . . . They found out that I've dropped around 40 to 45 percent of my breathing capacity since the last time I was tested . . . I went to see a specialist. He explained to me that all the stuff that got into my body down at Ground Zero—I didn't just inhale it into my lungs and bronchial tubes— I ingested it . . . And everything working together is keeping it constantly inflamed and infected . . . There's four to five hundred guys with breathing problems.

Salvatore Torcivia's problems were far from unusual. A 2007 study by the Albert Einstein College of Medicine and the New York City Fire Department noted a huge increase in the number of firefighters suffering from the lung ailment sarcoidosis. Some two thousand firefighters had at that point reportedly been treated for serious respiratory ailments.

"The World Trade Center dust," the college's Dr. David Prezant has noted, "is a combination of the most dense, intense particulate matter [first responders] were ever exposed to in an urban environment."

The respiratory ailments have continued to increase, affecting not only firefighters but policemen, emergency medical personnel, and those who worked on the rubble removed from Ground Zero.

Many have succumbed to their illnesses. In a landmark decision in 2007, the New York medical examiner ruled that the 9/11 dust cloud contributed to the death as early as five months afterward of a young attorney from sarcoidosis. As in the case of all victims of the attacks, the cause of her death was registered as homicide.

According to figures published in late 2008 by the New York congressional delegation, 16,000 9/11 responders and 2,700 people who lived near Ground Zero were at that time "sick and under treatment." Reports in 2009 suggested that some 479 people, from different walks of life, had died from illnesses that may be attributable to the condition of the air during and after the 9/11 attacks. One by one, news reports show, others continue to die.

In late 2010, when deaths from illness among first responders had risen to 664—many of them from causes suspected to be related to 9/11—Congress acknowledged the gravity of the problem.

The James Zadroga 9/11 Health and Compensation Act, named for a New York policeman who had died of pulmonary fibrosis at thirty-four, earmarked $4.2 billion to address the health needs of the long-term victims of 9/11.

"We will never forget the selfless courage demonstrated by the firefighters, police officers, and the first responders who risked their lives to save others," said President Obama when he signed the act. It seemed, though, that one category of sufferers might be forgotten. A study indicated that cancer rates had risen by 14 per cent among first responders—including more than three hundred members of the New York City police force. As of early summer 2012, it appeared that officialdom was clearing the way to ensure coverage for 9/11 survivors with cancer.

Back in September 2001, concern about the possible dangers of exposure to toxic dust and fumes had been swept aside. The Environmental Protection Agency declared after two days that initial tests were "very reassuring." Five days later, Assistant Secretary of Labor John Henshaw said it was "safe to go back to work in New York's financial district." The Stock Exchange reopened on September 17, with EPA administrator Christine Todd Whitman reassuring New Yorkers the next day that their air was "safe to breathe."

There had been pressure from the start, from the very top, to get the financial district up and running. At a National Security Council meeting not twelve hours after the attacks, according to counterterrorism co-ordinator Richard Clarke, President Bush said, "I want the economy back, open for business right away, banks, the stock market, everything tomorrow."

Those who knew the situation on the ground knew that opening the next day was an impossible fantasy. The President, however, had been removed from the realities.

AFTER HASTILY LEAVING Sarasota airport in Florida, at 9:55 on the morning of 9/11, Bush had spent the rest of the day aboard Air Force One, with brief stops at two U.S. military bases. "The President is being evacuated," press secretary Ari Fleischer told reporters on the plane, "for his safety and the safety of the country."

Key civil and military aides were at Bush's side, but circumstances wreaked havoc with the concept of round-the-clock presidential grasp of the levers of power. For all his power and all the modern technology at his disposal, it is not evident that the President had much influence—if any—on the government's reaction to the day's events.

Accounts conflict mightily as to whether communications aboard Air Force One functioned well or appallingly badly. Bush spoke with Dick Cheney around the time of takeoff, but it is far from clear with whom, and how usefully, he spoke once the plane was airborne.

In interviews conducted for the first anniversary of 9/11, chief of staff Andy Card repeatedly emphasized how efficiently the President had been able to communicate with the Vice President, National Security Adviser Condoleezza Rice, Defense Secretary Donald Rumsfeld, Transportation Secretary Norman Mineta, and the military.

Bush himself, though, said it proved difficult—time and again—to get through to Cheney. He recalled pounding his desk on the plane, shouting, "This is inexcusable! Get me the Vice President!" He "could not remain in contact with people," he was to say, "because the phones on Air Force One were cutting in and out." In Washington, senior aide Karen Hughes experienced the same difficulty getting through to the presidential plane. "The military operator came back to me and in—in a voice that sounded very shaken—said, 'Ma'am, I'm sorry. We can't reach Air Force One.' "

Given such contradictions, there is no way of knowing how Bush and Cheney or Bush and anyone else actually interacted that day. That issue, as will be seen, is central to the crucial matter of how the military responded to the hijackings.

Reporters traveling with the President watched the collapse of the towers on flickering television screens. At about 10:30, after the second tower fell, word came from the White House of a "credible," anonymous phone threat to "Angel," the insiders' word for Air Force One. Tension rose accordingly. Armed guards were posted at the cockpit door, and agents checked the identification of almost everyone on board. Reporters were told not to use their cell phones. F-16 fighters were soon to begin escorting Air Force One, and did so for the rest of the day. One escort plane flew so close, the President's press office would state, that Bush saluted through the window—and the F-16 pilot dipped a wing in reply. The warning of a threat to "Angel" had been just a base-less scare, but made a good story.

The President worried aloud about having literally vanished into the blue. "The American people," he reportedly said, "want to know where their dang President is." It was decided that he would land at Barksdale Air Force Base in Louisiana to make a television appearance. "Freedom itself," Bush said in a two-minute taped address at 1:20 P.M., "was attacked this morning by a faceless coward. And freedom will be defended." This was less than the reassurance he had wished to communicate, not least because the tape first hit the airwaves running backward.

Then the President was off again, this time heading for Offutt Air Force Base in Nebraska. Once aboard, in a conversation he did succeed in having with Cheney, Bush said: "We're at war, Dick. We're going to find out who did this and kick their ass." And: "We're not going to have any slap-on-the-wrist crap this time."

A rear admiral at Offutt, the underground head-quarters of U.S. Strategic Command, would say he thought the President "very much in control . . . con-cerned about what was happening . . . calm . . . articulate . . . presidential." In mid-afternoon, Bush took part in a videoconference with National Security Council members in Washington—Cheney, Rumsfeld, Rice, CIA director Tenet, and FBI director Robert Mueller.

The President, however, was by now preoccupied with the thought that his continued absence from the capital made him look bad. The Secret Service was still advising him to stay away from Washington. His staff wanted him to address the nation again from Offutt. Bush, however, would apparently have none of it.

"I'm not going to do it from an Air Force base," he

reportedly said. "Not while folks are under the rubble." And, in another account, "I don't want a tin-horn terrorist to keep me out of Washington." Press secretary Fleischer agreed that the President's whereabouts was becoming "an increasingly difficult issue to deal with."

Air Force One at last made the return trip to the capital. From the helicopter carrying him to the White House, Bush got his first glimpse of the reality of 9/11. There in the evening light was the Pentagon, partly veiled in black smoke, a deep gouge in its west side. "The mightiest building in the world is on fire," Bush muttered, according to Fleischer. "That's the twenty-first century war you've just witnessed." Then he was down, landing on the South Lawn and walking back into the White House almost ten hours after the attacks had begun.

Political Washington had begun to show a brave face to the world. More than a hundred members of Congress had gathered on the steps of the Capitol in a display of unity. "We will stand together," declared Speaker of the House Dennis Hastert—now back on the Hill—and he and colleagues broke into a chorus of "God Bless America." An hour and a half later, once he was anchored back in the Oval Office, Bush delivered a four-minute address to the nation. It is said that he had an audience of eighty million people.

"Evil, despicable acts of terror," the President said, "have filled us with disbelief, terrible sadness, and a quiet, unyielding anger." Though he could not have known it, he ended by citing the same passage from the Twenty-third Psalm to which United 93 passenger Todd Beamer had turned in a moment of terror: "Even though I walk through the valley of the shadow of death, I fear no evil . . ."

The address also included something Bush had added

himself just before going on air. "We will make no distinction," he said, after assuring Americans that those behind the attacks would be brought to justice, "between the terrorists who committed these acts and those who harbor them."

Afterward, in the underground bunker where Cheney and others had spent the day, Bush met with key officials—the group he was to call his "war council." The words "al Qaeda" and "Osama bin Laden" had been on everyone's lips for hours, and CIA director Tenet said al Qaeda and the Taliban in Afghanistan were essentially one and the same.

There was talk of reprisals and then, according to counterterrorism coordinator Clarke, Defense Secretary Rumsfeld came out with a remarkable comment. "You know," he said, "we've got to do Iraq."

PRESIDENT BUSH almost always went to bed early, and September 11 was no exception. He balked when the Secret Service asked him and the first lady to spend the night on a bed in the underground bunker, an old pullout couch. "The bed looked unappetizing," he recalled, "so I said no." The couple retired to their usual bedroom in the residence, only to be woken around 11:30 P.M. by a new security alert. "Incoming plane!" an agent told them. "We could be under attack. Come on. Right now!"

The President of the United States, he in T-shirt and running shorts and Mrs. Bush in her robe—with their dogs Barney and Spot—were rushed down to the basement to be confronted again by the unappetizing couch. The "incoming" plane, however, turned out to be merely a chartered airliner bringing FBI reinforcements from the West Coast. Back went the Bushes to their private quarters.

Two hundred and twenty-five miles away in New York City, in the glare of halogen lights, men worked on through the night in the tangle of steel and rubble that had once symbolized American prosperity. They were still looking hopefully for the living, and the hand of one more survivor—the last, as it turned out—would eventually appear through a hole to grasp that of a rescuer. It belonged to a young female clerk who had worked at the Trade Center and, though seriously injured, she was to recover.

That consolation aside, there would henceforth be only the dead, or fragments of the dead.

The pile at the scene of the attacks "heaved and groaned and constantly changed, was capable at any moment of killing again." The air smelled of noxious chemicals, and strange flames shot out of the ground, purple, green, and yellow. Fires were to burn on, underground, for three months to come.

An American apocalypse, a catastrophe with consequences—in blood spilled and global political upheaval—that continue to this day.

PART II

DISTRUST AND DECEIT

TEN

ONE CONSEQUENCE, A NATIONAL AND INTER-
national phenomenon, is that countless citizens do
not believe the story of September 11 as we have just told
it.

We have striven in these chapters to recount what is
firmly known. We have teased out detail, sorted the
reliable from the dross, often gone back to original
sources. Yet many would say our account is skewed, too
close to the "official version," or just plain wrong.

9/11 is mired in "conspiracy theory" like no previous
event in American history—more so even than President
John F. Kennedy's assassination. Doubt and disbelief as to
what really happened on 9/11, a *Time* magazine writer
noted in 2006, is "not a fringe phenomenon. It is a main-
stream political reality." By the end of George Bush's first
term as President, a more iconoclastic writer—Matt
Taibbi at *Rolling Stone*—concluded that Americans had
"no dependable authority left to turn to, no life raft in the
increasingly perilous informational sea. . . . Joe American
has to turn on the Internet and tell himself a story that
makes sense to him. What story is he going to tell?"

Americans, University of California history professor
Kathryn Olmsted has said, "tend to be particularly
receptive to anti-government conspiracy theories." Her

study of conspiracy theory notes not only the evidence of the polls—that in 2006 a third of the U.S. population believed the Bush administration was involved in 9/11—but that a majority of that third were aged eighteen to twenty-nine.

Significant, too, given the continuing global upheaval, is the degree of 9/11 conspiracy belief among Arab Americans (of whom there are more than three million), American Muslims, and Arabs worldwide. Taibbi, doing interviews in Dearborn, Michigan, was shocked to hear "well-educated, pious Lebanese Americans regurgitating 9/11 conspiracy theories like they were hard news." One woman he interviewed "could not be budged from her conviction that Bush had bombed the Twin Towers." In much of the Arab world, the author and longtime Middle East resident Jean Sasson has written, "conspiracy theories dominate public opinion."

As recently as 2009, persistent belief in such theories so concerned the U.S. government that it issued a fact sheet for global consumption, seeking to rebut "unfounded . . . popular myths" about 9/11. It was an acknowledgment that the authors of conspiracy theory, the "skeptics" as they like to be characterized, were a force hard to ignore. What are their principal theories and speculations, and is there substance to them?

AT THE CORE of conspiracy theory is the idea that we were all hoodwinked, that what we thought we saw on 9/11 was not the full picture. The Twin Towers may have been struck by airliners filled with passengers—though some doubt even that—but it was not the planes that brought them crashing down. Explosives, planted explosives, had been used to achieve that. The same went for the total collapse later in the day, the skeptics claim, of World Trade Center Building 7. As for the Pentagon, there were claims by some that it had been struck not by a plane but by a missile.

Why perpetrate such gross trickery? The overarching suspicion—for some the conviction—is that people at the heart of the United States government were behind the attacks. The doubters belong, essentially, to one of two schools of thought, broadly defined by the acronyms MIHOP—Made It Happen On Purpose—and, the alternative, LIHOP—Let It Happen On Purpose.

LIHOP proposes that elements in the Bush administration, aware that a terrorist onslaught was likely, and motivated by the opportunities for foreign intervention it might provide, turned a blind eye to warning signs and let the attacks happen. MIHOP adherents suspect— argue strongly—that elements in the U.S. government and military actually engineered the attacks.

Those, then, are the central planks of conspiracy theory. As late as January 2011, National Geographic Channel was rebroadcasting programming that covered the theories plugged by the people some call 9/11 "truthers."

CONSPIRACY THEORIES are nothing new, in America and much of the rest of the world. The growth and durability of 9/11 skepticism, though, was inseparably intertwined with the rise and rise of the Internet. For better or worse and for the first time in history, the Internet permits citizens to propagate ideas faster than traditional media and beyond the control of government.

The electronic murmur that was to reach millions seems to have begun not six hours after the first strike on the Trade Center. Boston-based David Rostcheck, a software consultant with a physics degree, had spent the morning watching the drama on television. "Eventually," he recalled, "I went to see what people were saying online. I belonged to the set of people who had been on the Internet for most of my adult life, before there was a Web and before the Internet became a household presence. . . . No one seemed to be commenting on the unusual aspects of the building collapses, so I wrote up an analysis and posted it."

"Is it just me," Rostcheck asked on the Net that afternoon,

> or did anyone else recognize that it wasn't the airplane impacts that blew up the World Trade Center? To me, this is the most frightening part of this morning . . . look at the footage—those buildings were demolished. To demolish a building, you don't need all that much explosive but it needs to be placed in the correct places. . . . Someone had to have had a lot of access to all of both towers and a lot of time to do this. . . . If, in a few days, not one official has mentioned anything about the demolition part, I think we have a REALLY serious problem.

There it was, almost instantaneously, the very first hint at the theory that for many has long since become an item of faith—that the fall of the Twin Towers was in reality caused by explosives planted within the buildings. Rapidly, the Internet became the forum for a great flood of skepticism.

"What happened after September 11," Rostcheck told the authors,

> is that American society bifurcated into two groups—call them America 1 and America 2. America 1 makes up much of America. It is depicted by and shaped by broadcast media. It thinks it occupies what it would consider to be "conventional reality," which is to say it thinks it

"is" America. It is barely aware of America 2, if at all.

America 2, by comparison, is what I'll roughly classify as the Internet domain. I don't mean that America 1 doesn't use the Internet—it does. . . . But America 2's concepts originate on the Internet, which is a different domain . . . The two Americas live together, work together, interact together, but they are not quite the same and they are not necessarily going in the same direction anymore. What happened after September 11 is that a whole group of Americans found themselves abruptly dumped into America 2 . . . the population of America 2 became huge—likely tens of millions.

America 1 is only dimly aware of America 2, and reflexively consigns any elements of thinking from America 2 that it becomes aware of into one bin marked "crazy," then dismisses it . . . By the standards of America 2, people from America 1 are profoundly and tragically uneducated—and reactionary.

Whatever one thinks of this concept of two Americas, the seeds of suspicion about 9/11 have flourished on the Internet ever since. Four years ago, it was said that almost a million Web pages were devoted to "9/11 conspiracy." As of early 2011, entering the phrase "9/11 conspiracy" into the Google search engine returned almost seven million hits.

"I don't believe the official story," wrote Jared Israel, a veteran anti–Vietnam War activist who had earlier started Emperor's Clothes—a website fired up by perceived American betrayal of the Serbs in Yugoslavia—within four days of the attacks. What he saw in "the semi-official *New York Times*," he told his readers, raised grave questions. Why had President Bush gone on listening to a children's story about goats when a third hijacked plane was aimed at Washington, D.C.? Wasn't there something odd about the military response to the hijackings, or the lack of it? Israel said he smelled—and this may have been the first mention of the word in the context of 9/11—"conspiracy."

Even to peer into the world we now enter requires suspending disbelief, giving houseroom to a mind-boggling range of views. It includes the "no-planers," people who question whether commercial passenger jets crashed into the Trade Center and the Pentagon at all. Talk of that began just two days after 9/11 on a website run by a man named Peter Meyer and intended—he told readers—"for thinking people." Meyer and others would eventually be expressing doubt as to whether some or all of the planes involved on 9/11 really existed as genuine passenger flights.

By early October, one Carol Valentine was declaring that "there were no suicide pilots on those September 11 jets. The jets were controlled by advanced robotics." Her account, which ran to twelve pages, suggested that air traffic controllers' records had vanished, that the alleged Arab hijackers' names were missing from airline passenger lists, and that an alleged hijacker's passport—reportedly found in the street near the Trade Center—had been planted. She believed, moreover, that Flight 93 was "without a doubt" shot down, to prevent its "electronic controls" being examined and to ensure the silence of its crew and passengers.

A character named Joe Vialls, meanwhile, cast doubt on the belief that there had been air-to-ground phone calls from the "electronically hijacked" planes. How was it, a certain Gary North asked, that no names of Arab hijackers appeared on early published passenger lists? The omission was "very strange . . . peculiar."

Over the years, the plot thickened. An academic named Alex Dewdney suggested in 2003 that the four aircraft were not really hijacked but "ordered to land at a designated airport with a military presence." Two "previously-prepared planes," painted to look like an American Airlines jet and a United Airlines jet, were "flown by remote control" along the designated flight paths of Flights 11 and 175 and on into the Twin Towers.

In Dewdney's version, it was a "fighter jet (under remote control), or a cruise missile" that crashed into the Pentagon. The passengers from the three genuine Boeings were transferred to Flight 93, which "flies towards Washington and is shot down by a U.S. Air Force jet over Pennsylvania." The three original Boeings were flown "by remote control out over the Atlantic," and then scuttled.

That is but a taste of the sort of theory many could read and some apparently believed—though there are more, yet more bizarre. Who are the theories' proponents? Dewdney is professor emeritus of computer science and adjunct professor of biology at Canada's University of Western Ontario. North holds a Ph.D. in history. Vialls, now deceased, said he was a "British aeronautical engineer." Valentine has described herself as a writer, researcher, and human rights activist. Meyer apparently holds a double honors degree in philosophy and mathematics from a leading Australian university.

There is more one should know about some of them. North describes himself as a Christian Reconstructionist and the magazine he edits as "an attempt to apply biblical principles to economic analysis." Cuba, Vialls declared as late as 2004, would "soon be used as 'point man' in a grand plan to deny American warships and other vessels safe transit through the Gulf of Mexico. . . . America will collapse in six months." The Southeast Asia tsunami that same year, he theorized, was a "nuclear war crime."

Carol Valentine, who ran a "Waco Holocaust Electronic Museum," claimed that Branch Davidian followers did not perish by fire in Texas in 1993. They had, rather, been secretly shot earlier, or shot while trying to escape, by the U.S. Army's Special Operations Command.

Peter Meyer, for his part, cheerfully acknowledges having indulged over a long period in the use of psychedelic drugs—including LSD. He developed computer software for "Timewave Zero," a program illustrating a "theory of time, history and the end of history" as revealed "by an alien intelligence." He reportedly "hopes to be present at the end of history in 2012."

AND THEN THERE ARE the books. As early as spring 2002 came one with a title that said it all—*9/11: The Big Lie.* This was the work of Thierry Meyssan, a Frenchman whose biographical note describes him as president of the Voltaire Network for freedom of speech and secretary of the Radical Left Party. According to the book's cover, *The Big Lie* was "based exclusively on documents published by the White House and the U.S. Department of Defense, as well as statements by American civilian and military leaders."

Meyssan's book was a best-seller, reportedly selling more than 200,000 copies in France and half a million internationally, and eighteen editions in other foreign languages. It was largely lambasted by the media in the West—ignored at first in France—and praised elsewhere, especially in the Middle East. In the United Arab Emirates, where Meyssan was invited to speak, he was introduced as a man "with the spirit of an investigative journalist, of a thinker." *Al Watan*, a prominent newspaper in Saudi Arabia, trumpeted the book on its front page.

The idea that the Pentagon had been struck by a Boeing airliner on 9/11, Meyssan claimed, was "nonsense," a "loony tale." "Only a missile of the United States armed forces transmitting a friendly code," he wrote, "could enter the Pentagon's airspace without provoking a counter-missile barrage."

The attacks on the World Trade Center had occurred "under the eye of the intelligence services, who observed but did not intervene." And: "We are asked to believe that these hijackers were Arab-Islamic militants. . . . The first question that should be asked is 'Who profits?' " Meyssan asked whether the ensuing FBI investigation was "meant to hide from view domestic American culpability and justify the military operations to follow." The 9/11 attacks, he concluded, were "masterminded from inside the American state apparatus."

That, the "truth" camp's dominant message, has been gotten over—couched in beguilingly moderate tones— by a theologian. David Ray Griffin, professor of religion and theology at Claremont School of Theology in California for more than three decades, has churned out no fewer than nine books on 9/11. He has become known as the "dean" of opposition to 9/11 orthodoxy.

Griffin makes stunning leaps, slipped in amidst phrases like "the evidence suggests" and "the many reasons to" in his books. The evidence on the destruction of the World Trade Center and other factors, he has said, "show that the attacks must have been planned by our own political and military leaders." He is evidently a full-fledged MIHOP man.

If the engine of the movement has been the Internet, it is the Web documentary film *Loose Change*—through its several incarnations since 2005—that has carried the message to a vast audience. The film is a fricassee of factoids, its ingredients largely clips from broadcast footage, laced with the voices of skeptics and served up over about two hours. While the film does not hand down a verdict in as many words, it makes no secret of its producers' belief in MIHOP. It is Ministry of Propaganda stuff delivered, ironically, via the Internet, the ultimate medium of free speech.

By mid-2010, the producers say, 125 million people had viewed *Loose Change* on Google alone. In the words of producer Korey Rowe, who served in the U.S. Army in Afghanistan and Iraq, "This is our generation's Kennedy assassination." Originally made for some $2,000 and available free on the Internet, the film has since gone into edition after edition. The latest update cost $1 million, and writer-director Dylan Avery moved to Los Angeles to write a feature film script.

In its most recent, 2009, edition, the makers of *Loose Change* no longer bothered to veil its message. They changed the title to *Loose Change 9/11—An American Coup*. "America was hijacked on September 11, 2001," an earnest voice intones at the end, "by a group of tyrants ready and willing to do whatever is necessary to keep their stranglehold on the United States of America. A group beyond any one man [a picture of President Bush appears on the screen], or any one administration [a picture of President Obama appears]. Until there is a new investigation into the events, we will not go away. We will not be silent. Ask questions. Demand answers."

David Griffin, usually careful to appear judicious, academically careful, at one stage acted as script consultant for *Loose Change*. He has, moreover, been quoted as saying he is doing what he can "to get the cabal who engineered 9/11 for imperialistic and plutocratic reasons stopped before they do still more damage to our country and our planet." The "cabal" he had in mind,

Griffin had long since made clear, was the Bush administration.

Many who have voiced support for the professor, to one degree or another, have been educated, professional people. Richard Falk, Princeton University's Milbank professor emeritus of international law—and currently the United Nations' special rapporteur on human rights in the occupied territories of Palestine—lent credibility to Griffin's first book with a glowing foreword. Falk has written, "It is not paranoid to assume that the established elites of the American governmental structure have something to hide, and much to explain."

PROFESSIONALS WITH IDEAS like Griffin's have associated themselves with Internet groups reflecting their expertise—Scholars for 9/11 Truth, the Scientific Panel Investigating 9/11, Architects and Engineers for 9/11 Truth, Veterans for 9/11 Truth, Pilots for 9/11 Truth, Medical Professionals for 9/11 Truth, and so on. Such skeptics include men and women from differing fields of expertise, some distinguished, some even prominent. Here is a sample.

Scholars for 9/11 Truth, originally headed jointly by James Fetzer, now professor emeritus at the University of Minnesota—a specialist on the philosophy of science—and Steven Jones, professor emeritus of physics at Brigham Young University, focused specifically on the collapses. Following a series of disagreements and a split into two separate groups—with perhaps a thousand members between them—Fetzer and Jones offer differing perspectives.

According to Fetzer, members of his group "believe that the government not only permitted 9/11 to occur but may even have orchestrated these events to facilitate its political agenda." Fetzer claimed that his group has "established beyond reasonable doubt that the Twin Towers were destroyed by a novel form of controlled demolition from the top down . . . and that, whatever may have hit the Pentagon, multiple lines of argument support the conclusion that it was not a Boeing 757." Perhaps, he theorized, "high-tech weapons of the directed energy kind" were used against the Trade Center.

Dr. Jones has called for "discretion and discipline" and strict adherence to "the Scientific Method." He, too, however, espouses the hypothesis that the Trade Center was brought down by controlled demolition. He, too, asserts that 9/11 was an "inside job," that "the case for accusing ill-trained Muslims of causing all the destruction on 9/11. . . just does not add up."

The academic doubters found apparently reputable allies in other walks of life. Glenn MacDonald, a former Army Reserve major who runs a Web journal called MilitaryCorruption.com, thought he could see something in the footage of the underside of Flight 175, as it tore toward the South Tower. "I have seen attachments that look like that—on military aircraft . . . It could have been even a missile . . ."

Morgan Reynolds, who served as chief economist in the Department of Labor under President Bush, has described the official wisdom on the collapse of the Trade Center as "bogus," explicable only as "professional demolition." "We know," said Paul Roberts, an assistant secretary of the treasury under President Reagan who himself has some engineering training, that "it is strictly impossible for any building, much less steel-columned buildings, to 'pancake' at free fall speed. Therefore, it is a non-controversial fact that the official explanation of the collapse of the WTC buildings is false."

Seven CIA veterans have found fault with the official

account. William Christison, a former director of the
Agency's Office of Regional and Political Analysis, has
been vocal on the collapses. In a lengthy article, he
declared himself impressed by the "carefully collected
and analyzed evidence" suggesting that the two Trade
Center Towers and Building 7 "were most probably
destroyed by controlled demolition charges placed in the
buildings before 9/11." He had time, too, for the theory
that the Pentagon was hit not by an airliner but perhaps
by a "missile, a drone, or . . . a smaller manned aircraft."

Military men and members of parliaments in several
foreign nations have raised questions about the towers'
collapse. A bevy of show business figures and
celebrities—including actors Charlie Sheen and Marion
Cotillard, director David Lynch, comedian Rosie
O'Donnell, and singer Willie Nelson—have drawn
attention to the issue. So has former Minnesota governor
turned television star Jesse Ventura, who showcased 9/11
on his television show *Conspiracy Theory*. Most
significant, however, have seemed the views of
professionals with seemingly relevant backgrounds.

Joel Hirschhorn, a former engineering professor who
has often testifued to congressional committees, believes
that studies by scholars and professionals in relevant
fields "reveal the collapse of the three World Trade
Center buildings was not caused by the two airplanes
exploding into the Twin Towers ... Why have the
government and official investigations not come to
the same controlled demolition conclusion?"

Dwain Deets, former director for aeronautical projects
at NASA's Dryden Flight Research Center, stated that
"The many visual images (massive structural members
being hurled horizontally, huge pyroclastic clouds etc.)
leave no doubt in my mind explosives were involved."
Larry Erickson, a retired aerospace engineer and

research scientist for NASA; David Griscom, a research physicist for the Naval Research Laboratory; and Robert Waser, a former research and development engineer with the U.S. Naval Ordnance Laboratory, all joined their names to a petition signed by a thousand architects and engineers requesting a new investigation.

Because the attacks began in New York, because they killed so many people, and because the Twin Towers were iconic, the strike on Washington, D.C., has tended to take second place in the public mind. The crash at the Pentagon has also preoccupied the skeptics, though, and appearances suggest they are in impressive company.

Colonel George Nelson, U.S. Air Force (retired), a former aircraft accident investigator, commercial pilot, and airframe mechanic, said that—on the evidence as he saw it in 2006—"any unbiased rational investigator" would conclude no Boeing 757 was involved in either the crash at the Pentagon or in Pennsylvania.

Air Force Lieutenant Colonel Jeff Latas, aerospace engineer, airline captain, and former president of an Air Force accident board, found discrepancies between the Flight Data Recorder information on Flight 77 and the 9/11 Commission's account.

Former Army Captain Daniel Davis, who served with Air Defense Command before becoming a senior manager at General Electric Turbine [jet] Engine Division, declared himself puzzled by the seeming lack of substantial airplane wreckage at the Pentagon. "Where," he wanted to know, "are all of those engines?"

Former Air Force Lieutenant Colonel Karen Kwiatkowski, who was at the Pentagon when it was hit on 9/11, later went public with a lengthy essay expressing her suspicions. "There was a dearth of visible debris on the relatively unmarked lawn, where I stood only minutes after the impact," she wrote. "There was no sign of the kind of damage to the Pentagon structure one would expect from the impact of a large airliner . . . It was, however, exactly what one would expect if a missile had struck the Pentagon."

From French author Thierry Meyssan to Lieutenant Colonel Kwiatkowski, that is the notion that has proved durable among the doubters. The Pentagon was hit not by an airliner but by a missile.

The perceived Pentagon mysteries have given the skeptics free rein. A group calling itself Citizen Investigation Team claimed in 2010 to have "proof " that "the plane that was seen flying low over Arlington on 9/11/01 did not in fact hit the Pentagon." Rather, it pulled up and flew over it at the last moment—all part, the authors would have us believe, of a "skilfully executed deception."

Only a tiny community of believers, perhaps, credit such bizarre hypotheses So influential have the skeptics proven, however, above all but not only thanks to the Internet, that many people are at least somewhat hooked.

The authors' contacts during the more than four years of work on this book—including both professional and social conversations with hundreds of people—seemed to confirm that many citizens, and not only young people, doubt that they have been given the full picture of what occurred on 9/11.

Such widespread doubt demands corroboration based on solid evidence—or rebuttal.

ELEVEN

THERE HAVE BEEN THREE MAIN OFFICIAL REPORTS ON the New York collapses. First, the World Trade Center Building Performance Study, compiled in 2002 by the Federal Emergency Management Agency, the Structural Engineering Institute of the American Society of Civil Engineers, and other bodies. Second, there was the far more thorough—248 pages coupled to forty-two companion reports—2005 report by the National Institute of Standards and Technology (NIST). There is also the institute's eighty-eight-page report on the collapse of Trade Center Building 7, issued in 2008.

More than two hundred technical specialists, eighty-five from NIST and the others from the private sector and the academic world, worked on the institute's report on the Trade Center. Its conclusion as to why the towers collapsed in essence differed from FEMA's earlier finding only in the detail of its analysis.

The impact of the planes, NIST's experts said, severed steel support columns and dislodged fireproofing—a vital factor—and started fires that reached temperatures as high as 1,000 degrees Celsius. The intense heat had the effect of weakening floors to the point where they sagged and pulled inward until outer columns— on the south face of the North Tower and the east face of the South Tower—in turn bowed inward.

That is the process, according to the NIST, that led the towers to collapse. The institute found "no corroborating evidence" for theories that the towers were brought down by controlled demolition using explosives planted in advance. It said that even the perception that the towers "pancaked," as a cursory look at video footage might suggest—and as is associated with films of demolition using explosives—is inaccurate. NIST's reading of the evidence, moreover, is that there was no failure of the floors—falling down one upon another one by one—but rather that the *inward* bowing, as described in the previous paragraph, initiated collapse.

What ammunition do the conspiracy theorists have to challenge the NIST account, and what is it worth? We came across a study of just that, dedicated solely to Professor Griffin's criticism of the NIST reports on the Trade Center, and written by a NASA research scientist named Ryan Mackey—in language anyone can understand. In his analysis of Griffin's work, Mackey applies what the astrophysicist Carl Sagan called a "baloney detection kit."

Vital tools in the kit include independent confirmation of the facts, not confining oneself at the outset to a single hypothesis, and adherence to Occam's Razor—the principle that precedence should be given to the simpler of competing theories.

The approach of Professor Griffin, the conspiracy author who presents himself as reasoned and judicious, in Mackey's view "violates every single tenet" of the baloney detection kit. Mackey demonstrates as much, successfully in our view, over some three hundred pages. Errors made by Griffin regarding the NIST report, Mackey writes, "are so numerous and substantial as to discourage further analysis of his claims." Here, large and small, are examples of Griffin's claims, Mackey's rebuttals, and on occasion points of our own.

Contrary to the NIST's finding that fires so weakened the Twin Towers as to cause their collapse, Griffin has claimed that the fires were not especially hot, that there was no evidence that the heat was "breaking windows." In fact, video and photographs show hundreds of windows broken, with either flame or smoke visible.

Griffin, who on the one hand argues that the fires in the Twin Towers were not hot enough to fatally weaken the steel columns, on the other hand asserts that molten steel was seen. For steel to have melted, he writes, "would be very strong evidence" that the columns were in fact "cut by explosives."

There is in fact no good evidence—*evidence*, as distinct from verbal eyewitness recollections—that any *steel*, as distinct from other metals like aluminum, melted. According to Mackey, moreover, explosives, "particularly those used in real controlled demolitions, do not melt steel. They destroy steel through impulse."

One possible scenario, Mackey writes, might support steel having melted at the very moment of collapse. That, he says, would fit not with the use of explosives but of "high-temperature incendiaries," such as thermite—the presence of which has been postulated by skeptic Dr. Steven Jones.

Jones has claimed to have discovered "thermitic" material in four samples of dust from Lower Manhattan. There are multiple problems with Jones's assertion, however, the first of them a problem that requires no scientific knowledge.

In all criminal investigations, a key factor is what detectives call the "chain of evidence" or "chain of custody." To be truly useful, evidence must have been handled with extreme care, to obviate questions as to its authenticity or origins. Dr. Jones's samples of dust emerged five years after 9/11, following an appeal by him for dust that might have been preserved.

One handful of dust reportedly came from a citizen who scooped it up on 9/11 from a handrail near the end of the Brooklyn Bridge, then preserved it in a plastic bag. Another was reportedly found the following day on a pile of laundry near an apartment window. Of the two other samples, both also picked up in Manhattan apartments, one had lain unretrieved—exposed to other particles entering through broken windows—for about a week.

To a detective—and in this case a scientist is indeed a sort of detective—such samples are interesting but much less than reliable. In a criminal case—and were the samples of, say, bloodstains containing DNA—they would be laughed out of court. There is no true chain of evidence in any of these instances.

Even were the provenance of the dust well established, moreover, some fellow scientists reject Jones's claim to have identified the incendiary thermite. Elements in the samples are as likely, they say, to have come from material one would *expect* to find in dust from the Trade Center—like paint.

There is disapproval, too, of the way Jones's thermite conclusions—grave, were they to be taken seriously— have been presented. The findings have not been subjected to peer review, the process under which a scholarly work is subjected to scrutiny by other experts in the same field. While most scientists consider peer review essential, Jones's thoughts on thermite seem first to have appeared in a paper he posted on a university website, then in the *Journal of 9/11 Studies*. The website of the *Journal*, of which Jones is coeditor, claims that it is "peer-reviewed." Fellow scientist Ryan Mackey dismisses that assertion as a "masquerade . . . cargo-cult science."

Thermite aside, Griffin and like-minded theorists espouse the idea that explosives of some sort were used to bring down the towers. They base their suspicion to a great degree on what witnesses said they saw and heard—understandably, or so one might think.

Wall Street Journal reporter John Bussey, for example, reported in a Pulitzer-winning article that from the *Journal* building near the South Tower he "heard metallic crashes and looked up out of the office window to see what seemed like perfectly synchronized explosions coming from each floor . . . One after another, from top to bottom, with a fraction of a second between, the floors blew to pieces."

Bussey later recalled having seen "individual floors, one after the other exploding outward." "I thought to myself, 'My God, they're going to bring the building down.' And they, whoever they were, had set charges." "It just descended like a timed explosion," said Beth Fertig of WNYC Radio, "like when they are deliberately bringing a building down."

The skeptics also pounced early on what Van Romero of the New Mexico Institute of Mining and Technology—unlike the reporters an expert on explosives—told the *Albuquerque Journal* on the day of the attacks. "My opinion is, based on the videotapes," he said, "that after the airplanes hit the World Trade Center there were some explosive devices inside the buildings that caused the towers to collapse."

Ten days later, however, Romero reversed himself. It had initially looked to him as though explosives triggered the collapses, he said, but a further look at the videotapes led him to agree with colleagues that—essentially as the NIST would conclude four years later—the buildings fell because fire weakened their steel structures.

There's the nub. So many people, with less expertise in

explosives than Romero or none at all, merely said what they *thought* they saw and heard. "Then we heard a loud explosion or what sounded like a loud explosion," Fire battalion chief John Sudnik recalled, "and looked up and I saw Tower Two start coming down." "First I thought it was an explosion," said firefighter Timothy Julian. "I thought maybe there was a bomb on the plane, but delayed type of thing, you know, secondary device."

"There was what appeared to be at first an explosion," said Chief Frank Cruthers, also describing the collapse of the South Tower. "It appeared at the very top, simultaneously from all four sides, materials shot out horizontally. And then there seemed to be a momentary delay before you could see the beginning of the collapse."

"The lowest floor of fire in the South Tower actually looked like someone had planted explosives around it," said battalion chief Brian Dixon. "Everything blew out . . . I thought, 'Jeez, this looks like an explosion up there.'"

Dr. Griffin seized on these accounts and more. On occasion, however, he was less than professorial in his editing. Griffin omitted, for example, what battalion chief Dixon said in his very next sentence, after recalling that he thought he was witnessing an "explosion." He had continued, "I guess in some sense of time we looked at it and realized, 'No, actually it just collapsed.' That's what blew out the windows, not that there was an explosion there."

Without having done a statistical study of the some five hundred formal interviews conducted with 9/11 emergency workers, it appears to the authors that the vast majority of them referred not to apparent explosions—as in detonations—but usually more vaguely, to loud bangs, thunder, rumbling, booms, or trainlike sounds.

There may even have been some actual explosions, but not ones indicating deliberate demolition. "You heard nothing but explosions all day," firefighter Salvatore Torcivia remembered. "The fires, the jet fuel burning. The nearby buildings had air conditioning and refrigerator units—they were all exploding from the super heat. It sounded like bombs going off. I believe the Secret Service had their armory in one of the towers. That stuff, ordnance, was going off."

After an analysis of Griffin's eye and ear witnesses to explosion, his critic Ryan Mackey notes that all were nonexperts, "relaying their impressions of a horrifically chaotic and deadly experience." There is no good reason to consider the witnesses' words evidence of the use of explosives.

To believe explosives were involved, moreover, one would have to account for how they were planted—in multiple locations—in advance of the attacks. Griffin states that demolition of the Twin Towers would have required more explosive than did that in 2000 of the Seattle Kingdome stadium—at the time the largest structure ever brought down by controlled implosion.

His tormentor Mackey, calculating that this would have meant bringing more than 60,000 kilograms of explosive into each tower, notes that the professor "produced no explanation of how such a staggering amount of explosives could have been smuggled into the Towers without detection, how it could have been placed without being seen, how many individuals would have been required to plant it all."

The 2005 report of the National Institute of Standards and Technology summed up the matter. Its experts had found no evidence, the report said, "for alternative hypotheses suggesting that the WTC towers were brought down by controlled demolition using explosives."

The authors have seen nothing, in all the verbiage of the skeptical literature, to persuade us otherwise.

IN 2010, Dr. Griffin came out with yet another book, on what he described as "The Official Account's Achilles' Heel." The "smoking gun" that he and others see is the collapse on the evening of September 11 of the forty-seven-story World Trade Center Building 7.

Though not struck by an airplane, Building 7 was catastrophically damaged by chunks of debris from the collapsing North Tower, caught fire, and burned all day. When it in turn fell, WTC 7 became the first known instance in the world of a tall, modern, steel-reinforced building brought down apparently as a result of fire.

It was, *The New York Times* reported later, "a mystery that under normal circumstances would probably have captured the attention of the city and the world"—had its collapse not been eclipsed by that of the Twin Towers themselves. The *Times* said engineers expected to spend months piecing together the "disturbing puzzle." In the event, it took the NIST's experts seven years.

According to the NIST, in its 2008 report, WTC 7 was brought down by "fire-induced progressive collapse," a chain of events technically unlike those in the Twin Towers, beginning with the failure of one key structural column. The NIST "found no evidence supporting the existence of a blast event."

There has long been witness testimony militating against the notion that the WTC 7 collapse was triggered by explosions. Fire Department interviewees recalled having anticipated the collapse of WTC 7 from early in the afternoon of September 11. Frank Fellini, a senior chief, said the building was a "major concern" because of the hit it took from the fall of the North Tower. "When it fell, it ripped steel out from between the third and sixth floors . . . We were concerned that the fires on several floors and the missing steel would result in the building collapsing. So for the next five or six hours we kept firefighters from working anywhere near that building."

"Early on," Deputy Chief Peter Hayden said, "we saw a bulge in the southwest corner . . . a visible bulge, it ran up about three floors . . . by about 2 o'clock in the afternoon we realized this thing was going to collapse."

Daniel Nigro, who succeeded as head of the department following the death of Chief Ganci, said he personally ordered a collapse zone cleared around the building three hours before the building tumbled, at 5:20 P.M.

Conspiracy theories on the fate of WTC 7, Nigro wrote in 2007, "are without merit."

ON, THEN, to the idea that the Pentagon was hit not by American Flight 77 but by a missile. Food for that thought has been photographs taken after the initial explosion—and before the collapse of a major portion of the facade more than half an hour later. The pictures appear to doubters to show a hole, amidst the smoke, only some eighteen feet wide.

A Boeing 757 like American's Flight 77 has a wingspan of 124 feet 6 inches and a tail 44 feet 6 inches tall. "How could such a big airplane have created such a small hole?" asked Dr. Griffin. The missile theory, he thought, "fits the physical evidence much better."

The apparent size of the hole does at first glance seem odd. It seems curious, too, that photographs do not show sizable airplane debris scattered around outside the building. To draw conclusions from those visual oddities, however, is to ignore the mass of eyewitness testimony from people who saw a low-flying airliner roar toward the Pentagon. It is to reject a wealth of other evidence and to spurn the opinion of technical experts.

As in New York, no formal National Transportation Safety Board (NTSB) accident investigation report was issued on the Pentagon crash, because the disaster was treated from the start as a crime scene. There could and probably should have been one, not least because— unlike the scene in the aftermath of the New York attacks—there was initially a crash site that air transport investigators could have examined. Both the remains of the airplane and rubble from the building collapse, however, were removed early on—the airplane debris reportedly to an FBI warehouse—for storage as evidence.

The nearest thing to an investigative probe into the Pentagon strike is the 2003 report by a team from the American Society of Civil Engineers (ASCE). Its title, "The Pentagon Building Performance Report," reflects the group's brief—to focus on the damage done to the nation's defense headquarters. The seven-month probe, however, inevitably also involved close study of the crash itself, and the resulting report reflects absolutely no doubt that the catastrophe was caused by an airliner.

To say otherwise, says Professor Mete Sozen, a member of the ASCE team, is "hogwash." "To look at only the photograph of what some people see as the 'small' entry hole in the facade," Sozen told the authors in 2010, "is to see only part of the reality. Much of the facade is obscured by smoke in the photos, and our work—judging by the locations of broken or heavily damaged columns in the wall—showed that the real damage consisted of a ragged series of holes stretching to a width of some ninety feet."

Why, then, do the photographs taken before the facade's collapse not show more clearly the virtually wingtip-to-wingtip entry gashes seen when similar planes hit the World Trade Center on 9/11?

Another, long-ago, New York City plane crash may offer an insight. A plane that smashed into the Empire State Building in dense fog in 1945—a B-25 bomber with a sixty-five-foot wingspan—created a hole only twenty feet wide. The Empire State is a reinforced masonry structure, as is the Pentagon—which was built during World War II. The walls of both make substantial obstacles, more substantial than the relatively fragile glass and steel sides of the Twin Towers.

Here is what the ASCE team's Sozen, professor of structural engineering at Purdue University in Indiana, believes happened to the Boeing that smashed into the Pentagon:

> Think of the external shell of the plane as a sausage skin, and the function of the structural frame as being mainly to contain the internal pressure at altitude. The plane's structure doesn't have much strength. What creates the power generated on impact is what we call its "mass and velocity." And much of the mass in the case of a Boeing 757–200 is in the fuel-filled wings.
>
> On September 11, the Boeing was reported to have approached the Pentagon flying very low, just a few feet off the ground, at some 530 mph. Eyewitnesses said the right engine hit a portable generator on the ground outside, the left engine a steam vault. Then the nose cone hit the limestone facade, and the facade's columns cut into the fuselage. The right wingtip, which hit next, would have been cut by the columns. But when parts of the fuel-filled wing close to the fuselage impacted—given the speed at which it was traveling and its greater mass—it was the *columns* that would have been destroyed or badly damaged. The same series of events would have happened when the left wing impacted (though in reverse order because of the angle at which the plane hit the

building). That is why the gash in the facade of the building was not as wide as the wingspan of the airplane.

By the time the aircraft's mass had penetrated the building—by about its own length—it had been transformed into a violent flow of small and large projectiles of solid and fluid that ricocheted off the internal parts of the building. The ensuing fire, we concluded, devoured the flammable part of the airplane's debris inside the building. The Boeing's tall tail and rudder assembly would have been shattered when it impacted with the edges of building slabs on the upper levels.

That may seem a compelling, credible explanation of what befell Flight 77. The skeptics, however, have long made much of the supposed lack of debris at the crash site. Photographs published in "Pentagon 9/11," the account of the day's events by the Defense Department's Historical Office, however, do depict some debris outside the building: mangled pieces of metal, one clearly marked "AA," for American Airlines, another evidently a part of the fuselage bearing part of the airline's livery, and smaller material—fragments rather than chunks.

The ubiquitous Griffin has suggested that evidence may have been "planted." Dr. Fetzer, cofounder of Scholars for 9/11 Truth, went further and suggested *how* the planting may have been achieved. "Don't be taken in," he said. "Debris begins to show up on the completely clean lawn in short order, which might have been dropped from a C-130 . . . or placed there by men in suits who were photographed carrying debris with them."

Preposterous. Reports, and photographs taken before removal by the FBI, reflect the finding of significant remains of the aircraft *inside* the building: seats, including one from the cockpit still attached to a piece of floor, cockpit circuitry, pieces of Rolls-Royce turbofan engines, landing gear, pieces of the nose gear, a wheel hub, a piece of the nose cone, a piece "the size of a refrigerator," a tire. Some parts, reportedly, bore Boeing part numbers consistent with the airplane that crashed.

Try telling Tamara "T" Carter that the debris at the Pentagon was planted. Carter, herself an American Airlines flight attendant, went to the scene two days later as a volunteer to serve refreshments to the cleanup crews. She has recalled seeing recognizable parts of a plane, the internal American upholstery with which she was familiar—and body parts. She and family members were also shown photographs of items that they might recognize, jewelry, clothing, and the like. "I'm here to tell you," she said a year later, "that my friend's arm with a bracelet exactly like this"—Carter held up a bracelet—"was found. We buried it in Washington, D.C."

The friend, a close friend, had been fellow flight attendant Renee May, who on 9/11 got through by phone from Flight 77 to alert authorities to the hijacking. To Carter, who knew all the crew members killed that day, the loss was personal. "I saw pieces of our American Airlines 757," she said. "If anyone thinks the plane did not go in there, then what happened to all my friends and where did all those body parts come from? Every crew member's body was found."

A random check supports this. Renee May's ashes were divided between her parents, who scattered them on the sea off San Diego, and her fiancé on the East Coast. Fellow flight attendants, married couple Kenneth and Jennifer Lewis, were interred in Virginia. Another colleague, Michele Heidenberger, was buried in Maryland. Their captain, Charles Burlingame, lies in Arlington Cemetery.

Such facts, in the view of the authors, render the claims voiced by the skeptics outrageous, cruel insults to the memory of the dead. Human remains were painstakingly collected and identified for all but five of Flight 77's sixty-four passengers and crew, and for all of the 125 people killed at the Pentagon. Have the "no-planers" seen the horrific photographs of bodies and body parts at the Pentagon, as carbonized and petrified in death as the victims of the eruption that destroyed Pompeii? No retrieval of human remains was more poignant than that of one of the children on board.

"A stillness fell over the recovery workers as a child's pajamas were pulled from the debris," recalled Lieutenant Colonel William Lee, a chaplain. A Barbie doll was pulled out next, followed by the foot of a child—probably part of the torn remains of eight-year-old Zoe Falkenberg, who had been traveling on the plane with her parents and little sister, Dana. Dana, aged three, was one of the five victims for whom remains were not identified.

In light of such realities, Griffin's musings—along with those of others, such as Professor Dewdney and a woman named Laura Knight-Jadczyk, who runs an Internet site called "The Cassiopaean Experiment"—might be thought to sink to the level of obscenity. The professor expressed doubt that "the bodies of the crew and passengers were really found in the Pentagon wreckage. "For all we know," he opined, "human remains from two different sites could have been combined by FBI and military personnel."

So it goes, in the face of all the evidence. Griffin, Dewdney, and Knight-Jadczyk have insisted for years that phone calls reportedly made from the hijacked planes—including Flight 77—are fabrications. His research, Dewdney wrote, showed that technologically, "cell phone calls alleged to have been made by passengers were essentially impossible" in 2001.

The suggestion is that the two conversations said to have been conducted from Flight 77—by flight attendant Renee May to her mother and by Barbara Olson to her husband, Theodore, the solicitor general—are official concoctions.

The issue of whether it was possible to make cell phone calls from airliners at the time turns out to be irrelevant. Detailed AT&T records now available make it clear that Mrs. Olson and May used seatback phones, not cell phones.

In a fatuous, callous account, Knight-Jadczyk suggests that Barbara Olson did not die on Flight 77, but may "have had a little plastic surgery and is waiting for Ted on that nice Caribbean island they have always wanted to retire to."

Theologian Griffin, who likes to write and talk about "voice transformers" and "voice morphing," techniques of flawlessly imitating voices that he thinks may have been used by the authorities on 9/11, does not emerge as having any consideration for the bereaved. Theodore Olson's account of having received calls from his wife on the morning of 9/11, he alleged, was only a claim.

"Either Ted Olson lied or else he, like many other people that day, was fooled by fake calls." The notion that the solicitor general told the truth, he said, "is based on the assumption that his wife Barbara Olson really died, and that he truly loved her."

The remains of Olson's wife, Barbara, were found in the ruins of the Pentagon, scattered in three separate locations. "It took a long time to provide an identification," her husband has said. "But finally they did release the remains of Barbara. And she's buried up in Door County, Wisconsin . . . because she loved that place so much. And she's there now."

Absent evidence for his claim about the Olson calls,

Griffin resorted to innuendo. One "cannot ignore the fact," he wrote, "that the information about Barbara came from Ted Olson, that he was working for the Bush-Cheney administration." It is the notion on which Griffin and the rest harp over and over—in his words that there is "overwhelming" supporting evidence that 9/11 was "an inside job." There was "a *prima facie* case for assuming that the Bush administration was involved."

THE SKEPTICS MAKE much of a document issued exactly a year before the attacks by the Project for the New American Century, a right-wing group that included men soon to hold senior posts in the Bush administration—Cheney, Rumsfeld, Lewis "Scooter" Libby, Paul Wolfowitz, and George Bush's brother Jeb, the governor of Florida.

The paper, entitled "Rebuilding America's Defenses," envisaged the removal of "regional aggressors" in the Middle East, and a continuing U.S. military presence in the Persian Gulf—"unquestioned military pre-eminence." Achieving such ambitions would be a lengthy process, the document noted, "absent some catastrophic and catalyzing event—like a new Pearl Harbor."

The luminaries of the New American Century group, all now appointed to positions in the new administration, got their catalyzing event within eight months. In a diary entry on the night of the attacks, President Bush reportedly called 9/11 "the Pearl Harbor of the 21st century." Later, he would draw the parallel to 1941 in public. The catastrophe of September 11 did predispose the American public for great military initiatives abroad, wars in Afghanistan and in Iraq—to topple regional aggressor Saddam Hussein.

The skeptics do not believe the September 11 attacks occurred by happenstance. They infer, rather, that those around Bush who yearned for "unquestioned military pre-eminence" must have been involved in 9/11. "Who benefits?" asked Griffin. "Who had the motive? Who had the means? Who had the opportunity? Certainly the U.S. government benefited immensely from 9/11 and cannot therefore be dropped from any rational list of suspect organizations."

MIHOP—Made It Happen On Purpose—adherents suggest that 9/11 was a false flag operation, a fabrication to justify foreign wars, and rattle off a string of supposed precedents. They cite U.S. provocation as having triggered the Mexican-American War of 1846, resulting in the acquisition of vast new territories from Texas to California. They point to the mysterious sinking of the battleship *Maine* in 1898. Though perhaps just a tragic accident, the sinking was used to justify the ensuing war with Spain—leading to U.S. dominance over the Philippines, Guam, and Puerto Rico.

MIHOP disciples also recall the argument that the orthodox history of Pearl Harbor itself is incorrect, that—though President Franklin Roosevelt had prior intelligence of a coming attack—he took no preemptive action. Roosevelt's motive? According to revisionist theory, he *needed* the day of Japanese "infamy" to ensure support for taking America into the war.

MIHOP people cite, too, the Gulf of Tonkin incident during Lyndon Johnson's presidency. Exposés have shown that the administration greatly exaggerated the facts about skirmishes in the gulf between North Vietnamese and U.S. ships in 1964. The inflated story was used, all the same, as pivotal justification for committing the United States to war in Vietnam.

Those who think the false flag ploy may apply to 9/11 also pounced, within days of the attacks, on an authentic recent revelation. Documents made public just months earlier showed that, back in 1962, the U.S. Joint Chiefs of Staff had worked up plans to stage phony acts of terrorism—including the staged downing of a U.S. airliner—that could be blamed on Fidel Castro.

The object, then, had been to provoke an American invasion of Cuba and—though the project never got beyond the planning stage—news of its existence led to fevered speculation among 9/11 skeptics. "We must wonder," one Web theorist wrote, "if the inexplicable intelligence and defense failures [surrounding 9/11] claimed by U.S. government agencies are simply part of some elaborate cover story."

Wonder one may, but the authors have seen not a jot of evidence that anything like a false flag scenario was used on 9/11. Nor, after more than four years' research, have we encountered a shred of real information indicating that the Bush administration was complicit in 9/11. Subjected to any serious probing, the suspicions raised by Professor Griffin and his fellow "truthers" simply vanish on the wind.

The investigative writer David Corn, a longtime Washington editor of *The Nation*, was on many matters a harsh critic of the President and those around him. As a serious investigative writer who specialized in intelligence coverage, though, he had no time for the skeptics' fancies. "I won't argue," he wrote six months after 9/11,

> that the U.S. government does not engage in brutal, murderous skulduggery from time to time. But the notion that the U.S. government either detected the attacks but allowed them to occur, or worse, conspired to kill thousands of Americans . . . is absurd.
>
> Would George W. Bush take the chance of being branded the most evil president of all time by countenancing such wrongdoing? Aren't these

conspiracy theories too silly to address? . . . Would U.S. officials be capable of such a foul deed? Capable, as in able to pull it off and willing to do so. Simply put, the spies and the special agents are not good enough, evil enough, or gutsy enough. . . . That conclusion is based partly on, dare I say it, common sense, but also on years spent covering national security matters . . .

Such a plot . . . would require dozens (or scores or hundreds) of individuals to attempt such a scheme. They would have to work together, and trust one another not to blow their part or reveal the conspiracy . . .

This is as foul as it gets—to kill thousands of Americans, including Pentagon employees . . . (The sacrificial lambs could have included White House staff or members of Congress, had the fourth plane not crashed in Pennsylvania.) This is a Hollywood-level of dastardliness, James Bond (or Dr. Evil) material . . . There is plenty to get outraged about without becoming obsessed with *X Files*–like nonsense.

Corn's piece attracted a howl of rage on the Internet from the busy scribblers he had characterized as "silly." Eight years of scribbling and talk show jawing later, though, their theories still look silly.

THERE IS NO REASON to doubt that a team of terrorists targeted four airliners on September 11. No reason to doubt that the doomed planes stood at their assigned gates, that passengers boarded, that the aircraft took off, for some time flew their allotted flight paths, were hijacked, and then—except for one that crashed following a brave attempt at resistance by its passengers —crashed into targeted buildings in New York and Washington. There is no good reason to suspect that the collapse of the Twin Towers and nearby buildings, and the resulting deaths, were caused by anything other than the inferno started by the planes' impact. There is no reason, either, to suspect that the damage and death at the Pentagon was caused by anything other than the plane striking the building.

The facts are fulsomely documented in the material available to the public—not just the 9/11 Commission Report but the reams of supporting documentation and the reports supplied by other agencies. The thousands of pages include: interviews of airline ground staff on duty that day, interviews with crews' families, flight path studies prepared by the National Transportation Safety Board, Air Traffic Control recordings—transcripts of verbatim exchanges between controllers and pilots—accompanying reports prepared by NTSB specialists, radar data studies, the transcript of the one Cockpit Voice Recorder recovered in usable condition, the two Flight Data Recorders recovered, and interviews and transcripts of staff of the FAA Air Traffic Control Centers involved on the day.

All that material is now available, part of the approximately 300,000 pages released by the National Archives —with national security and privacy-related redactions— since 2009. The authors have read as much of it as was feasible, and it provides no support for the naysayers.

The legacy of the spurious doubts, though, has been that far too little attention has been given to the very real omissions and distortions in the official reporting. The conspiracy theorizing in which the skeptics indulged, David Corn has rightly said, "distracts people from the actual malfeasance, mistakes and misdeeds of the U.S. government and the intelligence community."

There were certainly mistakes, and there may have been wrongdoing.

TWELVE

ALMOST THREE YEARS AFTER THE ATTACKS, IN 2004, the executive director of the 9/11 Commission—then in the final weeks of its work—dictated a memo. It was addressed to the inquiry's chairman and vice chairman, and it posed a very sensitive question. "How," Philip Zelikow wanted to know, "should the Commission handle evidence of possible false statements by U.S. officials?"

"Team 8," he reported, "has found evidence suggesting that one or more USAF officers—and possibly FAA officials—must have known their version was false, before and after it was briefed to and relied upon by the White House, presented to the nation, and presented to us. . . . The argument is not over details; it is about the fundamental way the story was presented. It is the most serious issue of truth/falsity in accounts to us that we have encountered so far."

The "story" that so provoked the Commission was the military and FAA version of their response to the 9/11 attacks, a response that failed utterly to thwart the terrorists' operation. The Commission's belief that it had been deceived would be lost in the diplomatic language of its final Report. Zelikow's memo on the subject would be withheld until 2009. The Commission's chairman, former New Jersey governor Thomas Kean, and the vice chairman, former congressman Lee Hamilton, however, gave a sense of their frustration in their later joint memoir. The military's statements, they declared, were "not forthright or accurate." To another commissioner, former congressman Tim Roemer, they were, quite simply, "false."

Former New Jersey attorney general John Farmer, who went on to become a senior counsel on the Commission, led Team 8's probe of the military's performance. He was shocked by the "deception," and explained why in a complex, mesmerizing account of his findings.

Farmer questioned not only how the military and the FAA had functioned on 9/11, but also the actions of the President and the Vice President. In his view, "The perpetuation of the untrue official version remains a betrayal of every citizen who demanded a truthful answer to the simple question: What happened?"

To ESTABLISH WHAT did happen, investigators found themselves plunging into a labyrinth of facts and factoids. Early official statements, made within days of the attacks, were clearly inconsistent.

Two days after the attacks, Air Force general Richard Myers testified to the Senate Armed Services Committee. Though the hearing had been scheduled before 9/11, questioning turned naturally to the crisis of the moment. For an officer of distinction, about to become chairman of the Joint Chiefs, Myers seemed confused as to when fighters had gone up to attempt to intercept the hijacked planes. Memory, he said vaguely, told him that fighters had been launched to intercept Flight 93, the plane that crashed before reaching a target. "I mean," he said, "we had gotten somebody close to it, as I recall. I'll have to check it out."

Twenty-four hours later, on the Friday, Deputy Defense Secretary Paul Wolfowitz seemed to confirm it. "We responded awfully quickly, I might say, on Tuesday," he said in a nationally broadcast interview, "and in fact we were already tracking in on that plane that crashed in Pennsylvania. I think it was the heroism of the passengers on board that brought it down, but the Air Force was in a position to do so if we had had to . . . it's the President's decision on whether to take an action as fateful as that."

The same day, though, another senior officer flatly contradicted Wolfowitz. Major General Paul Weaver, commander of the Air National Guard, gave reporters a detailed timeline of the military's reaction. According to him, no airplanes had been scrambled to chase Flight 93. "There was no notification for us to launch airplanes . . . We weren't even close."

What, moreover, asked Weaver, could a fighter pilot have done had he intercepted one of the hijacked airliners? "You're not going to get an American pilot shooting down an American airliner. We don't have permission to do that." The only person who could grant such permission was the President, the general pointed out, leaving the impression that Bush had not done so.

By week's end, however, that notion was turned on its head. Vice President Cheney, speaking on NBC's *Meet the Press*, said that George W. Bush had indeed made the "toughest decision"—to shoot down a civilian airliner if necessary. Fighter pilots, he asserted, had been authorized to "take out" any plane that failed to obey instructions to move away from Washington.

In spite of denials by General Myers and others, there were people who thought United 93 might in fact have been shot down. Bush himself had asked Cheney, "Did we shoot it down, or did it crash?" "It's my

understanding," Cheney had told Defense Secretary
Rumsfeld, that "they've already taken a couple of aircraft
out." Transportation Secretary Norman Mineta, who was
with the Vice President at the White House, recalled
thinking, "Oh, my God, did we shoot it down?"

At one base, a crewman saw a fighter returning without missiles, surmised that it had shot down Flight
93—then learned that the plane had never been loaded
with missiles in the first place. One F-16 pilot who flew
that day heard that the aircraft had been downed—only
to be told that the report was incorrect. Rumors would
still be circulating years later.

In the absence of good evidence to the contrary,
though, few now credit the notion that any pilot shot
down an airliner filled with helpless civilians on
September 11. No pilot would have fired without
authorization, could not have done so without fellow
officers, radio operators, and others being aware of it.
There was no way such an action could have been kept
secret.

Shoot-down aside, the statements by the military and
political leadership raised a host of questions. Had
fighters really gone up in time to intercept any of the
hijacked planes? If they did get up in time, what had they
been expected to do? Could they—would they—have
shot a plane down? If pilots were cleared to shoot, was
the order given in the way the Vice President described?
If so, when did he issue the order and when did it reach
military commanders?

Getting clear answers to these questions at first
seemed a manageable task. Why would it not be, given
that the military, the FAA, and the White House all kept
logs and records and taped hours of phone and radio
exchanges? The law establishing the Commission
"required" those involved to produce all records on

request. In the event, though, investigators were thwarted by delayed responses, irritating conditions, and actual obstruction.

The FAA said it had produced all relevant material, only for Commission staff to discover that was not true. It had failed to provide a large number of tapes and transcripts. What the Department of Defense and NORAD—North American Aerospace Defense Command—provided was, in the words of one Commission staff member, "incomplete, late, and inadequate to our purposes."

While key sources stalled, Commission investigators puzzled over further versions of what supposedly happened on 9/11—according to NORAD. Colonel William Scott suggested that fighters had been scrambled at 9:25 A.M., flying from Langley Air Force Base in Virginia to intercept the third hijacked plane, Flight 77, before it could reach Washington. Radar data, however, showed the fighters had headed away from Washington. As for the fourth plane, United 93, Scott appeared to corroborate the notion that the military had had notice of Flight 93's hijacking as early as 9:16, forty-seven minutes before it crashed at 10:03.

The senior officer who supervised NORAD's efforts on 9/11, Air Force Major General Larry Arnold, appeared to second what Scott had said about Flight 77— but in a very different context. "9:24," he said, "was the first time we had been advised of American 77 as a possible hijacked airplane. Our focus—you have got to remember that there's a lot of other things going on simultaneously here—was on United 93, which was being pointed out to us very aggressively, I might say, by the FAA." According to the general, fighters had been launched out of the base at Langley to "put them over the top of Washington, D.C., not in response to American

Airlines 77, but really to put them in position in case United 93 were to head that way."

There had been time to intercept Flight 93, Arnold indicated. The "awful decision" to shoot the plane down had been obviated only by the bravery of its passengers in storming the cockpit, and the ensuing crash. In one breath, however, General Arnold appeared to say that his airmen could have shot down planes as of 9:25, when all civilian airplanes were ordered to land, in another that shoot-down authority was not forthcoming until about 10:08, five minutes after the crash of Flight 93.

John Farmer and the Commission's Team 8 grew ever more leery of information offered by the military. Farmer stumbled on proof positive, too, that NORAD was failing to provide vital tapes. It took pressure at the very top, and a subpoena, to get them released. The more material team members obtained, the more they boggled in astonishment. Farmer heard one of his staffers, an Annapolis graduate named Kevin Schaeffer, muttering, "Whiskey tango foxtrot, man. Whiskey tango foxtrot." That phrase, Schaeffer and a colleague explained to Farmer, was a "military euphemism for 'What the fuck!'"

As the Commission zeroed in on the truth behind the military's failures, the phrase was used often.

THE MOST POWERFUL military nation on the planet had been ill-prepared and ill-equipped to confront the attacks. Time was, at the height of the Cold War, when NORAD could have called on more than a hundred squadrons of fighter aircraft to defend the continental United States. By September 2001, however, with the Soviet threat perceived as minimal—bordering on non-existent—the number had dwindled to a token force of just fourteen "alert" planes based at seven widely scattered bases. Only four of those fighters were based in the Northeast Air Defense Sector—NEADS—which covered the geographical area in which the hijackings took place.

Practice runs aside, moreover, the airplanes had never been scrambled to confront an enemy. They were used to intercept civilian aircraft that strayed off course, suspected drug traffickers, planes that failed to file a proper flight plan. Hijackings were rare, and countermeasures were based on the concept of hijacking as it had almost always been carried out since the 1960s—the temporary seizure of an airliner, followed by a safe landing and the release of passengers and crew. FAA security had recently noted the possibility that suicidal terrorists might use a plane as a weapon—but only in passing, without putting new security measures in place.

The cumbersome protocol in place to deal with a hijacking involved circuitous reporting, up through the FAA and on to the Pentagon, all the way up to the office of the defense secretary. At the end of the process, if approval was granted, NORAD would launch fighters. The pilots' mission would then be to identify and discreetly follow the airplane until it landed. Nothing in their training or experience foresaw a need to shoot down an airliner.

On September 11, faced with swift-moving, complex information about multiple hijackings, the FAA was overwhelmed. The internal communications mix—multiple Air Traffic Control Centers, Eastern Region Administration, a command center in Herndon, Virginia, an operations center and FAA headquarters in Washington—proved too muddled to be effective.

There was some confusion over operational language. At the FAA, a "primary target" denoted a radar return. At NORAD, it meant a search target. In FAA parlance, to speak of a plane's "coast mode" was to project its direction based on its last known appearance on radar. On 9/11, one NEADS staff technician interpreted the word "coast" as meaning that one of the hijacked flights was following the coastline, the eastern seaboard. One senior FAA controller admitted having not even known, on September 11, what NORAD was.

NORAD, for its part, ran into problems when units not designated for defense were called in. Such units had different training, different regulations and equipment, used a different communications net. In one area, NORAD fighter pilots found themselves unable to communicate with airmen from other units. Of three relevant radio frequencies, none worked.

Transcripts of FAA and NEADS conversations, when finally obtained by the Commission, were found to feature exchanges like this:

NEADS VOICE: In that book . . . we used to have a book with numbers [Dial tone]

NEADS IDENTIFICATION TECHNICIAN: Wrong one [Beeps] I can't get ahold of Cleveland. [Sigh] [Dial tone, dialing, busy signal] . . . still busy. Boston's the only one that passed this information. Washington [Center] doesn't know shit . . .

FA A BOSTON CENTER: . . . We have an F-15 holding . . . He's in the air . . . he's waiting to get directions . . .

NEADS IDENTIFICATION TECHNICIAN: Stand by— stand by one. Weapons? I need somebody up here that . . .

And so on. One NEADS technician would keep saying of Washington air traffic control, "Washington [Center] has no clue . . . no friggin' . . . they didn't know what the hell was going on . . . What the fuck is this about?" A staffer at the FAA's Command Center, speaking on the tactical net, summed up the situation in four words: "It's chaos out there."

"The challenge in relating the history of one of the most chaotic days in our history," a Commission analyst wrote at one point in an internal document, "is to avoid replicating that chaos in writing about it." So copious is the material, so labyrinthine the twists and turns it reflects, that a lengthy treatise would barely do it justice. Miles Kara, a member of the team that analyzed the military's failures—himself a former Army intelligence officer—was still producing learned essays on the subject as late as 2012. The Commission's basic findings, however, were in essence straightforward, and—based on the incontrovertible evidence of the tapes and logs— revelatory.

THE NERVE CENTER for the military on September 11 was an unprepossessing aluminum bunker, the last functional building on an otherwise abandoned Air Force base in upstate New York. From the outside, only antennas betrayed its possible importance. Inside, technicians manned rows of antiquated computers and radar screens. They did not, though, expect to have a quiet day on September 11. Their commander, Colonel Robert Marr, moreover, expected to have to respond to a hijacking.

A simulated hijacking. For the Northeast Air Defense Sector's headquarters was gearing up for its part in the latest phase of Vigilant Guardian, one of several large-scale annual exercises. This one, old-fashioned in that it tested military preparedness for an attack by Russian bombers, included a scenario in which an enemy would seize an airliner and fly it to an unnamed Caribbean island.

At 8:30 that morning, the exercise proper had not yet

got under way. The colonel was munching apple fritters. His mission control commander, Major Kevin Nasypany, was away from the ops floor—in his words, "on the shitter." The general to whom they answered, Larry Arnold, was at NORAD's regional command center in Florida.

On the ops floor at NEADS, Master Sergeant Maureen Dooley, Technical Sergeant Shelley Watson, and Senior Airman Stacia Rountree were chatting about furniture at the mall—wondering whether an ottoman and a love seat were on sale. To be sure, the orders for the day's training exercise provided for the team to be capable of responding to a "Real World Unknown," but no one expected much to happen.

Then the unknown arrived, in the form of a call from FAA controller Joe Cooper, at Boston Center, to Sergeant Jeremy Powell. It was 8:38.

COOPER: Hi, Boston Center TMU [traffic Management Unit]. We have a problem here. We have a hijacked aircraft headed towards New York, and we need you guys to, we need someone to scramble some F-16s or something up there, help us out.
SGT. JEREMY POWELL: Is this real-world or exercise?
COOPER: No, this is not an exercise, not a test.

The sergeant, and the women who moments earlier had been discussing home furnishings, needed some persuading. Fazed by the advent of real-life excitement, Shelley Watson even exclaimed, "Cool!" A moment later, after an "Oh, shit," she was all business. "We need call-sign, type aircraft. Have you got souls on board, and all that information? . . . a destination?" Boston Center could say only that the airplane seized was American 11—as would become clear, the first of the four hijacks.

No one could have imagined the destination its hijackers had in mind.

By 8:41, Colonel Marr had ordered the two alert jets at Otis Air National Guard Base, on Cape Cod, to battle stations. At 8:46, having conferred with General Arnold, he ordered them into the air—to no avail. Absent any detailed data, they were assigned merely to fly to military-controlled airspace off the Long Island coast. In the same minute, 153 miles away, American 11 smashed into the North Tower of the World Trade Center.

The NEADS technicians, who had glanced up at a TV monitor, saw the tower in flames. "Oh, God," one technician said quietly. "Oh, my God . . ." A colleague at her side cried, "God save New York."

FAA controllers had meanwhile lost contact with the second hijacked plane, United 175. "It's escalating big, big time," New York Center manager Peter Mulligan told colleagues in Washington. "We need to get the military involved." The military was involved, in the shape of the two NEADS fighters, but impotent.

The Air Force knew nothing of the second hijack until 9:03, the very minute that Flight 175 hit the South Tower. News of that strike reached the Otis pilots Lieutenant Colonel Timothy Duffy and Major Dan Nash while they were still holding off the coast of Long Island.

Five minutes after the second strike, NEADS mission commander Nasypany ordered his fighters to head for Manhattan. Now, though, there was no suspect airliner in New York airspace to intercept. When the pilots began to fly a Combat Air Patrol over Manhattan, as soon they did, there was no enemy to combat. As catastrophe overwhelmed the city, they could only watch from high above. "I thought," Nash remembered, "it was the start of World War III."

The Air Force officers and the FAA controllers rapidly began to fear—correctly—that they had seen only the start of *something*, that there were more strikes to come. Where might they come from? It was perhaps no coincidence, they figured, that both the planes so far hijacked had started their journeys from Logan Airport. "We don't know how many guys are out of Boston," mused mission commander Nasypany. "Could be just these two—could be more." An FAA manager voiced the same thought. "Listen," he said, "both of these aircraft departed Boston. Both were 76s, both heading to LA."

"We need to do more than fuck with this," Nasypany told Colonel Marr, urging him to scramble the other alert fighters available to them—at the Langley base, three hundred miles south of New York. Marr agreed at first only to put Langley on standby. Then, at 9:21, came a call with information that changed the colonel's mind—and later led to lasting controversy.

The caller was Colin Scoggins, an FAA controller at Boston Center who—in part because of his own previous military service—had special responsibility for liaison with the Air Force. On the phone to NEADS, he shared stunning news:

SCOGGINS: Military, Boston. I just had a report that American 11 is still in the air, and it's on its way towards—heading towards Washington.
NEADS: OK. American 11 is still in the air?
SCOGGINS: Yes . . . It was evidently another aircraft that hit the tower . . . This is a report in from Washington Center. You might want to get someone on another phone talking to Washington Center.

One of the technicians did check with Washington, more than once—only to be told that they knew nothing about American 11 still being airborne. "First I heard of that," said one supervisor. The source could not be Washington Center, another said. He added, correctly, that "American 11 is the airplane, we're under the premise, that has already crashed into the World Trade Center." Scoggins, however, insisted that he had heard "from Washington" that American 11 was still in the air, going "southwest."

After Flight 11's transponder was switched off, FAA controllers at New York Center had entered a new "track" for the flight into the system in order to alert other controllers to the airliner's *projected* southerly direction. The track remained in the system for a while even after the real Flight 11 had crashed into the Trade Center. 9/11 Commission staff conjectured that it was that track, and emerging information about the loss of Flight 77, that sparked the rumor that Flight 11 was still airborne.

Scoggins never has been able to recall his source of the erroneous information—only that he picked it up while "listening on a Telcon with some people at Washington HQ, and other facilities as well, but I don't know who they were."

The information was a red herring. In the chaos of the moment, however, no one knew for certain that it was Flight 11—as opposed to some other aircraft—that had hit the North Tower. If it had not, and if hijackers were taking the captured plane southwest—as Scoggins suggested—their target had to be Washington, D.C. The realization galvanized NEADS.

"Shit!" exclaimed Nasypany. Then, "OK. American Airlines is still airborne, 11, the first guy. He's heading toward Washington. OK. I think we need to scramble Langley right now ... Head them towards the Washington area."

So it was that at 9:30, chasing a plane that did not exist, three more Air National Guard fighters raced into the air—three, not just the two on alert duty, because NEADS had asked for every plane available. If a hijacked airliner was headed for Washington, Nasypany figured, he would send the fighters to the north of the capital, and block its way. NEADS duly ordered a course that would take them there, but the order was not followed. The tower at the base sent the fighters in another direction— east, out over the Atlantic. Where they were of no use at all.

Chaos prevailed. Four minutes into the fighters' flight, at 9:34, NEADS finally learned something American Airlines had known for more than half an hour and FAA controllers had known for even longer. "Let me tell you this," said Cary Johnson, the Washington Center operations manager. "We've been looking. We also lost American 77 . . . Indianapolis Center was working this guy . . . They lost contact with him . . . And they don't have any idea where he is."

Two minutes later, at 9:36, Scoggins came up on the phone again. "Latest report," he said. "Aircraft VFR [Visual Flight Rules, meaning the plane was not under the direction of Air Traffic Control], six miles southeast of the White House . . . We're not sure who it is." NEADS technician Stacia Rountree dialed Washington, only to be told, "It's probably just a rumor." This time, though, Scoggins's information was accurate. The plane maneuvering near the nation's capital was no phantom Flight 11. It was the very real, hijacked, American 77— lining up to strike.

In the NEADS bunker, mission commander Nasypany had no way of knowing that. What he knew, thought he knew, was that his Langley fighters were by now close to Washington, well positioned for an intercept. "Get your fighters there as soon as possible," he ordered.

Two minutes later, at 9:38, the major asked where the fighters were and learned that they were out over the ocean, 150 miles from where they were needed. Nasypany hoped against hope there was still time to respond. He urged them to fly supersonic—"I don't care how many windows you break." And, in frustration, "Why'd they go *there*? *Goddammit!* ... OK, push 'em back!"

Too late, far too late. Even before Nasypany asked the whereabouts of his fighters, American 77 had scythed into the Pentagon.

Then, and even before the devastating news reached NEADS, Colin Scoggins was back on the phone again from Boston Center—this time with information as misleading as had been his report that Flight 11 was still airborne. "Delta 1989," he said, "presently due south of Cleveland ... Heading westbound." Delta 1989 was a Boeing 767, like the first two planes seized, and like them it had left from Boston. "And is this one a hijack, sir?" asked Airman Rountree. "We believe it is," Scoggins replied.

They believed wrong. Boston Center speculated that Delta 1989 was a hijack because it fit the pattern. It had departed Boston at about the same time as the first two hijacked planes. Like them it was a 767, heavily laden with fuel for a flight across the continent. Unlike them, however, it was experiencing no problems at all—until the false alarm.

NEADS promptly began tracking the Delta plane— easy enough to do because as a legitimate flight it was transmitting routine locator signals. It was the only airplane the military was able to tail electronically that day for any useful period of time. On seeing that Delta 1989 was over Ohio, NEADS sent a warning to the FAA's Cleveland Center. For the airliner's pilots, already jolted out of their routine by what little they had learned of the attacks, hours of puzzlement and worry began.

First came a text message, instructing Captain Paul Werner to "land immediately" in Cleveland. When the captain sent a simple acknowledgment, back came a second message reading, "Confirm landing in Cleveland. Use correct phraseology." A perplexed Werner tried again—more wordily, but still too casually for Cleveland. Phrases like "confirmed hijack" and "supposedly has a bomb on board" began flying across the ether. Information from Delta 1989, a controller would report, was "really unreliable and shaky."

By 9:45, only six minutes after his initial warning, Scoggins was saying the plane "might not be a hijack . . . we're just not sure." By then, though, the Air Force was busy trying to get fighters to the scene, Cleveland airport was in a state approaching panic, and 1989's pilots feared they might have a bomb on board.

"I understand," Cleveland control radioed Captain Werner meaningfully, "you're a *trip* today." The word "trip" was an established code for hijack, and Werner assured control he was not—only to be asked twice more. Once on the ground, at 10:18, he was ordered to taxi to the "bomb area," far from the passenger terminal. Passengers and crew would not be allowed to disembark for another two hours, and then under the wary eyes of gun-toting FBI agents and a SWAT team in full body armor.

It had all been, a Cleveland controller would recall, like a "scene out of a bad movie." Even before the innocent Delta 1989 landed, however, the latest phase of the aviation nightmare had become real-life horror—for Cleveland, for the Air Force team in its bunker, and, for the fourth time that day, for the nation. At 10:07, a phone call between the FAA's Cleveland Center and NEADS produced a revelation.

> FAA: I believe I was the one talking about that Delta
> 1989 . . . Well, disregard that. Did you? . . .
> NEADS: What we found out was that he was not a
> confirmed hijack.
> FAA: I don't want to even worry about that right now.
> We got a United 93 out here. Are you aware of *that*?

NEADS was completely unaware. During the wild-goose chase after Delta 1989, NEADS had been told nothing of the very real hijacking, also over Ohio, of United 93. An FAA controller had heard screams from Flight 93's cockpit, followed by a hijacker's announcement about a "bomb on board," some seven minutes before Scoggins alerted NEADS to the imagined problem aboard Flight 1989.

The controller had reported the new hijack promptly, and word had been passed to FAA headquarters. Cleveland control then came up again, purposefully asking whether the military had been alerted. A quarter of an hour later, nevertheless, the following pathetic exchange took place:

> FAA COMMAND CENTER: Uh, do we want to think, uh, about scrambling aircraft?
> FAA HEADQUARTERS: Uh, God, I don't know.
> FAA COMMAND CENTER: Uh, that's a decision somebody is going to have to make, probably in the next ten minutes.
> FA HEADQUARTERS: Uh, you know, everybody just left the room.

Five minutes after that, at 9:53 and as United 93's passengers prepared to attack their captors, an FAA staffer reported that—almost twenty minutes after word of the hijack had reached the agency's headquarters—

senior FAA executive Monte Belger and a colleague were discussing whether to ask for fighters to be scrambled. Belger would tell the 9/11 Commission that he "does not believe the conversation occurred."

At 10:03, ten minutes after the reported discussion, a full half an hour after FAA headquarters learned of the hijack, United 93's passengers and crew all died when the airliner plunged into the ground in Pennsylvania. NEADS knew nothing at all of the airliner's plight until several minutes later—and were then given only vague, out-of-date information.

"In a day when we were already frustrated," the FAA's Colin Scoggins recalled, "we were always a day late and a dollar short. We just could never catch up."

THAT, THE LOGS and documents clearly show, is the true story of the effort to defend America on 9/11. Why, then, did senior military and political men say otherwise? Why, within days, did General Myers and Paul Wolfowitz suggest that fighters had been in pursuit of Flight 93 and would have been able to bring it down? Why did senior officers, and in particular General Arnold—who had been in charge at the NORAD command center in Florida on the day—make similar claims to the 9/11 Commission?

"We believe," Arnold wrote as late as 2008, "we could have shot down the last of the hijacked aircraft, United 93, had it continued toward Washington, D.C." It was a statement founded on sand, one that airbrushed out of history the inconvenient facts of the general's previous claims. Four months after the attacks, he asserted that NORAD had already been "watching United Flight 93 wander around Ohio" at the time the Trade Center's South Tower was hit. That strike had occurred at 9:03, twenty-five minutes before Flight 93 had even been attacked.

Two years later, as noted earlier, Arnold would claim
that NORAD's focus had been on Flight 93 by 9:24—
when the hijack "was being pointed out to us very
aggressively, I might say, by the FAA." This assertion also
suggested a magical feat by the military, that the Air
Force had been concentrating on United 93 before the
plane was seized. The documented reality—damning to
the FAA—is that no one at the agency reported the hijack
to NORAD in any way, let alone "aggressively," until
after it crashed.

General Arnold would eventually concede that his
testimony had been inaccurate. What he, General Myers,
and Deputy Defense Secretary Wolfowitz had said about
Flight 93 had been nonsensical—though just how nonsensical would emerge only after the disentangling by
Commission staff of a maze of logs and tapes—a
prodigious task.

Why the officers initially told inaccurate stories is
rather clear. In the fuzzy immediate aftermath of 9/11,
before the facts and the timings could be analyzed, they
conflated the flap over Delta 1989, the hijack that never
was, with the very real hijack of Flight 93. That does not
explain, however, why they continued to perpetuate the
fiction long afterward, when there had been ample time
to check the facts.

Former Commission analyst Miles Kara has likened
NORAD's account to an attempt to solve a Sudoku
puzzle—fated to fail if a single early mistake is made. He
put the inaccurate story down to shoddy staff work and
repeated misreadings of the logs.

Commission general counsel Daniel Marcus, though,
pointed to disquieting discrepancies, including the
"suspicious" omission of key times from an FAA document, the alteration of a NORAD press release, and a
disputed claim about the reason for a supposed tape

malfunction. Referring the matter to the inspectors general of both the Department of Defense and the Department of Transportation, he raised the possibility that the FAA and Air Force accounts were "knowingly false."

NORAD's commander-in-chief, General Ralph Eberhart, for his part, had assured the Commission he and his fellow officers "didn't get together and decide that we were going to cover for anybody or take a bullet for anybody."

Senator Mark Dayton, speaking at a hearing on the Commission's work, would have none of it. "NORAD's public chronology," he declared, "covered up ... They lied to the American people, they lied to Congress, and they lied to your 9/11 Commission, to create a false impression of competence, communication, co-ordination, and protection of the American people ... For almost three years now NORAD officials and FAA officials have been able to hide their critical failures, that left this country defenseless during two of the worst hours in our history."

The senator called on President Bush to fire "whoever at FAA or NORAD, or anywhere else who betrayed the public trust by not telling us the truth. And then he should clear up a few discrepancies of his own."

"At some level of the government, at some point in time ...," Commission counsel John Farmer has written, "there was a decision not to tell the truth about what happened." The troubling questions about the way the government really functioned on 9/11, Farmer made clear, also involved the White House.

THIRTEEN

WHILE THE FIRE AND SMOKE OF THE ATTACKS WERE still in the air, top Bush administration officials had hurried out statements on a highly sensitive issue—the decision made on 9/11 to shoot down civilian airliners if they appeared to threaten Washington. Who issued that momentous order, and when?

First there had been the flat statement by Deputy Defense Secretary Wolfowitz that—had United 93 not crashed—Air Force pilots had been poised to shoot it down. Next, on the Sunday, had come Vice President Cheney's account, in a *Meet the Press* interview, of how the shooting down of hijacked airliners had been authorized. Cheney said the "horrendous decision" had been made—with his wholehearted agreement—by the President himself. There had been moments, he said, when he thought a shoot-down might be necessary.

Bush took the decision during one of their phone calls that day, Cheney told *Newsweek*'s Evan Thomas. "I recommended to the President that we authorize . . . I said, 'We've got to give the pilots rules of engagement, and I recommend we authorize them to shoot.' We talked about it briefly, and he said, 'OK, I'll sign up to that.' He made the decision."

Bush himself, speaking with *The Washington Post*'s Bob Woodward, said Cheney had indeed suggested that he issue the order. His response, as he remembered it, had been monosyllabic. Just "You bet." Later still, speaking with the 9/11 commissioners, Bush recalled having discussed the matter in a call made to him by Cheney, and "emphasized" that it was he who authorized the shoot-down of hijacked aircraft.

By the time the President wrote his 2010 memoir, that call from the Vice President had become a call he made *to* Cheney. Bush's monosyllabic authorization, moreover, had transmogrified into a well thought-out plan.

"I called Dick Cheney as Air Force One climbed rapidly to forty-five thousand feet . . . ," the President wrote. "He had been taken to the underground Presidential Emergency Operations Center—the PEOC—when the Secret Service thought a plane might be coming at the White House. I told him that I would make decisions from the air and count on him to implement them on the ground.

"Two big decisions came quickly. The military had dispatched Combat Air Patrols—teams of fighter aircraft assigned to intercept unresponsive airplanes—over Washington and New York. . . . We needed to clarify the rules of engagement. I told Dick that our pilots should contact suspicious planes and try to get them to land peacefully. If that failed, they had my authority to shoot them down."

It would have been unthinkable for the U.S. military to down a civilian airliner without a clear order from the President, as commander-in-chief. In his absence, the authority belonged to the secretary of defense, Donald Rumsfeld. "The operational chain of command," relevant law decreed, ran "from the President to the Secretary of Defense," and on through the chairman of the Joint Chiefs to individual commanders. The Vice President was not in the chain of command.

The generals understood that. In an earlier exercise, one that postulated a suicide mission involving a jet aimed at Washington, they had said shooting it down would require an "executive" order. The defense secretary's authority, General Arnold told the Commission, was necessary to shoot down even a "derelict balloon." Only the President, he thought, had the authority to shoot down a civilian airliner.

The Commission made no overt statement as to whether it believed Cheney's assertion—that he recommended and Bush decided. Shown the final draft of the Report's passage on the shoot-down decision, however, Cheney was furious. For all its careful language, the Report dropped a clear hint that its staff had found Cheney's account—and Bush's—less than convincing.

"We just didn't believe it," general counsel Daniel Marcus declared long afterward. "The official version," John Farmer would say, "insisted that President Bush had issued an authorization to shoot down hijacked commercial flights, and that that order had been processed through the chain of command and passed to the fighters. This was untrue."

Why might a phony scenario have been created? "The administration version," Farmer noted, "implied, where it did not state explicitly, that the chain of command had been functioning on 9/11, and that the critical decisions had been made by the appropriate top officials. . . . None of this captures how things actually unfolded on the day."

THE POTENTIAL NEED to shoot down an airliner occurred to the man in the hot seat at NEADS, Major Nasypany, as early as 9:20 on 9/11— after two successful terrorist strikes and the realization that there might be more to come. "My recommendation if we have to take anybody out, large aircraft," he was taped saying, "we use AIM-9s [heat-seeking air-to-air missiles] in the face." Nasypany began asking his team whether they could countenance such an act. Everyone knew, though, that a shoot-down would require authorization from the top.

"I don't know," said Technical Sergeant Watson, on the line to the FAA, "but somebody's gotta get the President going." "I'm amazed," responded the operations manager at New York Center, "that we're not at a higher level of Defcon readiness already."

It was 9:30 by then. The President had yet to leave the school in Florida. Defense Secretary Rumsfeld, whose responsibility it was to set Defcon—the forces' Defense Condition, or military alert status—knew of the New York attacks but had so far taken no action. A few minutes later, when the Pentagon was hit at 9:37, that key figure in the chain of command would head off to view the damage—and have no contact with the President or Vice President until after 10:00.

Staff at the National Military Command Center, whose task it was to connect the President and the defense secretary to those charged with carrying out their orders, looked for Rumsfeld in vain. It was "outrageous," an unnamed senior White House official would later complain, for the man responsible for the nation's defense to have been "out of touch" at such a time.

Official reports disagree on what Rumsfeld did after leaving the scene of the crash and before his reappearance at the Pentagon's Executive Support Center around 10:15. Rumsfeld said in his Commission testimony that he had "one or more calls in my office, one of which I believe was with the President." The Defense Department's own report, however, states that he "tried without success to telephone the President."

When the President and Rumsfeld did finally speak, according to the secretary's communications assistant, the conversation covered only such questions as "Are you okay?" and "Is the Pentagon still intact?" The Commission decided that it was "a brief call, in which the subject of shoot-down authority was not discussed."

Rumsfeld was still "just gaining situational awareness"—as he put it—as late as 10:35, when he finally joined a conference call that included Vice President Cheney. Shoot-down authority had already been issued, Cheney said, and—as the transcript of the conversation makes clear—that was news to the defense secretary:

> CHENEY: There's been at least three instances here where we've had reports of aircraft approaching Washington—a couple were confirmed hijack. And, pursuant to the President's instructions, I gave authorization for them to be taken out . . . [Long pause] Hello?
> RUMSFELD: Yes, I understand. Who did you give that direction to?
> CHENEY: It was passed from here through the [Operations] Center at the White House, from the PEOC [shelter beneath the White House].
> RUMSFELD: OK, let me ask the question here. Has that directive been transmitted to the aircraft?
> CHENEY: Yes, it has.
> RUMSFELD: So we've got a couple of aircraft up there that have those instructions at this present time?
> CHENEY: That is correct. And it's my understanding they've already taken a couple of aircraft out.

Later, interviewed for his own department's report, Rumsfeld was asked whether shoot-down authorization "had come from the Vice President." "Technically," he replied, "it couldn't. Because the Vice President is not in the chain of command. The President and he were talking, and the President and I were talking, and the Vice President and I were talking. Clearly he was involved in the process."

That fuzzy answer was of no use in establishing when and by whom the shoot-down authority was issued. Rumsfeld's public testimony to the 9/11 Commission was no more useful. The record of what he told staff in closed session is still withheld, and his 2011 memoir added no substantive detail.

The White House itself ought to have been the best source of information on communications between Bush and Cheney, but the White House proved unhelpful. Though the Commission did manage to get clearance to interview a few of the staff members who had been around the President and Vice President that morning, what they learned on the shoot-down issue was of virtually no use.

"Very little new information has been gained in the five White House meetings conducted thus far," a frustrated staffer noted in the final months of the Commission's work. "To a person, no one has any recollection of the circumstances and details surrounding the authorization to shoot down commercial aircraft. . . . Our sense is that the White House will take the position that it is not possible to reconstruct—with any degree of accuracy or reliability—what went on that morning."

Investigators also asked for interviews with relevant Secret Service agents, but the White House stalled. Then it offered limited access to some of them, with an attorney present. It was next to impossible, the staffer reported, to probe beyond the vague stories told by Bush and Cheney in their media interviews.

Faced with this obstruction, the Commission team

concentrated on the paper trail. The White House famously keeps track of all high-level communications, maintains records of phone calls, logs of Secret Service operations, logs kept by military officers, a Situation Room log, a log of activity in the Presidential Emergency Operations Center—PEOC—the bunker in the bowels of the White House where Cheney spent much of the day on September 11, and logs kept aboard Air Force One. For the day of 9/11, there were also notes kept by individuals: President Bush's press secretary, Vice President Cheney's chief of staff, and his wife, Lynne Cheney.

Once again, however, the investigators found themselves stalled. White House personnel sought to limit the Commission's access to the contemporary record, while simultaneously insisting it was unreliable. Undeterred, Commission staff built a chronology as best they could from available logs and from what witness testimony they did manage to obtain.

The record, such as we have it, does not support the Bush/Cheney version of events, that the President gave Cheney shoot-down authorization during a phone conversation sometime soon after 10:00 A.M., after Cheney's arrival in the underground bunker.

The Bush/Cheney version, with its implication of the requisite line of command—Bush granted authority, Cheney transmitted it—does not mesh with events as they unfolded.

The emergency teleconferences that morning—one in the White House Situation Room, one at the Pentagon, another at the FAA—overlapped with one another, making for confusion rather than clarity. To participate in one, senior staff would temporarily have to drop out of another. The conference in the Situation Room—below the West Wing—was not linked to the part of the Pentagon dealing with the crisis, nor was it adequately linked to the Vice President in the PEOC, beneath the East Wing. "In my mind," one witness recalled of the teleconferences, "they were competing venues for command and control and decision-making."

It was not only the teleconferences that added to the fog. Some were to recall having seen staff members with a phone to each ear, reliance on runners to convey messages, and the use of personal cell phones to complete calls when landlines were unavailable. The cell phone system itself was at times overwhelmed.

Alerted to an aircraft approaching the city, just before Flight 77 struck the Pentagon, the Secret Service had hustled the Vice President toward the PEOC. Cheney had been logged in there at 9:58, having paused en route to use a phone in an adjacent passageway—and was to remain in the PEOC's conference room thenceforth.

It was from the PEOC, within moments of his arrival there, that the Vice President supposedly had his exchange with Bush about shoot-down authority. Yet, though many other key events of that morning are reflected in the contemporary record, there is no documentary evidence of the call. It is especially perplexing, moreover, that—assuming there was such a call and assuming the President did give shoot-down authority— the Vice President made no immediate move to pass on the order.

What the record does show occurred, at about the time the Cheney-Bush call is supposed to have been made, is that staff in the Situation Room received reports that further aircraft were missing, were told that a Combat Air Patrol had been established over Washington, and began attempting to reach the President.

At 10:03, in the Situation Room, NSC staffer Paul Kurtz made a note as follows: "asking Prez authority to shoot down a/c [aircraft]." That attempt to reach Bush, however, was apparently unsuccessful. The evidence is that calls reached not the President but only those with the Vice President in the PEOC. The weight of the written and spoken evidence indicates that it was beween 10:10 and 10:20—on being told of the progress of a suspect airplane supposedly headed for the Washington area—that Cheney twice rapped out a shoot-down order.

The Vice President's wife, Lynne, who was in the PEOC and not far from her husband, recorded some of the exchange about shoot-down authority in notes she made that morning.

Mrs. Cheney noted at "10:10":

Aircraft coming in from 80 miles out
Dick asked? Scramble fighters?

Navy commander Anthony Barnes, the senior military officer on duty in the PEOC that morning, told the authors in 2010, "A call comes into the PEOC. I'm talking to a general on a secure line. He asks for permission to engage confirmed terrorists on board commercial airplanes. I went into the conference room and I posed this question to the Vice President exactly the way it was posed to me. I received permission." Cheney's chief of staff, Scooter Libby, has recalled in an interview that the Vice President, asked whether fighters had authority to engage, barely paused before responding simply, "Yes."

At 10:12, Mrs. Cheney noted:

60 miles out—confirmed JOC [the Secret Service's Joint
*   Operations Center]*
hijacked aircraft
fighters cleared to engage

The Vice President's wife would recall feeling "a sort of chill up my spine, that this is the kind of things you only read about in novels . . . We had to shoot down those planes if they didn't divert."

"I asked for confirmation on what I was being allowed to pass back to the general," Barnes recalled. "It was twice. I said it the first time and he answered straight up. . . . It wasn't indiscriminately: 'Splat everything airborne!' It was 'If you can confirm there's another terrorist aircraft inbound, permission is granted to take it out.' . . . I went back to the phone and said to the general, 'The Vice President has authorized you to engage confirmed terrorist aboard commercial aircraft.'"

At 10:14, a lieutenant colonel at the White House passed word to the Pentagon that the Vice President had "confirmed" fighters were "cleared to engage the inbound aircraft if they could verify that the aircraft was hijacked." It was, another officer said, a "pin-drop moment."

A Libby note, timed as "10:15–18," read:

> *Aircraft 60 miles out, confirmed as hijack—engage? VP: Yes. JB: Get President and confirm engage order*

The initials "JB" referred to Joshua Bolten, the White House deputy chief of staff—who was also with the Vice President in the bunker. He suggested that Cheney call Bush, he told the Commission, because he "wanted to make sure the President was told that the Vice President had executed the order. He said he had not heard any prior discussion on the subject with the President."

Nor had press secretary Ari Fleischer, who was at Bush's side aboard Air Force One and keeping a record of everything that was said—at the President's request. His notes up to that point—like those of Scooter Libby and

Lynne Cheney at the White House—contain no reference to any conversation with Cheney about shoot-down authorization. They do show, however, that at 10:20—two minutes after a formally logged call from the Vice President—Bush told Fleischer that "he had authorized a shoot-down if necessary."

OTHER INFORMATION, reportable in detail now thanks to recent document releases, further suggests that the Vice President may have authorized the shooting down of suspect airliners without the President's say-so. It involves exchanges between Secret Service agents at the White House and Air National Guard officers at Andrews Air Force Base, just ten miles southeast of Washington. Though not an "alert" base, its units proudly styled themselves the "Capital Guardians."

Unlike the President—in his role as commander-in-chief—and those in the military chain of command, the Secret Service was not primarily concerned with countering the terrorist attacks. Its priority was the protection of the President and Vice President and those in the line of succession. On September 11, that meant trying to protect Air Force One and the White House itself from attack. On 9/11, according to Commission staff member Miles Kara, the missions of the military leadership—from the President as commander-in-chief on down—and the Secret Service were at times "mutually exclusive."

A Secret Service agent and his FAA liaison had, early on, after the two attacks on New York, discussed the need to get fighters over Washington. Once the Pentagon had been hit, the phones began ringing at Andrews. Brigadier General David Wherley, the National Guard commander at the base, arrived at a run to learn that Secret Service agent Ken Beauchamp had rung with the message, "Get anything you can airborne."

When he got back to Beauchamp, Wherley was help-
ful but cautious. He asked to speak with "someone a little
higher up the food chain," and was passed first to another
agent, Nelson Garabito. Garabito told him, "It's coming
direct from the Vice President." Still not satisfied, the
general then spoke with the agent in charge of
the Presidential Protective Division, Rebecca Ediger.
Ediger repeated the request—Wherley told the 9/11
Commission—"speaking for the Vice President."

The general asked to speak direct to Cheney, but
Ediger said the Vice President was on another line.
Wherley "wasn't going to get to talk to anyone he felt
comfortable getting the order from," he realized. So he
made do with Agent Ediger—and an "unidentified male
voice who took the phone from Ediger" and asked him to
"put aircraft over DC with orders to intercept any aircraft that approached within twenty miles and turn that
aircraft around. If the aircraft would not change course,
the interceptor should use 'any force necessary' to keep
that aircraft from crashing into a building." Wherley felt
the instructions were "understandable enough."

When did the Secret Service pass on this purported
order from the Vice President? Of the various documents
released, one heavily redacted Secret Service memo—
dated less than a month after 9/11—is tantalizing. It
states that:

After the crash at the Pentagon, Commander [Anthony
Barnes of the White House Military Office] in the
PEOC advised . . . that the Vice President had
authorized them to engage any other suspect aircraft. . . .
It was at about this time, I began fielding calls from
Andrews Air Force Base. I first got a call from [several
words redacted]. I verified that they had been requested
to do so with the PEOC. When I conveyed this to [words

redacted] I told him the Vice President [words redacted] Commander [Barnes] was more than a little incredulous. He had me tell the General to get it from the NMCC [National Military Command Center].

While Barnes cannot today pin down at what time this exchange took place, an Andrews control tower transcript shows that, beginning at about 10:04, a controller began repeatedly transmitting a warning that unauthorized flights entering the closed airspace around Washington would be shot down. Though one cannot be conclusive, the genesis of the warning was likely an instruction passed from the Secret Service.

Cheney would later tell the 9/11 Commission that he had not even been "aware that that fighters had been scrambled out of Andrews at the request of the Secret Service and outside the military chain of command." *The Wall Street Journal*, however, has reported conflicting claims. While White House officials said the Secret Service "acted on its own," the Secret Service issued a statement denying that it did so. To the contrary, the *Journal* reported, senior agents insisted that "the agents' actions on September 11 had been ordered by the Vice President."

Did Cheney give a shoot-down order on his own initiative, before consulting the President? The available evidence suggests he may have. To have done so, more-over, would certainly have been more sensible than sinister. At a moment the capital seemed to be in imminent peril, the two men properly heading the chain of command were out of touch—the secretary of defense away from his post and the President only intermittently in contact because of shaky communications. Many might think that Cheney, on the spot and capable, would have been justified in short-circuiting the system.

If he did so, and had he and the President soon acknowledged as much, it would have been pointless to blame the Vice President. If he did so and then persistently told a false story, however—and if the eventual release of all the records were to prove it—history will be less generous.

WHOEVER REALLY ISSUED the shoot-down order, it came too late to have any effect on events. At Andrews, General Wherley had no immediate way to respond to it—no planes were ready to take off, let alone planes armed and ready. He had, moreover, come away from his exchanges with the Secret Service less than certain about the Vice President's order. He sent up the first plane available, an unarmed F-16 summoned back from a training exercise, to "check out" the situation over Washington—with no explicit instructions. Four more fighters took off a little later, one pair also without armament, the other—at 11:12 and after a rushed loading process—fully armed with heat-seeking missiles. Their instructions were to fly "weapons free," which left the decision to fire up to the pilots.

Even then, an hour or more after the shoot-down order came to him via the Secret Service, General Wherley still felt "uncomfortable with the situation." He did not receive formal, detailed rules of engagement from the Defense Department until long after the real action was over, five hours after the start of the attacks.

The vice presidential authorization to shoot down airliners, meanwhile, had made its way down the designated chain of command from the Pentagon to NEADS, NORAD's Northeast Air Defense Sector—the nerve center for the two "alert" bases, as distinct from General Wherley's outfit at Andrews—by 10:31. When the harried men in the NEADS bunker received the order, however, they hesitated:

MAJOR STEVE OVENS: You need to read this . . . The Region Commander has declared that we can shoot down aircraft that do not respond to our direction . . . Did you copy that?
MAJOR JAMES FOX, WEAPONS DIRECTOR [A MOMENT LATER]: DO [Director of Operations] is saying "No."
OVENS: No? . . . Foxy, you got a conflict on that direction?
FOX: Right now, no, but . . .
OVENS: OK? OK, you read that from the Vice President, right? . . .Vice President has cleared us . . .
FOX [READING]: . . . to intercept traffic . . . shoot them down if they do not respond.

NEADS's Robert Marr, and Major Nasypany commanding the fighters from Otis and Langley, were unsure of the order's ramifications, did not know quite how to proceed. No new order was sent to the pilots at that point. General Eberhart, moreover, in overall command of NORAD, directed that pilots should not shoot until satisfied that a "hostile act" was being committed.

Not until 10:53 did Nasypany order that his pilots be sent the following tentative message:

Any track of interest that's headed toward the major cities you will I.D. If you cannot divert them away from the major cities you are to confirm with me first. Most likely you will get clearance to shoot.

THE STORIES TOLD by Cheney, Deputy Defense Secretary Wolfowitz, the FAA, and the military all seemed to fit neatly together after 9/11. Yet they distorted historical truths. The Air Force would not, as Wolfowitz claimed, have been in a position to shoot down United 93, because—had it not crashed—the hijacked airplane would have reached Washington before any fighter pilot in the air received a shoot-down order. The military and FAA versions were similarly misleading or inaccurate—so arousing the Commission's suspicions that it referred the matter to their respective inspectors general for further investigation.

The FAA's acting deputy administrator, Monte Belger, told the 9/11 Commission that his officials reacted quickly, "in my opinion professionally," on September 11. This in spite of the fact that for a full half hour—in a crisis when every moment counted—the agency failed to alert the military to the plight of Flight 93.

"In my opinion," NORAD's General Myers was to say in his prepared statement, "lines of authority, communication and command were clear; and the Commander in Chief and Secretary of Defense conveyed clear guidance to the appropriate military commanders."

That was the message they all wanted the world to hear—that the men who held power in America had been on top of the situation. What is clear, in fact, John Farmer pointed out in 2009, is that "the top officials were talking mainly to themselves. They were an echo chamber. They were of little or no assistance to the people on the ground attempting to manage the crisis." A thoroughgoing analysis, in Farmer's view, "would have exposed the reality that national leadership was irrelevant during those critical moments."

The testimony offered after 9/11, Farmer wrote,

> was not simply wrong about facts; it was wrong in a way that misrepresented the competence and relevance of the chain of command to the response. . . . It was difficult to

decide which was the more disturbing possibility. To
believe that the errors in fact were simply inadvertent
would be to believe that senior military and civilian
officials were willing to testify in great detail and with
assurance . . . without bothering to make sure that what
they were saying was accurate. Given the significance of
9/11 in our history, this would amount to an egregious
breach of the public trust. If it were true, however, that
the story was at some level coordinated and was knowingly false, that would be an egregious deception.

"History," Farmer wrote later in his book, "should
record that, whether through unprecedented admin-
istrative incompetence or orchestrated mendacity, the
American people were misled about the nation's response
to the 9/11 attacks."

AMERICA RESPONDS

FOURTEEN

AMERICANS KNEW, INSTANTLY ASSUMED THEY KNEW, who had attacked them on 9/11. The Arabs.

As soon as news of the attacks broke, before anything was known of the attackers, a woman phoned the FBI to report an experience she had had the previous evening. She had spotted a diary in a garbage can at Chicago's Midway Airport, she said, and the final entry had read: "Allah will be served." That, she thought, seemed sinister.

On an airliner en route to Australia, a flight attendant had kept an eye on a "Middle Eastern male passenger" who was busy on his laptop. Its screen carried a picture of a Boeing 747 and then, suddenly, the words "Mission failed." The attendant hurried to tell the captain. He in turn alerted the airline and the flight was diverted to the nearest airport—where it emerged that the swarthy passenger was from not the Middle East but Guatemala. The "suspicious" activity had been a video game.

In the turmoil at the Trade Center, even before the second tower fell, a New York fire chief witnessed what was almost certainly the first arrest of the day. As he led his men down to safety, Richard Picciotto remembered, he had come across a cluster of firemen and a police officer engaged in an encounter with "a middle-aged Middle Eastern man."

> The guy was dressed in a nice suit and carrying a nice briefcase, and as I pulled close to the commotion I could see there had been something of a struggle . . . One of the firemen on the floor had grown concerned at the man's sudden appearance; the firefighter had once been a police detective, and he felt there was something fishy about this guy, something about his still being on such a high floor.
>
> All kinds of speculation had been bouncing around on our radios regarding responsibility for these terrorist attacks, and the sight of a transparently Middle Eastern individual was suspicious . . . plus he had a briefcase, which could have contained a bomb . . . the "suspect" was in handcuffs and crying uncontrollably. He was claiming innocence of any wrongdoing. . . . In all likelihood, this guy was guilty of nothing more than foolishness and slowfootedness, but here we were, escorting him down as he cried and as we fought back our own terrors. . . . It was little over an hour since the first attacks, and already we were running scared.

The Arab with the briefcase would neither be charged with anything nor heard of again. If he was roughly interrogated, though, if he was even held in jail for some time, he was one of many. Some five thousand foreign nationals, most of them of Arab descent, were taken into custody at some point in the two years after the attacks.

According to a Department of Justice inspector general's report, detainees picked up after 9/11 "remained in custody—many in extremely restrictive conditions of confinement—for weeks and months with no clearance investigations being conducted . . . Those conditions included 'lock down' for at least 23 hours per day; escorts that included a '4-man hold' with handcuffs, leg irons, and heavy chains any time the detainees were moved . . . the evidence indicates a pattern of physical and verbal abuse by some correctional officers." None of those arrested in the United States was to be linked to the attacks, and only one man would be convicted of terrorism offenses. In the words of immigration commissioner James Ziglar, the period after 9/11 was "a moment of national hysteria."

Some innocent Arabs suffered humiliation or abuse simply on account of their ethnicity. In Brooklyn and Queens, districts where Arabs had long prospered, they suddenly faced open hostility from passersby. Anyone brown and foreign-looking was vulnerable, even at risk of physical violence. Four days after the attacks, a Sikh American was shot dead outside his convenience store by a man shouting that he was a "patriot." The previous day, the murdered man had made a donation to a charity for 9/11 victims.

Baseless prejudice aside, anything involving Arabs and air travel now triggered suspicion. An Egyptian pilot at a Manhattan hotel, overheard saying, "The sky's gonna change," faced a grueling interrogation. When the ban on civilian air travel was lifted, some passengers found themselves ordered off airliners before takeoff because they fit a profile—they were Arabs. On occasion, such incidents were defensible. For there were grounds for believing that, absent the order to ground all planes on 9/11, there would have been at least one more hijacking.

Several sources told of an incident that occurred at New York's Kennedy Airport that morning. It began as United Flight 23 waited its turn to take off, when an attendant told pilot Tom Mannello that there was something odd about "four young Arab men sitting in First

Class." Mannello, for the moment busy responding to the decision to ground all planes, took the airliner back to the gate and told all his passengers that they had to leave the aircraft.

"The Muslims wouldn't disembark at first," a United official said. "The crew talked to the Muslims but by the time the Kennedy Airport police arrived the individuals had deplaned ... they left the airport without being questioned." The Arabs' checked baggage, which they never reclaimed, reportedly contained "incriminating" material, including terrorist "instruction sheets."

One of the known 9/11 hijackers, Khalid al-Mihdhar, had reportedly told a cousin in Saudi Arabia sometime earlier that "five" hijacks were planned for September 11. "We think we had at least another plane that was involved," NORAD deputy commander Ken Pennie said later. "I don't know the target or other details. But we were lucky."

AROUND 1:00 P.M. on September 11, the President of the United States had a question for his CIA briefer on board Air Force One. "Who," he asked, "do you think did this?" "There's no evidence, there's no data," briefer Mike Morell replied, "but I would pretty much bet everything I own that the trail will end with al Qaeda and bin Laden."

In the Middle East as they spoke, some were celebrating. In contrast to most of their governments' expressions of sympathy, there were Arabs in Saudi Arabia, Egypt, and Lebanon who were openly jubilant. In Iraq, President Saddam Hussein said he thought Americans "should feel the pain they have inflicted on other peoples of the world." In Palestinian refugee camps across the region, men fired assault rifles into the air. People handed out candies to passersby, a tradition at times of joy. In the United Arab Emirates, a caller to a TV station claimed responsibility for the attacks in the name of the Democratic Front for the Liberation of Palestine. A DFLP spokesman swiftly issued a denial, surprising no one. For Arabs, knowledgeable or otherwise, shared the view of Bush's CIA briefer.

In the Gaza Strip, two men marched through the streets carrying an enormous blowup of Osama bin Laden. Messages circulated on Saudi mobile phones, according to a leading Saudi dissident, reading: "Congratulations. . . . Our prayers to bin Laden!" "This action," said Dr. Sayid al-Sharif, an Egyptian surgeon who had once worked with bin Laden in the underground, "is from al Qaeda."

Osama bin Laden.

Al Qaeda.

The day before the attacks, September 10th, the Congressional Research Service had published its 2001 report on terrorism in the Near East.

"Al Qaeda (Arabic for 'the base')," it said, "has evolved from a regional threat to U.S. troops in the Persian Gulf to a global threat to U.S. citizens and national security interests." It was "a coalition of disparate radical Islamic groups of varying nationalities to work toward common goals—the expulsion of non-Muslim control or influence from Muslim-inhabited lands." Cells had been identified or suspected in more than thirty-five countries, including the United States. On an activity scale of Low to High, al Qaeda was the only organization rated "Extremely High."

Osama bin Laden—"Usama bin Ladin" in officialese—got a page to himself in the report. It noted that he was forty-four years old, the seventeenth of twenty sons of a Saudi construction magnate. He "had gained prominence during the Afghan war against the Soviet Union," after which his "radical Islamic contacts caused him to run afoul of Saudi authorities ... As a result of bin Ladin's opposition to the ruling Al Saud family, Saudi Arabia revoked his citizenship in 1994 and his family disavowed him, though some of his brothers reportedly have maintained contact with him ...

"In May, 1996, following strong U.S. and Egyptian pressure ... he returned to Afghanistan, under protection of the dominant Taliban movement ... Bin Ladin is estimated to have about $300 million in personal financial assets, with which he funds his network of as many as 3,000 Islamic militants." The report linked the bin Laden network to attacks on U.S. forces in Somalia in 1993 and to a dozen terrorist operations or plots—including the devastating bombing of the U.S. Navy destroyer the USS *Cole* the previous year. In 1999, it noted, "bin Ladin was placed on the FBI's 'Ten Most Wanted' list, and a $5 million reward is offered for his capture."

CBS News fingered bin Laden half an hour after the first strike on the World Trade Center. U.S. intelligence, it said, had "for some time been warning that Osama bin Laden has not been heard from ... they believed it was only a matter of time." Half an hour after that, the National Security Agency—which spies on international communications—picked up the first indication that the intelligence had been accurate. A known bin Laden operative, talking on a phone in Afghanistan, was overheard speaking of having heard "good news." Also intercepted were the words: "We've hit the targets."

Airline computers were by now starting to disgorge printouts of passenger manifests for the hijacked flights. "Although in our collective gut we knew al Qaeda was behind the attacks, we needed proof," recalled CIA director George Tenet. "So CTC [the Agency's

Counterterrorism Center] requested passenger lists . . . the initial response from some part of the bureaucracy (which parts since mercifully forgotten) was that manifests could not be shared with CIA. There were privacy issues involved. Some gentle reasoning, and a few four-letter words later, the lists were sprung."

The manifests satisfied Tenet "beyond a doubt" that al Qaeda was involved. For thousands of FBI agents, they opened the way to a massive investigation that was to last far into the future—but immediately bore fruit.

THE VERY FIRST LEAD was provided by the two flight attendants who phoned from Flight 11 in those last fraught minutes before the airplane hit the World Trade Center. Betty Ong and Amy Sweeney had between them provided the seat numbers of three of the five hijackers. "We could then go to the manifest," FBI director Robert Mueller said later, "find out who was sitting in those seats, and immediately conduct an investigation of those individuals, as opposed to taking all the passengers on the plane and going through a process of elimination."

The three passengers identified by the flight attendants were Satam al-Suqami and two brothers, Wail and Waleed al-Shehri, all Saudis. Among the Anglo, Russian, East European, and Latino names of the eighty-one passengers aboard Flight 11, two other names stood out: Moham—the computer had failed to complete the name "Mohamed"—Atta, and Abdul al-Omari.

A bright U.S. Airways employee in Portland, Maine, was already focusing on passengers Atta and Omari. On learning of the Trade Center crashes—two crashes at the same location in seventeen minutes had to be terrorism—security coordinator Diane Graney pulled the records to see if any passengers had left Portland for Boston that morning on the first leg of a longer journey. There were those two same names: Atta and Omari, booked to fly on to Los Angeles aboard American Flight 11.

Graney talked with the customer service representative who had checked in the two men. He remembered them, remembered that Omari had seemed not to know any English, that he had kept quiet and tagged along behind Atta. He remembered that, told he would have to check in again at Boston, Atta had "clenched his jaw . . . looked like he was about to get mad." He remembered, too, that Atta had checked two bags. Graney called her manager, and together they called corporate security.

Before 6:00 A.M., it would emerge, a security camera at Portland airport had recorded the pair, Atta in a blue shirt and dark pants, Omari in lighter clothing, retrieving hand baggage from the X-ray machine at the security point. Nothing about their demeanor, nothing in the expressions on their faces, had betrayed what they were about to do.

It would be a long time before the pieces of the jigsaw would be found and seen to make sense. From Portland, it would be discovered, Atta had called two key fellow conspirators; Marwan al-Shehhi, a citizen of the United Arab Emirates, whose name appeared on the manifest of United Airlines Flight 175, the second plane hijacked; and a Lebanese man named Ziad Jarrah, who had flown on Flight 93, the fourth plane hijacked.

The Nissan rental car Atta had used, found where he had left it in the parking lot, contained a rental agreement in Atta's name, maps of Boston and Maine, fingerprints and hairs—and a Chips Ahoy! cookie package. At other airports, however, and in other hotels and parking lots, there would be evidential treasure.

At Boston's Logan Airport, where two of the hijacker teams had boarded their target airliners, the FBI found two cars, a blue Hyundai Accent and a white Mitsubishi Mirage. The Hyundai had been rented in the name of "Fayez Ahmed," the two first names of Flight 175 hijacker Banihammad, from the United Arab Emirates. Phone records linked him, too, to Atta—they had spoken three times early on 9/11. Hotel stationery left in the Hyundai identified one of the Boston area hotels the hijackers had used, the Milner on South Charles Street. Banihammad had been ticketed for overstaying his time on a parking meter across the street from the hotel.

The white Mitsubishi at Logan was found rapidly, thanks to the man who had pulled up alongside and—as described earlier—reported the strange behavior of the three Arabs seated in it. The car had been rented by Flight 11 hijacker Wail al-Shehri, who had on the eve of the hijackings shared Room 433 at the Park Inn Motel near the airport with his brother Waleed and Satam al-Suqami. One of them, agents concluded, had slept in the bathtub.

Two comrades, Hamza and Ahmed al-Ghamdi— members of the same Saudi tribe but apparently not brothers—had stayed first at the upmarket Charles Hotel, just behind the John F. Kennedy School of Government, found it too pricey, and moved to a Days Inn. The Ghamdis were truly parsimonious. They tipped the driver of the cab that took them to the airport, on the way to hijack Flight 175, just 15 cents.

The contents of the cars at the airports and the hotel rooms, and the contacts the hijackers made, revealed an unexpected side of the Arabs—unexpected, that is, in supposed Muslim zealots. Muslims living according to their religious tenets are forbidden to engage in *zināa*— premarital sex or adultery. Even masturbation is *harām*— forbidden—except in certain circumstances. Anecdotal evidence suggests that some of the future hijackers respected these rules. In one of the rooms they had used at a seaside motel in Florida, a witness was to recall, two of the men draped towels over pictures on the wall of women in bathing suits. These were all young men, however—most of them in their twenties—and probably knew they were soon to die.

English-language reading the hijackers left behind ranged from what the FBI inventory calls "romance-type" books to an old copy of *Penthouse*, found under a bed. Among the toiletries found in one of the cars were a dozen Trojan condoms. It would turn out that several of the terrorists had sought out prostitutes in their last days alive.

Many other, evidentially significant, clues came out of Boston. From tracking the phone records, it early on began to look as though Atta had headed the operation in the field. In both Portland and Boston, agents got started on a key element in the case—the money trail. A FedEx bill in a trash can, calls to the United Arab Emirates, calls to Western Union, an attempt to send money from a TravelX office—all were clues that contributed to understanding how the 9/11 attacks had been funded. Much of the money had come through two key contacts in the Emirates and—faithful to the Muslim precept that prohibits squandering wealth—the men about to die were returning what was left over.

There were ominous indications, too, that the hijackers had had associates in the United States. Agents puzzled over a strange incident involving a hotel room the hijackers had used. "A maid at the Park Inn," an FBI report noted, advised "that an Arabic male answered the door of the room at approximately 11:00 A.M. on the morning of 9/11/01. The man asked her to come back later to clean because someone in the room was sleeping." Who was the unknown Arab still in a hijacker's room more than two hours *after* the hijackers had carried out their mission and gone to their deaths? And if there was a second man in the room, who was *he*? Were fellow terrorists, "sleepers," at large in the United States?

In one of the hijackers' cars, agents found a piece of paper with a name and a phone number, 589-5316, and—scrawled on a map in yellow highlighter—a second name and two numbers, 703–519–1947 and 703–514–1947. The names related to men who could be traced—leading to manhunts, arrests, and protracted investigations.

Washington's Dulles Airport, where the five American 77 hijackers had boarded, was replete with clues. Security camera pictures, and a detailed account by a security guard, seemed to indicate that several of the terrorists had reconnoitered a secure area of the airport the evening before the attacks. They may, too, have had the use of an electronic pass—another indication that the hijackers may have had accomplices.

There were major finds in the blue, California-registered Toyota Corolla found parked at Dulles. The vehicle was registered to Flight 77 hijack suspect Nawaf al-Hazmi, yet another Saudi, and he (and perhaps another man) had left their personal belongings in the vehicle. There was clothing—T-shirts, pants, shorts, belts, socks, and briefs. There were toiletries—Nivea cream, Dry Idea deodorant, Dr. Scholl's foot powder, Breath Remedy tongue spray, and Kleenex tissues. There was a broken pair of sunglasses, a hairbrush, an electric razor, no fewer than three alarm clocks, a compact disk entitled *The Holy Qur'an*, and worry beads.

As well as the bric-a-brac of daily life, though, there was also investigative treasure: fragments of torn paper relating to Flight 77, which, reassembled, revealed hand-written notes; a receipt for a driver's license issued to

Hazmi in San Diego, banking information for him and fellow Saudi Hani Hanjour—another Flight 77 suspect— and a doctor's prescription written for Hazmi's Saudi comrade Khalid al-Mihdhar. There were mailbox receipts; a flyer for a library in Alexandria, Virginia; addresses in Virginia, Maryland, New Jersey, and Arizona; and a hand-drawn map pointing to an address in a suburb of San Diego.

Also, and this was a key to a whole world of inform- ation that would keep agents swarming across the country for months, here were the first traces of the suspects' involvement in aviation: Hanjour's ID card for the Pan Am International Flight Academy in Phoenix; a receipt from Caldwell Flight Academy in Fairfield, New Jersey; and four color diagrams of the instrument panels in a Boeing 757, the type of airliner that Nawaf al-Hazmi and his brother Salem, Hanjour, Mihdhar, and Majed Moqed—yet another Saudi—had boarded on 9/11.

There would be much more. Two duffel bags left at the Ayah Islamic Center in Laurel, Maryland—apparently by Hazmi and Mihdhar—contained pilot logbooks, evidence that they had attended a flight school as early as 2000, receipts for aviation headsets, and a chart kit. In the rental car at Portland Airport there was an Arabic- language flight manual and the name of another flight school, Huffman Aviation in Venice, Florida. Boeing 757 manuals would also be found at a motel the terrorists had used in Florida.

Even as news of the attacks was breaking, people at Huffman Aviation remembered their encounters with Atta and Shehhi. "Everybody was gathered around the hotel lobby television," said Mark Mikarts, a former Huffman instructor who had taught the pair, "and lo and behold there's Mohamed Atta's picture and Marwan al- Shehhi's picture up on the TV screen. I felt myself just pooling into a puddle . . . I was speechless, aghast. I just could not believe that these were the people I had sat next to, had given primary instruction to."

In southern England, former Huffman student pilot Ann Greaves recognized Atta's picture the moment it was shown on television. "It was the sort of face that once you'd seen it you would never forget it," she remembered. "His bearing was that of someone very much in command."

Rudi Dekkers, the Dutchman who ran Huffman, was soon besieged by journalists from around the world. He said he had assumed Atta and Shehhi had been at the school, like his many other foreign students, just to get their pilot's licenses. There had been no reason to inquire about their longer term plans.

By MIDNIGHT on September 11, agents had evidence that appeared to dispel any doubt as to the suspects' guilt and what their purpose had been—in Mohamed Atta's luggage. Atta and Omari had checked two suitcases when they arrived at Portland Airport, a green one and a black pull-along. When they made their connection to American 11 at Boston, however, the suitcases did not. The baggage reached the plane too late to be loaded. Atta, already on board and waiting for takeoff, had apparently been concerned about the bags—a flight attendant, presumably at his behest, had asked ground staff whether the bags safely made the transfer. If Atta did worry that the suitcases would be found later and searched, he worried with good reason.

Atta's pull-along bag turned out to be a window on his life—and on the nature of the 9/11 attacks. It contained his Egyptian passport and ID, which revealed his full name, a report card from the Faculty of Engineering at Cairo University, and an addressed envelope indicating that he had lived in Germany. There were videotapes of Boeing 747 and 757 operating procedures, flight simulator information, and a flight computer in a case. A copy of the Qur'an, a prayer schedule, and Atta's will— written and signed when he was only twenty-seven — revealed him to be intensely religious.

The significance of all that, however, paled beside that of another document. Seventeen days after the attacks, the FBI released four pages of Arabic script that had also been found in Atta's bag. Further copies were recovered, moreover, one in the car Hazmi abandoned at Dulles Airport, another—apparently a remnant—at the United 93 crash scene in Pennsylvania. Neither the 9/11 Commission Report nor a Commission staff document— released later—even mentions the find. An obscure footnote lists the various other contents of the retrieved baggage, but not the document.

The omission is extraordinary, unconscionable, for the telltale pages were important evidence. Scholars who have translated and analyzed them have described them as nothing less than a "Spiritual Manual" or "Handbook" for the 9/11 attacks. Intensely religious in tone from beginning to end, the document is a mix of counsel, comfort, inspiration, and practical instruction—complex in many ways, replete with references obscure to the non-Muslim Westerner—but its thrust is clear. The pages offered the hijackers detailed advice on how to prepare for the attacks—and for death.

The manual opens with instructions for its readers' "Last Night," a time to stay awake, to meditate, pray, renew the "mutual pledge to die," to contemplate "the eternal blessing God has prepared for the believers, especially for the martyrs."

As physical preparation, readers were reminded of the importance of "shaving off excess hair from the body and

The "Spiritual Manual," apparently written to steel the resolve of the hijackers for the 9/11 attack.

perfuming oneself " and "Performing the greater ritual ablution [washing thoroughly]." The manual urged the old custom of *nafth*—spitting—to bring protection. Readers were to spit on "the suitcase, the clothing, the knife ... equipment ... ID ... *tdh* [probably an abbreviation of *tadhkira*, ticket] ... passport ... all your papers." "Each one of you must sharpen his knife."

The car journey to the "*m*" [the abbreviation, probably, of *matar*, airport] was to include further prayers, the prayer for travel, the prayer for arriving. Then the prayer: "O God, protect us from them ... O God, we throw you against their throats and we seek refuge in you from their evil ... Those who are enchanted by Western civilization are people who have drunk their love and reverence with cold water ... Therefore do not fear them; but fear you Me, if you are believers" [Qur'an 3:175].

Readers were to recite repeatedly the first part of the Islamic creed, *lā ilāha illā llāh*—"There is no god but God." Care was to be taken, however, to appear to be silent, to ensure that "nobody takes notice." "Don't show signs of confusion or tension, but be happy, cheerful, bright and confident, because you carry out an action that God loves and approves ... Smile in the face of death, young man, for you will soon enter the eternal abode.

"When you board the '*t*' [the abbreviation, probably, for *tā'ira* airplane]," the manual continued, "proceed with the prayer ... and consider that it is a raid on the path [of God] ... When the '*t*' begins to move slightly and heads for the '*q*' [perhaps standing for the Arabic word for 'takeoff position,' or perhaps for *Qiblah*, the direction of Mecca, toward which the planes did point once diverted], recite the prayer of travel because you are traveling to God the Most High, for you are traveling to Allah ...

This is the moment of the encounter of the two camps. Recite prayers . . . 'Our Lord, pour out upon us patience, and make firm our feet, and give us aid against the people of the unbelievers.'

"Pray for victory, assistance and the hitting of the target for yourself and for all your brothers, and don't be afraid. And ask God to grant you martyrdom . . . In close combat, strike firmly like heroes who do not wish to return to this world. Exclaim loudly *Allāhu akbar*, because the exclaiming of *Allāhu akbar* strikes fear into the un-believers' hearts . . . the heavenly virgins are calling you, saying, 'O friend of God, come!'

"And when God grants any of you a slaughter," the text counseled, "you should dedicate it to your father and mother."

Those to be killed were the passengers and crews of the airliners. The Arabic word used for "slaughter" in the text is *dhabaha*—the word used for the cutting of an animal's throat.

"If everything has come off well, each of you is to pat his apartment brother on the shoulder. And in the *m* [airport] and in the *t* [plane] and in the *k* [perhaps the abbreviation for *kābīna*—cockpit] (each of you) should remind him that this operation is for the sake of God . . .

"When the true promise and zero hour approaches," the manual's readers were told, "tear open your clothing and bare your chest, welcoming death on the path of God. Always mind God, either by ending with the ritual prayer—if this is possible—starting it seconds before the target, or let your last words be, 'There is no God but God, and Muhammed is his Prophet.' After that, God willing, the meeting in the highest Paradise will follow."

So powerful is this document, so revelatory of the planning for the 9/11 hijackings—and the religious mind-set that drove them—it seems incomprehensible that the official U.S. account did not mention it at all. Professor Hans Kippenberg, coauthor of the most thorough study of the hijackers' manual, has a theory.

"To those who investigated the events of September 11," said Kippenberg, who is professor of Comparative Religious Studies at Jacobs University in Bremen, Germany,

> the terrorists were people without any conscience or moral compass, intentionally attacking civilians. In fact, far from being devoid of morality, the terrorists had an excess of it. They sought to bring summary justice to bear on those who—the way they saw it—inflicted injustice on their people.
>
> Civilians did die in the process. But the real targets, in the hijackers' minds, were the power centers of the United States: the financial hub by striking New York's Trade Center, the military hub by hitting the Pentagon, and—if as many think the plane that crashed in open country was meant to hit the Capitol or the White House—the heart of political power. I don't think the Americans could quite handle the concept that the attackers went ahead with what they did impelled by what they believed their religion required. No one who reads the hijackers' "manual," though, can do so without seeing that it, certainly, is totally driven by faith.

ALL OTHER EVIDENCE ASIDE, the "Spiritual Manual" must surely close off all doubt as to whether Atta and his comrades committed the hijacking. How the attacks were planned, and who was behind them, was another question. Was Osama bin Laden the éminence grise of 9/11, as President Bush's advisers had promptly told him?

In the days and weeks after 9/11, the man himself issued a string of denials, equivocations, and lofty comments. "We believe," bin Laden said the very day after in a message sent through an associate, "what happened in Washington and elsewhere against Americans, it was punishment from Almighty Allah. And they were good people who have done it. We agree with them." According to the go-between, bin Laden had "thanked Almighty Allah and bowed before him" on hearing the news, but had "no information or knowledge about the attack."

Four days later, on the Qatar-based television channel Al Jazeera, an announcer read out a first-person statement from the exiled Saudi: "I would like to assure the world that I did not plan the recent attacks, which seem to have been planned by people for personal reasons," it said. "I have been living in the Islamic emirate of Afghanistan and following its leader's rules. The current leader does not allow me to exercise such operations." A spokesman for the Taliban regime, for its part, said it accepted bin Laden's denial.

Late in September, he denied it yet again. "As a Muslim," he told a Pakistani newspaper, "I try my best to avoid telling a lie. I had no knowledge of these attacks. . . . Islam strictly forbids causing harm to innocent women, children and other people . . . even in battle. . . . We are against the American system, not against its people."

A few weeks later, though, the denial was blurred, the outright rejection of killing civilians dissipated. "Whenever we kill their civilians," he told Al Jazeera, "the whole world yells at us from East to West. . . . I say to those who talk about the innocents in America, they haven't tasted yet the heat of the loss of children and they haven't seen the look on the faces of the children in Palestine and elsewhere . . . Who says our blood isn't blood and their blood is blood?"

For bin Laden, the 9/11 hijackers were heroes. "As concerns [America's] description of these attacks as terrorist acts," he said, "that description is wrong. These young men, for whom God has created a path, have shifted the battle to the heart of the United States. . . . We implore God to accept those brothers within the ranks of the martyrs, and to admit them to the highest levels of Paradise. . . . They have done this because of our words—and we have previously incited and roused them to action—in self-defense, defense of our brothers and sons in Palestine and in order to free our holy sanctuaries. If inciting for these reasons is terrorism, and if killing those that kill our sons is terrorism, then let history witness that we are terrorists."

Three weeks after 9/11, a single intelligence report—leaked to the media—seemed to speak as loud as the man's own denials. On the very eve of the attacks, *The New York Times* and NBC News reported, bin Laden had made a telephone call to his mother, Allia. He had always spoken affectionately of her, and she for her part had visited him in Afghanistan. She was on vacation in Syria in early September, and reportedly hoped he might be able to join her there. In the phone call, though, bin Laden said he would not be joining her.

"In two days," he reportedly told his mother, "you're going to hear big news." After the big news broke, he added, "You're not going to hear from me for a long time."

The story seemed loaded with sinister implication, but was it true? NBC could quote only "sources" who said the information—apparently gleaned by electronic eavesdropping—came from "a foreign intelligence service."

Just weeks later, in a rare interview, bin Laden's mother said the story was false. Her son had not risked phoning for the past six years. "I would never disavow him," she went on. "Osama has always been a good son to me . . . very kind, very considerate and very sweet . . . I love him and care about him." Allia was convinced, she said, that bin Laden was not responsible for 9/11.

In November, two months after the attacks, bin Laden gave the Pakistani newspaperman Hamid Mir a lengthy interview—one of only two interviews he granted in the past decade. He had talked with Mir twice before, seemed to think his reporting had been fair, and arranged for the journalist to be brought to him—trussed up and blindfolded during a lengthy jeep ride—at a secret hideout.

Bin Laden responded to most of the journalist's forty prepared questions, but on occasion made it clear he did not wish to go on the record. "I asked Osama whether he had done 9/11," Mir said in 2009, "and he asked me to turn off my recording machine. Then he said, 'Yes.' But when I turned on my machine again, he said, 'No.'"

FIFTEEN

THE TRUTH OFFICIALDOM GAVE US, THAT YOUNG MEN loyal to al Qaeda and bin Laden were responsible for carrying out the attacks, is not the full story. The 9/11 Commission varnished the story for public consumption, spared the American people knowledge of troubling factors and issues—perhaps because they were highly sensitive, perhaps because pursuit of them involved banging on doors that seemed best left closed, perhaps simply because they remained unresolved.

The Nation's David Corn, rightly dismissive of most of the skeptics' ramblings, has made the point that serious matters have yet to be explained. "Without conspiracy theories," he wrote, "there is much to wonder about September 11th ... official answers ought not to be absorbed automatically without questions." Others agreed that what Corn saw as the failings of the U.S. government and the intelligence community should be exposed—and this well after publication of the 9/11 Commission Report.

No one at all, reportedly, has been held accountable for the mis-steps that preceded the September 11 attacks. There were no known dismissals, demotions, or even formal reprimands—at any level in the government or in government agencies. "No one has taken the fall for the failure to prevent attacks that killed 2,819 people," former Bush White House aide Richard Falkenrath noted following publication of the Report. "They could perhaps have been prevented . . . the starting point in any after the fact analysis should always be the concept of personal responsibility."

"Why did 9/11 happen on George Bush's watch," Senator Patrick Leahy asked in 2006, "when he had clear warnings that it was going to happen? Why did they allow it to happen?" Just what the President and his senior aides had been told, when they had been told it, and how they responded, had long been a vexatious issue. Why did CIA director Tenet tell the Commission that he had not briefed Bush in August 2001, only for it to emerge that he in fact saw him twice?

The previous month, according to Tenet, he and top aides had met with National Security Adviser Condoleezza Rice to deliver a dire warning that a major al Qaeda attack was imminent. According to one of America's most distinguished reporters, she responded by giving them the "brush-off." Rice said she could not recall the meeting. The record shows the 9/11 Commission was told of the meeting, but there was no mention of it in the 9/11 Commission Report. Why not?

"As each day goes by," Senator Max Cleland had said shortly before resigning as a member of the 9/11 Commission, "we learn that this government knew a whole lot more about these terrorists before September 11 than it ever admitted." Such doubts proved durable.

The agency most directly responsible for protecting the almost two million people who took flights every day in the States, the Federal Aviation Administration, seems to have been at best ineffectual, at worst fatally irresponsible, in the months and years before the attacks. The 9/11 Commission heard shocking testimony, which went unmentioned in its Report, from an experienced FAA team leader whose job it was to conduct undercover tests on airport security.

After September 11, said Bogdan Dzakovic, "officials from FAA as well as other government agencies made defensive statements such as, 'How could we have known this was going to happen?' The truth is, they did know. . . . FAA very deliberately orchestrated a dangerous facade of security . . . They knew how vulnerable aviation security was. They knew the terrorist threat was rising, but gambled nothing would happen if we kept the vulnerability secret and didn't disrupt the airline industry. Our country lost that bet."

In the spring and summer of 2001, half of the FAA's daily summaries had mentioned bin Laden or al Qaeda. In July, it had "encouraged" all airlines to "exercise prudence and demonstrate a high degree of alertness." There was little or no real drive to ensure that better security was enforced, however, no sense of urgency at the level that mattered.

The US Airways ticket taker who checked in Atta and Omari in Portland for the first leg of their journey, Michael Touhey, would recall having had a "bad feeling" about them. They arrived just minutes before departure and carried expensive one-way, first-class tickets— though most business travelers fly round-trip. Had he received instructions to be more vigilant, he said later, he thought he would have acted differently. He might have ordered a search of the men's bags, which could have turned up suspicious items. There had been no such instructions, however, and Touhey let the men go on their way.

"I've been with American for twenty-nine years," said Rosemary Dillard, whose husband died aboard Flight 77. "My job was supervision over all the flight attendants who flew out of National, Baltimore or Dulles. In the summer of 2001, we had absolutely no warnings about any threats of hijacking or terrorism, from the airline or from the FAA." A key part of the FAA's mandate is to keep air travelers safe, and in that it signally failed.

The intelligence agencies failed, too, in ways that could perhaps have changed the course of history. The CIA and the FBI were both at fault, in part because of sheer inefficiency. The most scathing criticism of the FBI has come from insiders.

"September the 11th," said FBI agent Robert Wright, who had long been assigned to a Terrorism Task Force in Chicago, "is a direct result of the incompetence of the FBI's International Terrorism Unit. No doubt about that. . . . You can't know the things I know and not go public." Wright was joined in his protest—over the bungled handling of a counterterrorist operation two years earlier—by a fellow agent and a former assistant U.S. attorney.

In July 2001, exactly two months before the attack, an FBI agent in Phoenix had reported his suspicion that it was "more than a coincidence that subjects who are supporters of [bin Laden] are attending civil aviation universities/colleges in the state of Arizona. . . . Phoenix believes that it is highly probable that [bin Laden] has an established support network in place in Arizona." The memo recommended checks on flight schools and on the visa details of foreign students attending them, not only in Arizona but around the country.

After 9/11, the agent's apprehension was proven to have been entirely justified. One of the four hijacker pilots had indeed trained in Arizona, the other three at Florida flight schools. Two others, already known to the CIA as terrorist suspects, had for a while taken flight training in California. FBI headquarters, however, had virtually ignored the agent's prescient memo. No effective action was taken or planned.

Another, even more glaring FBI failure occurred just before the attacks, when agents in the Minneapolis field office reported their grave concern about a then-obscure French Moroccan flight student named Zacarias Moussaoui. The flight school at which he was studying had reported that he was behaving suspiciously, and a check with French intelligence revealed that he had links to extremism.

The Minneapolis agents, who wanted clearance to search the suspect's baggage, were rebuffed time and time again with legalistic objections sent from headquarters. Only on September 11, after the strikes on the Trade Center, was the search warrant approved. Moussaoui is now serving a life sentence for conspiracy to commit acts of terror and air piracy. Evidence found in his belongings and detainee statements would link Moussaoui to two of the most significant of the 9/11 conspirators.

Information that emerged in 2005 suggested that the Defense Intelligence Agency had failed to inform the FBI of intelligence on four of the future hijackers, including their leader, Mohamed Atta, when it was obtained in early 2000. The lead, provided by a U.S. Army officer, and initially supported by several other members of the DIA operation concerned, went nowhere. The Defense Department refused to allow those involved to testify to a Senate committee, and relevant documents have been destroyed. The Bush White House had allegedly been briefed on the matter within weeks of 9/11, as— much later—9/11 Commission staff had been. The episode went unmentioned, however, in the 9/11 Commission Report.

And then there is the CIA. The month before 9/11, the Agency's inspector general produced a report lauding the CIA's Counterterrorist Center as a "well-managed component that successfully carries out the Agency's responsibilities to collect and analyze intelligence on international terrorism." In 2007, however, and then only when Congress demanded it, the Agency belatedly produced an accountability review admitting that—before 9/11—the Counterterrorist Center had been "not used effectively."

It got worse. Most of those in the unit responsible for bin Laden, the inspector general reported, had not had "the operational experience, expertise and training necessary to accomplish their mission." There had been "no examination of the potential for terrorists to use aircraft as weapons," "no comprehensive analysis that put into context the threats received in the spring and summer of 2001."

Senator Bob Graham, who in 2001 was chairman of the Senate Intelligence Committee—and later chaired the House-Senate Joint Inquiry into the intelligence community's pre-9/11 failures—has cited a dozen "points at which the plot could have been discovered and potentially thwarted." "Both the CIA and the FBI," he wrote, "had information that they withheld from one another and from state and local law enforcement and that, if shared, would have cracked the terrorists' plot."

One item the CIA withheld from the FBI has never been satisfactorily explained. Agency officials had to admit—initially on the afternoon of 9/11 to a reportedly irritated President Bush—that the CIA had known a great deal about two of the future hijackers for the best part of two years. They had known the men's names, where they came from, the fact that they were al Qaeda operatives, that they had visas to enter the United States—and that one of them certainly, perhaps both, had long since actually arrived in the United States.

226 THE ELEVENTH DAY

Why did the CIA hold this knowledge close, purposefully avoiding sharing it with the FBI and U.S. Immigration until just before the attacks? The CIA has attempted to explain the lapse as incompetence—human error. The complex available information on the subject, however, may suggest a different truth. Some at the FBI came to suspect that the Agency held what it knew close because it had hopes of turning the two terrorists, in effect recruiting them.

Or did the CIA contemplate keeping the men under surveillance following their arrival in the United States? Absent special clearance at presidential level, it would have been unlawful for the Agency to do that. Domestic surveillance is properly a task for the FBI. Alternatively, could it be that the CIA relied on an information flow from another, foreign, intelligence organization? If so, which organization?

One candidate, some might think, is the Israeli Mossad, a service uniquely committed to and experienced in countering Arab terrorism. Fragments of information suggest Mossad may indeed have had an interest in the 9/11 plotters before the attacks. Another candidate, though few would have thought it, is the General Intelligence Department—or GID—the intelligence service of Saudi Arabia. The Saudi element of the 9/11 story is multifaceted, complete with internal contradictions—and highly disquieting.

Saudi Arabia: leading supplier of oil to the United States in 2001, with reserves expected to last until close to the end of the century, a nation that has spent billions on American weaponry, in many ways America's most powerful Arab friend in the Middle East—and the birthplace of Osama bin Laden and fifteen of the nineteen 9/11 hijackers.

Though bin Laden was an exile, a self-declared foe of

the regime, disowned in public statements by the Saudi royals and by his plutocrat brothers, many believed that was only part of the story—that powerful elements in his homeland had never ceased to support his campaign against the West in the name of Islam.

The Saudi GID, said since 9/11 to have fed inform-ation on the future hijackers to its counterparts in Washington, had long been regarded by the CIA's bin Laden specialists as a "hostile service." If the GID did share information, was it genuine? Or was it, by design, bogus and misleading?

The Saudi factor is one of the wild cards in the 9/11 investigation. Suspicion that Saudi Arabia had supported the hijack operation was rife for a while after 9/11, then faded—not so much because there was no evidence but because the suspicion was snuffed out. The possibility of Saudi involvement, a vital issue, will be a major focus in the closing chapters of this book.

In the immediate aftermath of September 11, only those in the inner councils of government and the intelligence services were mulling the deeper questions. The loud public call was for hitting back, striking those believed to have been the organizers, those who had been in direct command, hard and swiftly.

SIXTEEN

ON SEPTEMBER 14, 2001, THREE DAYS AFTER THE attacks, the words marching across the great, glittering signboard in Times Square had read: "BUSH CALLS UP 50,000 RESERVISTS." President Bush's motorcade drove past the sign that evening at the end of a day of prolonged high emotion—a memorial service at the National Cathedral in Washington, a visit to the pulverized ruins of the World Trade Center in New York, and a gut-wrenching two hours talking with relatives of the hundreds of firefighters and police who were missing and believed dead.

"After all the sadness and the hugging and the love and the families," the President's aide Ari Fleischer recalled thinking as the White House motorcade rolled down 42nd Street, "you could just feel the winds of war were blowing."

The way America would react to the al Qaeda assault had rapidly become clear. Evident within forty-five minutes of the first strike on the World Trade Center, when Bush spoke to the nation from the schoolroom in Florida, promising to "hunt down and to find those folks who committed this act." Evident two hours later at an Air Force base in Louisiana, away from the microphones, when he told aides, "We're gonna get the bastards."

Evident in everything he said thereafter, in private or in public.

The vast majority of the American people agreed that there must be severe retribution. The symbol of their resolve appeared within eight hours of 9/11, when a firefighter named Dan McWilliams took a national flag from a yacht moored in the Hudson nearby and—helped by fellow firemen—raised it high in the rubble at Ground Zero. The photographer who snapped them doing it realized instantly how the image would resonate. Right down to the angle of the flag as it went up, it resembled the raising of the Stars and Stripes by U.S. Marines during the battle of Iwo Jima in World War II.

At a memorial service on the 14th, with four U.S. presidents in the congregation, the National Cathedral reverberated to the roar of almost a thousand people singing "The Battle Hymn of the Republic": "He hath loosed the fateful lightning of His terrible swift sword . . . the watch fires of a hundred circling camps . . . the trumpet that shall never call retreat . . . Let us die to make men free."

The September 11 onslaught had been an act of war, and the response was to be war. Many tens of thousands—the vast majority of them not Americans—were to die or be wounded in what Bush described as the coming "monumental struggle between good and evil." He made clear from the start that bin Laden and his followers would not be the only targets. Speechwriter Michael Gerson, briefed on the message the President wanted to convey in his address to the nation on the night of 9/11, has recalled writing in a draft that the United States would "make no distinction between those who planned these acts and those who permitted or tolerated or encouraged them."

Bush insisted that the language be clearer. In the final,

amended version, he said the U.S. would "make no distinction between those who planned these acts and those who *harbor* them." Within an hour of the television appearance, he was discussing what that would mean with his war council—by now comprising Cheney, Rumsfeld, Secretary of State Colin Powell, Tenet, Rice, Richard Clarke, FBI director Robert Mueller, Attorney General John Ashcroft, key generals, and a few others.

In Afghanistan, by contrast, Taliban foreign minister Wakil Muttawakil had been asked whether he was certain bin Laden had not been involved in the attacks. "Naturally," he said. Were his government's restrictions on bin Laden's military activity on Afghan soil still in force? "Naturally," he said, and played down the likelihood of U.S. retaliation against Afghanistan.

Seven thousand miles away, though, the talk in the Situation Room at the White House was uncompromising. The Taliban were soon to propose trying bin Laden in Afghanistan or handing him over for trial in another Muslim country, but America was to turn a deaf ear. "We're not only going to strike the rattlesnake," Bush said at this time. "We're going to strike the rancher."

The administration never even considered negotiating with the Taliban, Rice said later. Washington would eventually issue a formal ultimatum—promptly rejected —demanding that Afghanistan hand over the Saudi exile, or "share in his fate."

The posture of Afghanistan's neighbor Pakistan—with its schizophrenic mix of ties to the Taliban, dependence on Washington, and divided religious and tribal loyalties— would now be pivotal. As Secretary of State Powell would recall it, Pakistan's president, Pervez Musharraf, "had to be told in no uncertain terms that it was time to choose sides." The way Musharraf remembered it being reported to him, those terms included being told that "if we chose the terrorists, then we should be prepared to be bombed back to the Stone Age." He bent to almost all the American demands for cooperation.

There were voices in Washington raising the notion of retaliation against nations other than Afghanistan. "Need to move swiftly," Rumsfeld's aide Stephen Cambone, noting the defense secretary's comments on the afternoon of 9/11, had jotted: "Near term target needs—go massive—sweep it all up . . . need to do so to get anything useful . . . thing[s] related or not." "I know a lot," Rumsfeld would say publicly within days, "and what I have said, as clearly as I know how, is that states are supporting these people."

That first night at Bush's war council, the 9/11 Commission determined, Rumsfeld had "urged the President and the principals to think broadly about who might have harbored the attackers, including Iraq, Afghanistan, Libya, Sudan, and Iran." Though bin Laden was a Saudi and most of the hijackers Saudis, the possibility of that country's involvement was apparently not raised.

It was then, though, that Rumsfeld jumped at what he saw as the need to "do Iraq." "Everyone looked at him," Richard Clarke recalled. "At least I looked at him and Powell looked at him, like, 'What the hell are you talking about?' And he said—I'll never forget this—'There just aren't enough targets in Afghanistan. We need to bomb something else to prove that we're, you know, big and strong and not going to be pushed around by these kind of attacks.' And I made the point certainly that night, and I think Powell acknowledged it, that Iraq had nothing to do with 9/11.

"That didn't seem to faze Rumsfeld. . . . It shouldn't have come as a surprise. It really didn't, because from the first weeks of the administration they were talking about

Iraq. I just found it a little disgusting that they were talking about it while the bodies were still burning in the Pentagon and at the World Trade Center."

President Bush kept the immediate focus on bin Laden and Afghanistan, but he did not ignore Rumsfeld. On the evening of the 12th, Clarke recalled, Bush quietly took aside his counterterrorism coordinator and a few colleagues to say, "Look . . . I want you, as soon as you can, to go back over everything, everything. See if Saddam did this. See if he's linked in any way . . . Just look. I want to know any shred."

"Absolutely, we will look . . . again," Clarke responded. "But, you know, we have looked several times for state sponsorship of al Qaeda and not found any real linkages to Iraq. Iran plays a little, as does Pakistan, and Saudi Arabia, Yemen."

Bush looked irritated. He replied, "Look into Iraq, Saddam," and walked away. Clarke's people would report that there was no evidence of cooperation between al Qaeda and Iraq. Pressure on the President to act against Iraq, however, continued. His formal order for military action against terrorism, a week after 9/11, would include an instruction to the Defense Department to prepare a contingency plan for strikes against Iraq—and perhaps the occupation of its oilfields.

THE WEEKEND FOLLOWING the attacks, after the frenzy of the first fearful days, Bush flew his war council to the presidential retreat at Camp David. Their deliberations began, as always during his presidency, with a moment of devotion. The meeting the day before, the Friday, had opened with a prayer spoken by Defense Secretary Rumsfeld. He had asked the Lord for "patience to measure our lust for action," for resolve and patience. In the wooded peace of Camp David, nevertheless, the debate focused on the storm of violence that was coming.

Across the vast table from the President, CIA director Tenet and his counterterrorism chief Cofer Black briefed their colleagues on the Agency's plan for "Destroying International Terrorism." They described what they called the "Initial Hook," an operation designed to trap al Qaeda inside Afghanistan and destroy it. It was to be achieved by a numerically small CIA paramilitary component and U.S. Special Forces, working with Afghan forces that had long been fighting the Taliban. The chairman of the Joint Chiefs, General Hugh Shelton, outlined the crucial bomb and missile strikes that would precede and support the operation. "When we're through with them," Black had assured Bush, the al Qaeda terrorists would "have flies walking across their eyeballs."

The war planners dined that evening on what the President called "comfort food," fried chicken and mashed potatoes. Afterward, Attorney General Ashcroft accompanied Condoleezza Rice on the piano as she sang "Amazing Grace." Treasury Secretary Paul O'Neill sat in an armchair in the corner perusing the briefing documents the CIA had brought along that day. He read of measures to track and cut off the flow of money to terrorists, his special interest—and of draconian measures of a different sort.

The CIA proposed the creation of Agency teams to hunt down, capture, and kill terrorists around the world. It would have the authority to "render" those captured to the United States or to other countries for interrogation—effectively establishing a secret prison system. It would also be authorized to assassinate targeted terrorists. Two days later, the President signed a secret Memorandum of Notification, empowering the Agency to take such measures without the prior approval of the White House or any other branch of the executive.

Bush was by now referring to the coming fight as a "war on terrorism." By the following week, when he addressed a joint session of Congress, it had become the "war on terror"—the label for the conflict that was to endure until the end of his presidency.

So far as Osama bin Laden personally was concerned, the White House set the tone. "I want justice," the President told reporters on September 17, "and there's an old poster out West, I recall, that said, 'WANTED— DEAD OR ALIVE.'" Vice President Cheney said on television that he would accept bin Laden's "head on a platter." If he intended this figuratively, others did not.

Three days later, the CIA's Cofer Black gathered the team that was to spearhead the covert operation in Afghanistan. He dispensed with any notion of taking the terrorist leader alive. "Gentlemen, I want to give you your marching orders and I want to make them very clear. I have discussed this with the President, and he is in full agreement. . . . I don't want bin Laden and his thugs captured. I want them dead. Alive and in prison here in the United States, they'll become a symbol, a rallying point. . . . They must be killed. I want to see photos of their heads on pikes. I want bin Laden's head shipped back in a box filled with dry ice. I want to be able to show bin Laden's head to the President. I promised him I would do that."

"The mission is straightforward," Black told a colleague at headquarters. "We locate the enemy wherever they are across the planet. We find them and we kill them."

In the field, three men led the operations that targeted bin Laden, two veteran CIA officers, and a Special Forces officer with the unit popularly known as Delta Force. Their teams in the early months numbered only some seventy men, including a dozen Green Berets, Air Force tacticians, communications experts, and a small group of elite British commandos.

Asked by his wife why he was accepting the mission—he was on the verge of retirement—the CIA's Gary Schroen had picked up a newspaper with a picture of a Manhattan firefighter, his arm at the salute, tears running down his cheeks. "This is why I'm going," he said. "We all feel the pain. . . . Everyone wants to strike back." Schroen's successor, Gary Berntsen, told that some Afghan officers favored negotiating with al Qaeda, would merely snap, "Tell them your commander is from New York. I want them all dead!"

The U.S. generals' requirement, recalled Dalton Fury, the major in command of the military component, was a little less exorbitant than the demand for bin Laden's head in a box. "A cloudy photograph would do, or a smudged fingerprint. A clump of hair or even a drop of blood. Or perhaps a severed finger wrapped in plastic. Basically, we were told to go into harm's way and prove to the world that bin Laden had been neutralized, as in 'terminated with extreme prejudice.' In plain English: stone-cold dead."

The first CIA team was on the ground in Afghanistan just two weeks after 9/11, armed with not only their weapons but $3 million in $100 bills. "Money," Schroen has wearily noted, "is the lubricant that makes things happen in Afghanistan." The cash, lugged around in duffel bags, was used mostly to grease the palms of anti-Taliban warlords. For a mission that targeted the Taliban as much as bin Laden, buying their loyalty was essential. Brilliant American management of the warlords and their forces, combined with devastating use of airpower, would defeat and decimate the Taliban soldiers—though they were often valiant fighters—in little more than two months. Getting Osama bin Laden was another matter altogether.

He had continued to address the world as he had for years, by videotape. On October 7, the day of the first U.S. airstrikes, the terrorist leader was all defiance—and lauding the 9/11 attacks. "God has struck America at its Achilles' heel and destroyed its greatest buildings," he said. "What America is tasting today is but a fraction of what we [Arabs] have tasted for decades. . . . So when God Almighty granted success to one of the vanguard groups of Islam, He opened the way. . . . I pray to God Almighty to lift them up to the highest Paradise."

A few days earlier, in a letter to Taliban leader Mullah Omar that was to be retrieved later, bin Laden forecast that the coming U.S. campaign in Afghanistan would cause "great long-term economic burdens . . . force America to resort to the former Soviet Union's only option: withdrawal from Afghanistan." Two weeks on, with the bombing continuing, the Taliban's military commander—a longtime bin Laden ally—claimed his soldiers were holding their ground. Bin Laden was "safe and sound . . . in good spirits."

Thus far, the CIA team had only poor intelligence on bin Laden's whereabouts. There were attempts to persuade them that he had left the country soon after 9/11. Other reports put him either in the capital, Kabul, or at Jalalabad, nearer to the border with Pakistan. He was indeed in Kabul, or was there in early November, when he gave the first of his two post-9/11 interviews. Bin Laden was still talking tough, but his situation had clearly changed. He was in the capital that day to pay tribute to two comrades who had been killed, one of them his military chief—and close friend—Mohammed Atef. Enemy forces were closing on Kabul, and would take the city within the week.

Bin Laden did now head for Jalalabad, some ninety miles to the east. He and a large group of fighters were seen arriving in a convoy of white Toyota trucks. American bombs were already falling on the city, and their stay was brief. Dressed in the camouflage jacket familiar to Western television viewers, their leader appeared at the Saudi-funded Institute for Islamic Studies and addressed those brave enough to come to listen. "God is with us, and we shall win the war," he reportedly said. "Your Arab brothers will lead the way. . . . May God grant me the opportunity to see you and meet you again."

Bin Laden, said to have been upset, apparently spoke of wanting to stay and fight. He was dissuaded. The convoy left soon afterward, a Jalalabad witness later told the BBC, and it now consisted of as many as three hundred vehicles filled with tall, thin Saudis, muscular men who said they were from Egypt, and blacks who may have been from Sudan. They were, he said, "good Muslims, carrying the Qur'an in one hand and their Kalashnikov in the other." Bin Laden and his close companions, seated in the third vehicle, had covered their faces. At least one of those in the group said they were on their way "to their base at Tora Bora."

Tora Bora, which translates as "Black Widow," lies almost sixteen thousand feet above sea level on Towr Ghar—the "Black Dust"—a series of rocky ridges and peaks, ten precipitous miles from the border of Pakistan's Tribal Areas. A legend now, it was at the time a media fantasy. By November 27, a British newspaper was reporting that it was a "purpose-built guerrilla lair . . . 350 yards beneath a solid mountain. There are small rooms and big rooms, and the wall and floor are cemented. . . . It has its own ventilation system and its own power, created by a hydro-electric generator

. . . driven by water from the peaks of the mountains."

The reality was far more primitive. Bin Laden's first wife, who had spent time there, remembered a place with no electricity and no running water, where life was hard at the best of times. In early December of 2001, in the icy Afghan winter, it became a desolate killing ground.

From their base at an abandoned schoolhouse, the pursuing Americans struggled with multiple obstacles. Tora Bora is not one place but a series of natural ramparts and cave complexes, a frustratingly difficult place to attack. Afghan generals, whose troops were key to the mission, were often intransigent, rarely dependable, and partial to negotiating with an al Qaeda enemy that the Delta Force and CIA commanders wanted only to destroy. The Afghan inhabitants of the mountains were at best uncertain sources of information. The Americans could dole out cellophane-wrapped cash from duffel bags, but these were people who had enjoyed bin Laden's largesse for years. Some locals had named their sons Osama, in his honor.

Berntsen, heading the CIA detachment, encountered reluctance when he begged for more U.S. military support. The operation to hunt down bin Laden, the team was told, was "flawed," too high-risk, and the reluctance to commit American ground forces was only going to get worse. What the United States could and did promptly deliver was the bludgeon of pulverizing airpower. Often guided by forward observation teams, waves of bombers flew from bases in the United States and carriers in the Persian Gulf to bombard the al Qaeda positions. AC-130 Spectre gunships, with their lethal firepower, pounded them by night.

The Americans became sure their quarry was there. A Lebaneseborn former Marine with the CIA group, who had fluent Arabic and knew bin Laden's voice from tapes and intercepts, made a discovery on the morning of December 5. In the wreckage of a bombed encampment, he found a working radio clutched in the hand of a dead fighter. It was tuned to the al Qaeda frequency and soon, amidst the to-and-fro between harried men calling for water and supplies, he heard the familiar voice urging his followers to fight on.

On the 7th, a source who had been in among the enemy reported having encountered an "extremely tall" Arab—bin Laden was between six foot four and six foot six—near some large cave entrances. Berntsen called for the dropping of a BLU-82, the largest nonnuclear bomb in the U.S. arsenal, an eight-ton weapon the size of a Volkswagen Beetle. Used earlier to break Taliban lines on the plains, its primary target now was to be a single man in the mountains.

In the early morning of the 9th, CIA and Delta Force operatives watched through binoculars as an MC-130 airplane delivered the BLU-82. B-52s followed minutes later, dropping bombs guided by GPS. A desperate fighter was soon heard on a radio intercept saying, "Cave too hot. Can't reach others." There were calls for the "truck to move wounded." Another fighter, captured later, would speak of a "hideous" explosion that had vaporized men even deep inside the caves.

Decimated but not yet finally broken, the defenders held out a few days longer. Intercepts picked up an al Qaeda commander giving movement orders, ordering up land mines, exhorting his men to "victory or death." There was talk of "Father" moving to a different tunnel. Then, on the afternoon of December 13, Delta Force's Major Fury and his men listened to a voice they were sure was that of bin Laden. "His Arabic prose sounded beautiful, soothing, and peaceful," Fury recalled. "I paraphrase him . . . 'Our prayers have not been answered.

Times are dire. . . . Things might have been different. . . . I'm sorry for getting you into this battle. If you can no longer resist, you may surrender with my blessing.'"

According to the ex-Marine expert at recognizing the Saudi's voice, bin Laden then gathered his men around him in prayer. There was the sound of mules, used for transport in the high mountains, and people moving around. Then silence.

BY THE TIME the bombing and the shooting stopped, Tora Bora was devastated, a wasteland of shattered rocks and broken trees. The detritus of war: spent ammunition, bloody bandages, torn fragments of documents in Arabic script—and not a trace of Osama bin Laden.

Had he died in the onslaught from the air? Or, in Fury's words, had a bomb "punched his ticket to Paradise"? Troops flown in months later by helicopter found the cave entrances impenetrably blocked by tons of rubble. Exhumations at a fighters' graveyard turned up nothing that was identifiable with bin Laden.

Long since convinced that their quarry escaped, those who risked their lives to kill him cast bitter blame on those from whom they had taken their orders. The Delta Force operatives, Fury said, had not been allowed to engage in "real war fighting." Had they been, he thought, things could have turned out differently. Being held back had been like "working in an invisible cage."

The CIA's Gary Berntsen had in vain requested a force of eight hundred U.S. troops—to block the "back door," the mountain escape route to Pakistan. "We need Rangers [Special Operations combat troops] now!" he had begged with increasing urgency. "The opportunity to get bin Laden and his men is slipping away!" He had been rebuffed every time.

Why were the troops refused, and who was responsible

for the refusal? Military decisions were transmitted by the generals, directly to Berntsen by the officer commanding Joint Special Operations Command, Major General Dell Dailey, who in turn answered to General Tommy Franks, commander-in-chief at U.S. Central Command, the man running the Afghanistan operation.

"We have not said," Franks remarked at a press briefing just before the fighting at Tora Bora, "that Osama bin Laden is a target of this effort." It was a strange comment, even taking into account security considerations, given what Fury and Berntsen have said of the explicit orders they had been given. In a 2004 memoir, Franks skirted any discussion of the decision not to use U.S. troops to trap bin Laden. As recently as 2009, the general said he had doubted whether bin Laden was even at Tora Bora. Notwithstanding the certainty expressed by the CIA and Delta Force commanders on the spot, he claimed the intelligence had been "conflicting."

Delta Force's Major Fury placed responsibility elsewhere. "The generals," he said, "were not operating alone. Civilian political figures were also at the control panel. . . . I was not in those air-conditioned rooms with leather chairs when they came up with some of the strangest decisions I have ever encountered. . . . At times, we were micromanaged by higher-ups unknown, even to the point of being ordered to send the exact grid coordinates of our teams back to various folks in Washington."

The two civilian higher-ups involved with Franks in the decision making were Defense Secretary Rumsfeld and the man ultimately responsible as commander-in-chief, President Bush. Bush, who six days after 9/11 had indicated that he wanted bin Laden "dead or alive."

The President "never took his eye off the ball when it

came to bin Laden," according to General Franks. Through October and into November, Bush had appeared still keen to "get" bin Laden. In late November, at a CIA briefing, he was told Tora Bora had become the focus, that Afghan forces were inadequate to do the job, that U.S. troops were required. "We're going to lose our prey if we're not careful," the CIA briefer warned. The President seemed surprised. In Afghanistan in early December, shortly before the massive BLU-82 bomb was unleashed on Tora Bora, those heading the fight in the field were told that POTUS had been personally "asking for details."

According to CIA sources, Bush would reportedly remain "obsessed" with the hunt for bin Laden even months after Tora Bora. In public, though, far from talking of getting him dead or alive, he seemed to downgrade his importance. "Terror's bigger than one person," the President said in March 2002. "He's a person who has been marginalized. . . . I don't know where he is. Nor, you know, I just don't spend that much time on him really, to be honest with you. . . . I truly am not that concerned about him."

THE RECORD, PERHAPS, explains the sea change in the priority given to the hunt for Osama bin Laden. On November 21, a couple of weeks before the final battles in the mountains and bin Laden's disappearance, the President had taken Rumsfeld aside for a conversation that he insisted must remain secret. He wanted a war plan for Iraq, and insisted that General Franks get working on it immediately.

Franks, already up to his eyes dealing with the conflict in Afghanistan, could barely believe what he was hearing. "Goddamn!" he exclaimed to a fellow general. "What the fuck are they talking about?" From then on, not least in early December, when there were repeated appeals for U.S. troops to block bin Laden's escape route, the general was constantly plagued with requests for plans as to how to attack Iraq. At a crucial stage of the Tora Bora episode, Bush's primary focus had begun to shift—and a shift in the commander-in-chief's focus meant distracting the attention of his overworked general from developments in Afghanistan.

FOR A LONG TIME, for almost three years, Osama bin Laden remained neither dead nor a prisoner—the options the President of the United States had initially contemplated—but an elusive, at times illusory, ghost.

A story in the Pakistan *Observer*, published on December 25, quoted a Taliban official as saying the fugitive had died "a natural and quiet death" of "serious complications in the lungs." He had supposedly been buried with military honors, according to his faith, in an unmarked grave. The story was clearly inaccurate—and perhaps a diversionary tactic, given that he in fact survived. A story that bin Laden made his escape after suffering a wound to the shoulder seems entirely possible.

Reports that became available in 2011, meanwhile, offer two versions of his escape. One holds that he headed north, to a remote part of Afghanistan, and remained there for months. The other suggests that, just as the CIA's man at Tora Bora had feared he would, he escaped over the snow-covered passes to Pakistan with the assistance of a Pakistani militant commander.

While the force guarding the border was commanded by a Pakistan army general, most of the troops involved were drawn from tribes in the region who answered to tribal chiefs, most of whom bin Laden had cultivated and who to one degree or another approved his cause.

Good evidence that he had survived came gradually: a handwritten letter, scanned and posted on islamonline.net in August 2002; weeks later, another letter; an audiotape, followed by two others in 2003— one of them, triumphal in tone, describing how "the forces of faith" had beaten back "the evil forces of materialism" at Tora Bora; in October 2003 a videotape urging on the fighters resisting the American occupation of Iraq, encouraging the people of Palestine to continue their struggle; in 2004 three further audiotapes and—on October 29, days before the U.S. presidential election— a videotape addressed to the American people.

Bin Laden wished to tell Americans, he said, how "to avoid another Manhattan." September 11 had been a response to the United States' "great injustices"— especially in Iraq and Israel. He invoked God's blessing on "the nineteen" [there had been nineteen hijackers on 9/11], and openly admitted his personal involvement. "We agreed with the general commander Mohamed Atta, may God bless his soul, to carry out all operations within twenty minutes, before Bush and his administration could be aware of them."

Until he saw that videotape, the former Delta Force commander at Tora Bora had not been sure what to think. Some had believed the previous bin Laden tapes authentic. Some had suspected they were fakes. Fury had preferred to think them fakes, until he saw the fall 2004 appearance.

"I knew immediately that the tape was the real thing. His posture, the voice, his thin body, and the aged beard that seemed frosted of snow were unmistakeable. Unfortunately, the man was still alive."

Not long before, far off in Afghanistan, a local militiaman named Faqir Shah had accompanied reporter Tim McGirk back to Tora Bora. "This was where Osama lived," Shah said as they walked the shattered battlefield. "We fought al Qaeda here for two weeks in the snow. . . . See that hole? An American soldier tossed a piece of concrete in there from the World Trade Center, because he thought al Qaeda was all finished . . .

"I didn't think so."

PART IV

PLOTTERS

SEVENTEEN

Two decades earlier, when the Twin Towers of the World Trade Center had been a relatively new phenomenon—years before the earliest official concern that they would make a prime target for terrorists—an improbably tall young Saudi, still in his early twenties, had flown into the United States with his pregnant wife and two infant children. His visit, in 1979, passed without notice, for he was neither famous nor infamous.

Osama bin Laden's activity in America appeared entirely peaceful. The fact that he came at all was not firmly established until 2009, when his wife Najwa—nine babies later and separated from her husband by force of circumstance—published a memoir. She recalled having thought that Americans in general were "gentle and nice . . . easy to deal with. . . . My husband and I did not hate America, yet we did not love it."

An incident on the final day of their stay, as the family sat in an airport departure lounge, showed Najwa how little some Americans knew of other cultures. "I saw an American man gawking at me . . . jaw dropped open in surprise, curious eyes growing as large as bugs popping from his skull . . . I knew without asking that his unwelcome attention had been snagged by my black

Saudi costume . . . face veil, head scarf, and *abaya*. . . . That man gave us a good laugh."

Bin Laden had been busy during the trip, but Najwa was the good Arab wife. "Since my husband's business was not my business, I did not ask questions." She asked no questions when bin Laden took off for Los Angeles for a week to talk with unknown men. Nor did she press for details when he said he was meeting—elsewhere—with "a man by the name of Abdullah Azzam."

By mentioning Azzam, bin Laden had provided a first pointer to the direction his life was going to take. Azzam lectured and led prayers in the mosque at King Abdul Aziz University in the Saudi city of Jeddah, where bin Laden was a third-year student of economics and management. Often described as a "cleric" or "scholar," Azzam was more than that. A Palestinian, whose village had been overrun by the Israelis in the Six Day War, he was on his way to becoming the "Emir of Jihad."

"Jihad" is a religious duty for Muslims. It can be interpreted in several ways—its basic sense is "struggle," or "striving"—but what Azzam meant by it was very clear. He preached the need for jihad to liberate Muslim lands from foreign occupation. "Humanity," he was to say, "is being ruled by Jews and Christians. The Americans, the British, and others. And behind them, the fingers of world Jewry."

In the late 1970s Azzam, an imposing figure and a fine speaker, was raging especially about Egyptian president Anwar al-Sadat's peacemaking visit to Israeli-occupied Jerusalem, a visit that millions in the Middle East saw not as statesmanship but betrayal.

With Azzam at Abdul Aziz University was Mohammed Qutb, brother of a writer and thinker who in death, following his execution in Egypt, became the guiding light of Islamic extremism. Sayid Qutb had been the

leading voice of the Muslim Brotherhood, deplored the
corruption of secular regimes in the Middle East, and
advocated using violence to remove them. He excoriated
Western society as he had seen it in the United States and
poured verbal vitriol on the Jews and Zionism. Osama
bin Laden read Sayid Qutb, and attended his brother's
lectures.

Azzam and Qutb were free to spread their message at
will in the Saudi Arabia of the 1970s, and what they said
about Israel accorded perfectly with Saudi doctrine. For
all his anti-Zionist speechifying, moreover, the United
States welcomed Azzam. From 1979, the year the young
bin Laden met with him in the States, he was perceived
as an ally in a common cause, the struggle to expel Soviet
forces from Afghanistan. For both Saudi intelligence—
the GID—and the CIA, Azzam was useful, a man to
manipulate.

An irony, then, that—after 9/11—Azzam's name would
be joined to that of Osama bin Laden. The dedication to
a so-called *Encyclopedia of Jihad*, a sort of how-to manual
for terrorists in eleven volumes, would read: "To our
much loved brother Abu Abdullah Osama bin Laden,
who shared in the jihad of Sheikh Abdullah Azzam . . .
Who has committed himself every day to jihad."

Azzam, bin Laden himself would say, was "a man
worth a nation." For he, with bin Laden and a few
comrades, was to found a movement that would shake the
Western world and change history: al Qaeda.

In 1979, when the preacher from Palestine and the
Saudi economics student got together in Indiana,
the seeds were being sown. For the student, then and
for the rest of his life, the driving force was always religion.

"God Almighty was gracious enough for me to be
born to Muslim parents in the Arabian Peninsula in

al-Malazz neighborhood, in al-Riyadh, in 1377 hegira . . ."

Bin Laden, perorating—he was always long-winded—on his early life and parentage. The year of his birth, 1377 hegira, is the Muslim calendar's rendering of the year most of the world refers to as 1957. The actual birthday appears to have been February 15.

Nineteen fifty-seven was the year that President Dwight Eisenhower took office for a second term, and that a rebel named Fidel Castro—previously rumored to have been killed—surfaced to fight on against the Cuban government. The nations of Western Europe began forming a unified economic bloc. The Soviet Union launched the Sputnik satellite into orbit and began catching up with U.S. missile technology.

The Saudi newborn's full name was Osama bin Mohammed bin Awad bin Aboud bin Laden al-Qatani—"bin" meaning "son of." He would one day tell his own children that "al-Qatani," which denotes those who trace their ancestry to Yemen, was their true family name. "Osama" means "Lion," apt for a man who came to see himself as a warrior.

"I was named," bin Laden himself said, "after one of the venerable Companions of the Prophet, Osama bin-Zeid . . . He was someone whom the Prophet, God's peace and blessings be upon him, has loved and has loved his father before him." That Osama was an Islamic hero, a commander said to have defeated a Roman army.

"My father was born in Hadramaut," bin Laden said in 1999. "He went to work in Hejaz at an early age, more than seventy years ago. Then God blessed him and bestowed on him an honor that no other contractor has known. He built the holy Mecca mosque where the holy Ka'bah is located and at the same time, because of God's blessings to him, he built the Holy Mosque in Medina.

... [Then] the Dome of the Rock in Jerusalem. ... It is not a secret that he was one of the founders of the infrastructure of the Kingdom of Saudi Arabia."

The father, Mohamed bin Laden, had been a legend in his time. The Hadramaut was a sparsely populated region of what is now Yemen, which borders on Saudi Arabia, and the young Mohamed made his way the thousand miles to Jeddah penniless and hungry. He started out portering for pilgrims, moved on to lowly work in the construction trade, worked incessantly, thrived as a manager, and eventually—though almost illiterate, he had a phenomenal memory for facts and figures—rose to become a fabulously wealthy construction magnate.

The key to the rise of bin Laden Sr. was the patronage of the all-powerful Saudi elite, the rulers of a land that emerged from obscurity to gilded affluence in the space of a few decades. He hit his prime just as American money for Saudi oil began to bring the royal princes unparalleled riches. From the reign of King Abdul Aziz in the 1930s to that of King Faisal in the 1960s, he built palaces, roads across the desert, reservoirs, power stations. He catered to every royal whim, from providing the ramp that delivered the wheelchair-bound Abdul Aziz to his throne room to—a measure of his wealth—bailing out Faisal when the royal coffers ran dry for a while.

Nothing enhanced bin Laden Sr.'s prestige so much as his work on Islam's religious sites. "Religion in Saudi Arabia is like gravity," bin Laden family biographer Steve Coll has written. "It explained the order of objects and the trajectory of lives. The Qur'an was the kingdom's constitution and the basis of all its laws. The kingdom ... evolved into the most devout society on earth."

Religion and Saudi royalty are inseparable. The Saud family had gained power in the eighteenth century thanks to a deal with a reformist preacher named

Mohammed ibn Abdul Wahhab. He and his followers insisted on the most austere interpretation of Islam, banned the arts, music and dancing, celebration of holidays, and memorials to the dead.

The author Stephen Schwartz has defined Wahhabism as a "form of fascism" built on "a paramilitary political structure comparable to the Bolsheviks and Nazis" and "a monopoly of wealth by the elite, backed by extreme repression and a taste for bloodshed." In Saudi Arabia, someone who had lived there for many years told the authors, "Everything comes down to money. The extent of the greed is beyond the understanding of the ordinary Westerner."

Under the extreme form of shari'a—Islamic law—applied in today's Saudi Arabia, theft may be punished by amputation of a hand. Public beheading remains the designated penalty for murder, drug trafficking, rape, and adultery. In some cases a beheading is followed by crucifixion of the body, and placing of the head upon a pole. Human rights are severely limited. Women cannot attend university, have bank accounts, or take employment without permission of a male relative.

The Yemeni immigrant Mohamed bin Laden had no quarrel with Saudi ways. A devout Muslim himself, he would invite prominent clerics to his home to debate religion. His renovations and innovations at the three holy shrines of Medina, Mecca, and the Dome of the Rock in Jerusalem—before the Israeli occupation of 1967—earned him high honors in Saudi Arabia. He was appointed a minister of state by royal decree, and the letter appointing him to the Jerusalem work styled him "Your highness, Sheikh Mohamed bin Laden."

Mohamed's son Osama was the eighteenth of some two dozen sons sired by his series of some twenty-two wives. He was the product of a short-lived marriage to a

Syrian girl named Allia who was fourteen years old to her husband's forty-nine. In the year Allia gave birth to Osama, her new husband fathered seven children.

Even by Saudi standards, Mohamed behaved bizarrely in the marital home. According to Osama, his mother confided that he had had "a shocking habit of asking his wives to take off their veils and stand in a line, sending for his male servants to look upon their faces . . . like harlots on view . . . and point out his most beautiful wife." Allia asked for a divorce, for reasons unknown, and went on to marry one of her husband's employees. Osama, who lived principally with her from then on, is said by his son Omar—one of the children of his first wife, Najwa—to have loved his mother "more than he loved his wives, his siblings, or his children."

Mohamed, Osama was to tell his own family, would usually summon his sons to see him as a group, and only a few times a year. "In my whole life," Osama said, "I only saw your grandfather five times . . . brief meetings, all but one with my large clan of brothers."

Mohamed had a strict rule, Osama told Omar, that "when he met with his sons, we must stand in a very straight line, organized according to height, rather than age. . . . Before I became a teenager, I was not the tallest . . . [One day] two of my older brothers, taller than me, locked me between them. . . . Your grandfather noticed. Furious, he marched to stand in front of me and without one word of warning struck me across the face with his strongest force. . . . I've never forgotten the pain." "Most of us were afraid of him," said Yeslam, one of Osama's half-brothers.

Bin Laden Sr. believed that Palestine belonged to the Arabs, not the Jews, and was accordingly "very, very, very anti-Israel, anti-Jewish." In June 1967, when Israel seized East Jerusalem and King Faisal made bellicose noises,

Mohamed suggested a contribution he could make. He would, he said, convert the 250 bulldozers he used in his building operations into army tanks.

Three months later, Osama's father was dead. Ten thousand people reportedly attended the ceremonies that followed his death in an airplane crash. His myriad sons and daughters and wives, separated according to sex of course, gathered for the days of mourning. King Faisal, who said his protégé had been his "right arm," declared that he would henceforth act as father to the bin Laden children.

This was not only because the king had held the dead man in great affection. The bin Laden companies were important to ongoing government operations, and Faisal decreed that they must continue to function. The overall value of Mohamed's estate was in the region of $150 million, almost a billion dollars at 2010 values. His children, the sons as stipulated by law entitled to twice as much as the daughters, all instantly became millionaires.

The son named Osama, still in the care of his doting mother, was ten at the time. His most recent memory of his father was of a patriarch who—in spite of the boy's tender age—had recently given him a car as a present. Though of course not allowed to drive it, he remained crazy about cars for years to come.

The sparse memories of Osama's early life, however, recall a child who was "shy . . . aloof . . . gentle . . . polite . . . obedient . . . quiet, to the point of timidity." Briefly, before his father's death, he had been sent as a boarder to a Quaker school in Beirut. Not long afterward, back in his homeland, he began the first of eight years at a school for the Saudi elite founded by the king himself. An Englishman who taught there, Brian Fyfield-Shayler, remembered a pupil who was "extraordinarily courteous . . . not pushy in any way . . . pleasant, charming, ordinary, not very exceptional."

Fyfield-Shayler thought Osama's command of English mediocre, though a person who met him years later found him fluent enough in the language. His science teacher judged him "normal, not excellent." In arithmetic, he had inherited his father's flair. According to his son Omar, "No calculator could equal my father's remarkable ability, even when presented with the most complicated figures." Given the school's top national ranking, Fyfield-Shayler thought, Osama was probably "one of the top fifty students" in his age group.

Away from class, he was a boy like other boys. His schoolfriend Khaled Batarfi recalled him taking part in soccer games, near the Pepsi factory. Taller than most of his pals, Osama would "play forward to use his head and put in the goals." Off the pitch, he and his peers enjoyed watching cowboy and karate movies.

Batarfi recalled an incident when his friend was confronted by a bully. "I pushed him away from Osama, and solved the problem. But then Osama came to me and said, 'You know, if you waited a few minutes I would have solved the problem peacefully.' . . . This was the kind of guy who would always think of solving problems peacefully."

IN SUMMER during his childhood, Osama traveled to his mother's seaside home in Syria. There were camping trips, long hikes with a male cousin, and a special friendship with the cousin's young sister—Najwa. To her he seemed "soft-spoken, serious . . . delicate but not weak . . . a mystery—yet we all liked him." She had these impressions, by her account, before either child turned ten.

By the time Najwa turned thirteen, in 1972, "unanticipated emotions began to swirl" between her and Osama. He seemed "shyer than a virgin under the veil," said nothing directly to her. Instead he spoke to his mother and the respective parents spoke to each other. There was a wedding and a celebratory dinner—male and female guests carefully segregated, no music, no dancing—when Osama was seventeen and Najwa fifteen.

The teenage husband brought his wife home to Jeddah swathed in black, her face totally veiled. "Osama," she recalled in a 2009 memoir written with her son Omar, "was so conservative that I would also live in purdah, or isolation, rarely leaving the confines of my new home." Her husband explained "how important it was for me to live as an obedient Muslim woman. . . . I never objected because I understood that my husband was an expert regarding our faith."

It was decided that Najwa would no longer go to school. Instead she sat in the garden reading the Qur'an while Osama went to school. Her husband, she discovered, could recite the sacred texts by heart. Proudly, he took her to pray at the mosque in Mecca that his father had rebuilt. He fit attendance at school, and occasional arduous work for the family construction company, around praying at the mosque several times a day.

Najwa soon had a first baby, to be followed not long after by another. The obedient Muslim wife would bear eleven children over the years. The devout Muslim husband, meanwhile, observed his faith to the letter. Muslims should in principle avoid shaking hands with a person of the opposite sex or of a different religion, but Osama took things further than that. When a woman— his European sister-in-law Carmen bin Ladin—opened the front door of her home unveiled, he averted his gaze and ducked speaking to her. He did not allow Najwa to feed her baby from a bottle, because it had a rubber teat.

His rules extended to male company. Osama slapped

one of his own brothers for ogling a female servant. He stared in disapproval when a male friend arrived in shorts, on the way to a soccer game. In the broiling heat of Saudi Arabia, he even urged his brothers not to wear short-sleeved shirts. In Syria, offended by the sound of a woman singing in a sexy voice, he ordered a driver to turn off the car radio.

"Around eighteen or nineteen or so," his half-brother Yeslam would say of Osama after 9/11, "he was already more religious than the average person or the average member of the family." Most Westerners might think that comment a gross understatement and dismiss Osama as having been an obsessive, a religious nut. To be super-strict about religion, however, was not—is not—unusual in Saudi Arabia. Far from alienating everyone, Osama's zealotry earned him respect. "His family revered him for his piety," his sister-in-law Carmen said. "Never once did I hear anyone murmur that his fervor might be a little excessive." Osama would rise to pray even during the night, Batarfi remembered. It was not compulsory for Muslims, but it was "following the example of the Prophet." When he went on from school to university— he would start but not complete his economics degree—Osama became close to a fellow student named Jamal Khalifa, one day to become his brother-in-law. "I was almost twenty, and he was nineteen," Khalifa remembered. "We were religious . . . very conservative; we go to that extreme side."

Osama no longer watched movies. He did not watch television, except for news programs, and he avoided music with instruments, which some religious advisers deemed sinful. He disapproved of art, so no pictures hung on the walls. He avoided being photographed, though this was a matter on which he was to vacillate.

The shift to the extreme had not happened overnight.

Looking back, Najwa remembered how—even while still at school—her husband had regularly gone out at night "for impassioned discussion of political or religious topics." Even before his marriage, a schoolfriend revealed, Osama and a half dozen other boys had begun studying Islam after school hours, taught by a Syrian teacher on the staff who was a member of the Muslim Brotherhood. It was at his urging that Osama memorized the Qur'an, under his tutelage that Osama and friends themselves began attending secret meetings of the Brotherhood.

In their impressionable teenage years, meanwhile, bin Laden and his contemporaries lived through a decade that destabilized the Arab world. The running sore of Palestine remained a concern for everyone. When Osama watched the news on television, he wept.

At his house, Batarfi recalled, they and their friends would "sing religious chants about Muslim youth and Palestine." The 1973 war, when Israel managed to beat back invading Arab forces, had been a great humiliation. Saudi Arabia's participation in the oil embargo that followed, the first use of the oil weapon against the West, had been a temporary consolation.

The year 1979, when Osama turned twenty-two, marked the start of a new century in the Islamic calendar, a time said to herald change. Sure enough, upheaval piled on upheaval. First, and in the name of Islam, came the toppling of the monarchy in Iran, a monarchy that had long been sustained by the United States. Then, in November, came a bloody event in Saudi Arabia itself, one in which Osama may have played a minor role.

"For forty years," Osama would say years later, "my father kept on waiting for the appearance of Hazrat Mahdi. He had set aside some twelve million dollars for the Mahdi." The Mahdi, according to some Islamic texts, is an Islamic Messiah who will return to earth, bring justice in a time of oppression, and establish true Islamic government.

In 1979, a Saudi religious zealot claimed that the Mahdi had arrived—in the shape of his brother-in-law, a university drop-out named al-Qahtani. They and some five hundred heavily armed comrades then committed the unprecedented outrage of seizing the Grand Mosque in Mecca—one of the three holy places that bin Laden Sr. had renovated. They entered the mosque, indeed, through an entrance used by the bin Laden company, which was still completing construction within the complex.

This was more than sacrilege. It was sedition. The zealots accused the Saudi royal house of being pawns of the West, traitors to the faith. The government crushed the insurrection, but only after a bloody standoff that lasted for two weeks. Hundreds died in the battles, and sixty-eight prisoners were later beheaded.

The Mahdi did not survive to be executed. He had believed, until the fatal moment that he discovered otherwise, that he could pick up five live hand grenades and not be harmed.

THE MONTH AFTER the battle at the mosque, forty thousand Soviet troops began pouring into Afghanistan, the vanguard of an army that would eventually become a hundred thousand strong. The invasion marked the start of a savage conflict that would last almost a decade, kill a million Afghans, and drive some five million into exile. Long before it ended, it became a trial of strength between the Soviet Union and the United States—at the time underreported and minimally understood by the American public.

The war got scant attention not least because it did not

involve the commitment of American troops. It was, rather, a purposeful, secret war to push back communism. Covertly, the United States committed cash and weaponry on a grand scale, using Afghans and foreign irregulars to do the fighting. Appropriately for a secret war, the conflict was orchestrated by the intelligence agencies of three nations: America, Pakistan, and Saudi Arabia.

So it was that, very relevantly for the 9/11 story, the Afghan saga that began in 1979 drew in two men, Osama bin Laden and Abdullah Azzam.

"MY FATHER," bin Laden would one day tell a visitor, "was very keen that one of his sons should fight against the enemies of Islam. So I am the one son who is acting according to the wishes of his father."

He had been called, he also believed, by a higher power. "Just remember this," he was to tell his son Omar. "I was put on this earth by God for a specific reason. My only reason for living is to fight the jihad. . . . Muslims are the mistreated of the world. It is my mission to make certain that other nations take Islam seriously."

IN 1979, the day bin Laden would be taken truly seriously was still more than two decades away. It was then, however, that—as his friend Batarfi has said—"the nightmare started."

EIGHTEEN

ON EVERY LEG OF THE JOURNEY TO 9/11—OVER ALL the twenty-one years that followed the Soviet invasion of Afghanistan—there would never be a time when several intelligence agencies were not involved.

Truth for public consumption is not a tool much favored by intelligence services. Those who direct the agencies prefer not to share information at all, except—in principle—with their own governments. It may, on occasion and in democracies, be useful to offer information to others—to investigating commissions, congressional and parliamentary committees, and the like, even to the media—but rarely can it be wholly relied upon.

Only rarely does an intelligence agency reveal facts inimical to its own interests. Most often, intelligence sources share only information that it is useful to share—in other words, self-serving. Such information is not necessarily truthful.

The natural impulse of the general public in the West may be to give credence to accounts provided by "our" intelligence—publicly and officially or through "sources." Such trust, though, may be misplaced. Like any story told by humans, an account given by an intelligence agency—domestic or foreign—may be only partially true. It may even be an outright lie.

*

WHAT IS CLEAR is that Saudi Arabia's intelligence service, the GID, reached out for bin Laden early in the Afghan confrontation with the Soviets—through his former school science teacher, Ahmed Badeeb. Badeeb had kept an eye on his pupil during his days on the school's religious committee, had liked him, thought him "decent . . . polite," and—now that bin Laden was in his early twenties—saw a role for him.

Badeeb had gone up in the world. He was no longer a science teacher but chief of staff to GID's director, Prince Turki al-Faisal. Turki was in the second year of what was to be a long career as chief of the agency. He was American-educated, a man who could relate easily to his U.S. counterparts. The GID and the CIA liaised closely with each other from the moment he became director—on his terms, not Washington's.

For the United States, the coming struggle with the Soviets was a pivotal confrontation in the Cold War. For the Saudi government in 1980, it was much more than that. Afghanistan was a fellow Muslim nation over-whelmed by catastrophe. Uncounted numbers of its citizens were swarming into Pakistan as refugees. To bring aid to the Afghans, and being seen to do it, was to aid the cause of Islam.

That aside, it was feared that the Soviet thrust heralded an eventual threat to Saudi Arabia itself. Prince Turki was soon shuttling between Riyadh and Pakistan, networking with Pakistan's Directorate for Inter-Services Intelligence—ISI—triggering a relief effort that was to last far into the future.

On another tack, and in great secrecy, the GID and the CIA worked together to support the Afghan rebels' fight against the Soviets. Thanks to huge sums of money funneled through a Swiss bank account, modern

weaponry began to make the rebels a more viable fighting force.

"When the invasion of Afghanistan started," bin Laden
once said, "I was enraged and went there at once. I
arrived within days, before the end of 1979." At GID
headquarters, Prince Turki and his aide Badeeb noted bin
Laden's potential. Youthful though he was, as a member
of the bin Laden conglomerate he had clout. He had,
above all, religious drive and commitment.

"To confront those Russian infidels," bin Laden said,
"the Saudis chose me as their representative in
Afghanistan. When they decided to participate actively in
the Islamic resistance they turned to the bin Laden
family . . . which had close links to the royal family. And
my family designated me. I installed myself in Pakistan,
in the frontier region bordering on Afghanistan. There I
received the volunteers who arrived from Saudi Arabia
and all the Arab and Muslim countries."

Prince Turki has admitted having met bin Laden a
couple of times in that early period, while avoiding going
into detail. His former chief of staff Badeeb has been
more forthright. Bin Laden, he has said, "had a strong
relation with the Saudi intelligence and with our embassy
in Pakistan. . . . He was our man. . . . We were happy with
him. . . . He had a good relationship with the ambassador,
and with all Saudi ambassadors who served there. At
times, the embassy would ask bin Laden for some things
and he would respond positively. . . . The Pakistanis, too,
saw in him one who was helping them do what they
wanted done there."

According to one of the most well-informed sources
on the conflict, the journalist Ahmed Rashid, Pakistan's
ISI had wanted Turki "to provide a royal prince to lead
the Saudi contingent." In bin Laden, with his family's
links to the Saudi royals, they got the next best thing.

What was required of him in the early 1980s was not to fight but to travel to-and-fro, spread money around, cultivate Afghan contacts, make sure that cash got to the right people. Then his activities became entwined with those of Abdullah Azzam, the jihadist whose lectures he had attended at university. The duty of jihad "will not end with victory in Afghanistan," Azzam was heard to declare. "Jihad will remain an individual obligation until all other lands that were Muslim are returned to us."

With Saudi support, Azzam moved full-time to Pakistan, and so eventually did bin Laden—at his mentor's request. By 1986 they were running the office that processed Arab donations and handled recruits rallying to the cause. Funded with money from Saudi Arabia and the Gulf, and his own wealth, bin Laden ensured that arrivals were housed, cared for if they were sick or wounded, and fed Islamic propaganda.

Newcomers stayed initially at a building called Beit al-Ansar, which translates as Place of the Supporters. That was a reference to an episode in the story of the Prophet Mohammed, but it resonates today in another way. Twelve years later, some of the future 9/11 hijackers would give their apartment that name. Azzam, for his part, toured the United States regularly, raising funds and starting what eventually became a nationwide support system.

At some point, according to a source quoted by Barnett Rubin, now a senior State Department adviser on Pakistan and Afghanistan, the CIA "enlisted" Azzam. Did the Agency have any involvement with bin Laden himself?

The CIA had significantly ratcheted up its support for the anti-Soviet forces by the mid-1980s. U.S. funding, $470 million in 1986, continued to soar, and the agency saw to it that more and better weapons reached the

Afghans. Under a supposedly strict, immutable arrangement, however—necessary to the United States to ensure deniability, to Pakistan to retain control—all this assistance was handled by the ISI, Pakistan's intelligence service. officials of the day have played down the notion that there was American contact with bin Laden, or anyone else in the field.

Reputable authors have reported how the CIA on occasion circumvented the rules. While the bulk of the mujahideen were trained by Pakistani officers, some of the officers were trained in the States. U.S. and British Special Forces veterans entered Afghanistan and operated alongside the fighters. American cash went to at least one Afghan commander who collaborated with bin Laden.

Other voices claim there was an early link between the CIA and bin Laden himself. Michael Springmann, who in 1986 and 1987 headed the Non-Immigrant Visa Section at the U.S. consulate in Jeddah, said that the CIA forced him against his will to issue visas to people who would otherwise have been ineligible. "What I was protesting was, in reality, an effort to bring recruits, rounded up by [the Agency and] Osama bin Laden, to the U.S. for terrorists training by the CIA. They would then be returned to Afghanistan to fight against the Soviets."

Simon Reeve, a British author, cited a "former CIA official" as saying that "U.S. emissaries met directly with bin Laden." According to this source it was bin Laden, acting on advice from Saudi intelligence, who suggested that the mujahideen be supplied with the Stinger missiles that proved devastatingly effective against Soviet airpower.

"Bin Laden," wrote former British foreign secretary Robin Cook, "was a product of a monumental miscalculation of Western security agencies. Throughout the 80s he was armed by the CIA and funded by the Saudis to wage jihad against the Russian occupation of Afghanistan."

In a little-known interview, bin Laden himself appeared to offer a revelation. "I created my first camps," he said in 1995, "where these volunteers underwent training, instructed by Pakistani and *American officers* [authors' italics]. The arms were provided by the Americans and the money by the Saudis."

Then, a year later, bin Laden reversed himself. "Personally," he said in 1996, "neither I nor my brothers saw evidence of American help."

Statements by Osama bin Laden—and for that matter those of intelligence officials—rarely contribute much to historical clarity.

THE USE THE GID SAW for bin Laden initially put him nowhere near the combat zone. "The Saudi government," he would recall, had "officially asked me not to enter Afghanistan, due to how close my family is to the Saudi leadership. They ordered me to stay in Peshawar [Pakistan], because in the event the Russians arrested me that would be a proof of our support for the mujahideen. . . . I didn't listen to them, and went into Afghanistan for the first time."

Quite early in the 1980s, back in Jeddah, Najwa bin Laden heard her husband tell other family members that he had entered the Afghan war zone. He mentioned, too, that he had handled the controls of a helicopter. She began to probe a little but he merely said, "Najwa, stop thinking." As a dutiful Saudi wife, she knew it was not her place to ask what her husband did outside the home.

Many Arabs who answered the call to jihad never saw actual fighting, but bin Laden saw to it that some of them did. He eventually set up a base at Jaji, ten miles inside

Afghanistan and not far from a Soviet base, and called it Maasada, or the Lion's Den. It was there that he and his Arabs had their baptism of fire.

One of Azzam's sons recalled how, greenhorn that he was, bin Laden initially reacted to explosions by running away. Soon, however, he and his men gained a reputation for breathtaking bravery in terrifying circumstances—for a reason that Westerners can barely begin to understand. One observer saw a man in tears because he survived an attack. For jihadis, Azzam would say, had a "thirst for martyrdom." The fact that he himself had not taken part in the fighting earlier, bin Laden said, "requires my own martyrdom in the name of God."

"As Muslims," he explained to the British journalist Robert Fisk, "we believe that when we die we go to heaven. Before a battle, God sends us *seqina*, tranquillity." "I was so peaceful in my heart," he said of one experience under bombing in Afghanistan, "that I fell asleep."

In 1989, after the deaths of more than a million Afghans and some fifteen thousand Soviets, the Russians pulled out of Afghanistan. With the Afghan communist regime still in place, however, the conflict merely entered a new phase. Bin Laden and an Arab force, who took part in an attempt to take the eastern city of Jalalabad, suffered appalling casualties. Their contribution had been botched and ill-planned, but Saudi propaganda mills continued to profile bin Laden as a champion of Islam.

He "took charge of the closest front lines to the enemy," trumpeted *Jihad* magazine, "started attacking with every hero that God gave him. Their number increased in view of their desire to take part in the deliverance of Jalalabad under the command of Osama bin Laden." And: "the land of Jalalabad swallowed one lion after another. Osama had pain every time he said goodbye to one mujahid. And every time he would say goodbye a new rocket would come and take another."

Bin Laden had for some time been having disagreements with his mentor, Azzam. That year, however, their differences became moot. Azzam and two of his sons were assassinated as they drove to the mosque to pray. Who was behind their murder was never established, let alone the motive. Bin Laden had left for Saudi Arabia a few weeks earlier, to be met with a hero's welcome.

He was greeted in Jeddah, by one account, by the crown prince himself, Abdullah bin Abdul Aziz. The great and the good of Jeddah feted bin Laden, threw feasts to celebrate his prowess. He gave talks on his experiences at the mosque and in private homes. Bin Laden recordings about the Afghan campaign circulated on audiocassette, and he featured largely in a film that was being made.

Heady stuff for a man who had just turned thirty-two. For a while, to Najwa's relief, he went back to work for the bin Laden construction company. Since the start of Osama's involvement in Afghanistan, there had been many changes in their domestic life.

He had taken a second wife, then a third, then a fourth. Though it is proper under religious law to take up to four wives, this had at first troubled Najwa. She reconciled herself to the new arrangements, she said, when her husband explained that "his aim was purely to have many children for Islam." Religion did dominate bin Laden's thinking, but—with male acquaintances—he joked about his polygamy. "I have four wives waiting for me," he would say. "Time for some fun."

The fun certainly produced his quota of bin Laden children for Islam. There were eleven children by late 1989, and more would follow. A total as of 2001—with one intervening divorce, an annulment, and one more wife along the way—of twenty.

His friend Jamal Khalifa thought bin Laden was good with his children. "I never saw him shouting at his kids, hitting his kids. Even his wives, they never say he has treated them bad . . . his wives, they like him so much." As time passed, meanwhile, it became clear that—wealthy though he might be—bin Laden believed that being "a good Muslim" required severe austerity. He decreed, Najwa has said, "that our home furnishings should be plain, our clothes modest in number." He considered Islamic beliefs to have been "corrupted by modernization," and forbade his wives to use the air-conditioning or the refrigerator. To ensure a supply of fresh milk, he kept cows.

Bin Laden was more severe with his children than Khalifa saw. "We were allowed to speak in his presence," recalled his son Omar, "but our voices must be kept low. . . . We were told that we must not become excited. . . . We should be serious about everything. . . . We were not allowed to tell jokes. . . . He would allow us to smile so long as we did not laugh. If we were to lose control of our emotions and bark a laugh, we must be careful not to expose our eye teeth. I have been in situations where my father actually counted the exposed teeth, reprimanding his sons on the number their merriment revealed."

The entire family was supposed to "live just as the Prophet had lived, whenever possible." Unless a family member were to become mortally ill, they were forbidden to use modern medicines. For asthma, which afflicted all the boys, bin Laden insisted on a natural remedy—breathing through a honeycomb rather than using an inhaler. Instead of toys, Omar recalled, "Father would give us some goats to play with, telling us that we needed nothing more than God's natural gifts to be happy . . .

"From the time we were toddlers, he demanded that we be given very little water. . . . Our father would transport his sons into the dry desert . . . bin Laden sons must be physically immune to inhospitable desert heat." Bin Laden was teaching them, Khalifa has said, "how to be a mujahid, trying to bring them up on jihad, on jihad thinking." He had taken his eldest son, Abdullah, into the Afghan war zone when he was only ten years old.

The "shy" side of bin Laden was no longer so evident. His experience in Afghanistan had given him confidence. At meetings there, speaking clearly in elegant, classical Arabic, "like a university professor," he had sat at the head of the table handing down decisions. "We will do this," he would say. "We will do that . . ."

Canadian journalist David Cobain, who had encountered bin Laden outside Afghanistan, noted his "still, silent intensity," the way he would sit "gazing unblinkingly at everything. . . . He had the extraordinary quality of attracting and holding one's attention inactively, by his presence, by the impression he gave of other-worldliness."

As THE STRUGGLE against the Soviets ended, the CIA thought the most radical Islamic groups—backed by Pakistan's ISI—would be most effective in the effort to remove the residual communist regime. Far from showing gratitude for the U.S. contribution to beating the Soviets, however, the fundamentalists proved virulently anti-American.

Working with the United States, bin Laden was to say, had all along been only a "tactical alliance." America's motive in Afghanistan had merely been self-interest. "The United States was not interested in our jihad. It was only afraid that Russia would gain access to warm waters [i.e., the Gulf]. . . . The United States has no principles.

"In our struggle against the communists, our aim was the Islamic revolution, whoever our allies might be. . . . We got involved as Muslim fighters against Soviet atheism, not as American auxiliaries. The urgent thing was to deal with communism, but the next target was the United States. . . . I began by allying myself with them, and I finished without them."

"Every Muslim," bin Laden was to claim, "hates Americans, hates Jews, and hates Christians. This is a part of our belief and our religion. For as long as I can remember, I have felt tormented and at war, and have felt hatred and animosity for Americans."

Three firsthand accounts indicate that bin Laden was hostile to Westerners by the time the Soviets left Afghanistan.

Dana Rohrabacher, former Reagan White House aide and future congressman, recalled coming across an unusual encampment near Jalalabad. "We could see these tents, luxurious tents . . . more like a modern-day camping expedition by some rich people with SUVs than a mujahideen camp. . . . I was told immediately that that was the camp of the Saudis and that I should keep my mouth shut and no English should be spoken until we were far away . . . because they said there was a crazy man in that camp who hated Americans, worse than he hated the Soviets. . . . They said, 'That man's name is bin Laden.' "

A few months later, two experienced war reporters had separate encounters with bin Laden near Jalalabad. Edward Girardet, a Swiss American with long experience of the conflict, found himself confronted by "a tall, bearded man flanked by armed men," demanding in English, with a slight American accent, "to know who I was and what I, a *kafir* [infidel], was doing in Afghanistan. For the next forty-five minutes we had a heated debate about the war, religion, and foreigners. Haughty, self-righteous, and utterly sure of himself, he proceeded to lambast the West for its feebleness and lack of moral conviction." When Girardet held out his hand to say goodbye, the tall man refused to shake. Instead, he threatened, "If you ever come again, I'll kill you."

The BBC reporter John Simpson and his crew also had an unpleasant encounter with the tall, bearded figure. This time, the man actively urged the mujahideen present to kill Simpson and his colleagues. No one obliged—the group around bin Laden included more moderate Afghan fighters. The driver of an ammunition truck, offered $500 to run down the "infidels," also declined.

The murderous threats aside, Girardet and Simpson both thought there was something peculiar about the man in white. "The best description I can give," Girardet said, "is that he sort of came across as being a rather spoiled brat, like he was sort of 'playing at jihad.' Kind of an 'I'm here now, look at me,' sort of thing."

John Simpson, for his part, witnessed something bizarre. Toward the end of the encounter, when the tall Arab ran off toward the mujahideen sleeping area, the BBC crew followed—only to find their would-be nemesis "lying full-length on a camp-bed, weeping and beating his fists on the pillow."

Looking back, Simpson vividly remembered how the Arab who wanted him dead had looked at that moment. He remembered especially the eyes: with that "crazy, handsome glitter—the Desert Sheikh meets Hannibal Lecter."

Only years later, when the news was filled with stories and photographs of bin Laden, did Girardet and Simpson realize just who the menacing Arab had been.

*

THE MEN AROUND bin Laden had indeed long since deferred to him, as they had to his mentor, Azzam, before his death, as sheikh. Azzam had said jihad needed a "vanguard," a leadership that would give the dreamed-of future Islamic society a "strong foundation." The Arabic words he used for "strong foundation" were "*al-qaeda al-sulbah*."

A few months later, in 1988, Azzam, bin Laden, and a handful of comrades had discussed plans for how to make progress once the Soviets finally left. Initially, they planned, they would maintain a militia of some three hundred men. Those who enlisted would make a pledge, "so that the word of God will be the highest and his religion victorious." The camps in which they would train would be "*al-qa'ida al'askariyya*"—the Military Base.

Those who do not understand Arabic—these authors included—might interpret these utterances as the birth of the dragon that the Western media now calls "al Qaeda." Not so, recent scholarship suggests. The word does mean "the foundation" or "the base"—and other things, for such is Arabic. More than one future bin Laden militant, though, would say he never heard the name "al Qaeda"—referring to an organization or fighting entity—before 9/11. Bin Laden himself would not refer to "members of al Qaeda" until shortly before 9/11.

"He rang me to explain," Saudi journalist Jamal Khashoggi said of a call from bin Laden after the anti-Soviet conflict. "He said al Qaeda was an organization to record the names of the mujahideen and all their contact details: a database. . . . So wherever jihad needed fighting, in the Philippines or Central Asia or anywhere in the world, you could get in touch with the fighters quickly."

All the same, a seed had been sown.

The ISI chief of the day, Hamid Gul, was asked in 1989 whether it had not been "playing with fire" to bring in Muslim radicals. "We are fighting a jihad," Gul replied. "The communists have their international brigades, the West has NATO, why can't the Muslims unite and form a common front?"

Gul was replaced as head of ISI by Benazir Bhutto, the moderate, Western-educated prime minister who had come to power in Pakistan the previous year. At a private meeting with President George H. W. Bush, she remembered saying that "in our common zeal to most effectively combat the Soviets in Afghanistan, our countries had made a strategic decision to empower the most fanatical elements of the mujahideen. . . . I sadly said to President Bush, 'Mr. President, I'm afraid we have created a Frankenstein's monster that could come back to haunt us in the future.' "

THE FUTURE CAST OF 9/11's characters was now waiting in the wings. Ayman al-Zawahiri, a doctor by training, led a clique of militant Egyptians in Afghanistan. Though his specialty was eye surgery, he had dealt with every sort of injury and ailment during the conflict—including bin Laden's chronic low blood pressure. One day, he would become bin Laden's principal cohort. Bin Laden and Mohammed Atef, who would become his strategist and senior commander, had fought side by side. All three of them knew Omar Abdel Rahman, the incendiary preacher later to be known in the West as the "Blind Sheikh."

Khalid Sheikh Mohammed, who would one day claim to have been the principal planner of 9/11, was in his mid-twenties in 1989. Ramzi Yousef, who would lead a frst attempt to destroy the World Trade Center, was still at college. Both of them were passionately hostile to the United States because of its support for Israel.

Mohamed Atta, who was to lead the 9/11 hijackers,

was just twenty-one and studying architecture at Cairo University. His future fellow "pilots," Hani Hanjour, Ziad Jarrah, and Marwan al-Shehhi, were seventeen, fourteen, and eleven.

As a little boy, Jarrah had lived near the refugee camp where hundreds of Palestinian refugees had been slaughtered—by Christian militiamen with the knowledge of Israeli commanders—during Israel's 1982 invasion of Lebanon.

The plight of the Palestinians, the rise and rise of Israel, and America's consistent support of Israel pre-occupied bin Laden from very early on. His mother has recalled him, as a teenager, being "concerned, sad, and frustrated about the situation in Palestine in particular." It was essential, bin Laden said even then, "to reclaim Palestine."

By the mid-1980s, bin Laden was already speaking out publicly about boycotting American products. He would not drink Coca-Cola, Pepsi, or 7-Up, or allow his children to drink such beverages. "The Americans take our money," he recalled saying, "and give it to the Jews so that they can kill our children with it in Palestine." "Our" children, because Palestinians were fellow Arabs, part of the wider Arab community. He was to raise the Palestine issue and excoriate American support for Israel time and again—until as recently as 2009.

The 1982 Israeli assault on Lebanon, bin Laden said after 9/11, made a lasting impression on him. "America allowed the Israelis to invade Lebanon," he declared. "They started bombing, killing and wounding many. . . . I still remember those distressing scenes: blood, torn limbs, women and children massacred. . . . It was like a crocodile devouring a child, who could do nothing but scream. . . . The whole world heard and saw what happened, but did nothing."

It was then, bin Laden asserted, that something like 9/11 first occurred to him. He watched, presumably on television, as Israel bombarded the high-rise apartment blocks that housed many Palestinians in Beirut. "The idea came to me," he asserted, "when things went just too far with the American-Israeli alliance's oppression and atrocities against our people in Palestine and Lebanon. . . . As I looked at those destroyed towers in Lebanon, it occurred to me to punish the oppressor in kind by destroying towers in America, so that it would get a taste of its own medicine."

"The events of Manhattan," he would say on an audio-taped message broadcast after 9/11, "were retaliation against the American-Israeli alliance's aggression against our people in Palestine and Lebanon."

PERHAPS so. While he was still the hero home from the war, though, a further grievance against the United States arose on his home territory—one that, for bin Laden and many other Saudis—loomed at least as large as Palestine.

NINETEEN

IN AUGUST 1990, OSAMA BIN LADEN STOCKED UP ON food supplies, candles, gas masks, and portable communications equipment. In the event of the need for a quick getaway, he had a more powerful engine fitted to the boat he kept at the family marina. At home, he got his sons to help him cover the windows with adhesive tape. The tape, he explained, was in case of bombing, to protect the family from broken glass.

Bombing was a possibility. Saddam Hussein's army had overrun neighboring Kuwait and appeared poised to push on into Saudi Arabia. Bin Laden despised the Iraqi president, whom he considered an unbeliever. Saddam, he predicted, "will attack Saudi Arabia for possession of the oilfields in the eastern province."

Oil was what mattered, the one thing that really mattered, to all the nations involved. It was the only reason, certainly, that Saudi Arabia had ever mattered to the Americans. "The defense of Saudi Arabia," President Franklin Roosevelt had said back in 1943, "is vital to the defense of the United States." Half a century on and within twenty-four hours of the Iraqi invasion, the first President Bush now made a promise. "If you ask for help from the United States," he told Saudi ambassador Prince Bandar, "we will go all the way with you."

Four days later, at King Fahd's seaside palace in Jeddah, a senior U.S. delegation told the monarch what a request for help would mean. Some 300,000 Iraqi troops and almost three thousand tanks were threatening the border. To drive them back and throw them out of Kuwait, General Norman Schwarzkopf explained, would mean "flooding his airfields, harbors and military bases with tens of thousands more Americans than Saudi Arabia had ever seen."

To allow a foreign and overwhelmingly Christian army to enter the country—the sacred land of the Prophet— would be seen by much of the Saudi population as heinous sacrilege. Everything in the country, everything, revolved around religion. "This is something that a Westerner will never understand," one of the royals, Prince Amr, later explained to a foreigner. "Religion is the law. . . . It is rooted in the history. It is part of the DNA, if you like, of the Saudis."

At least a third of the Saudi school curriculum was devoted to religious study. Holy writ, children were taught, held that "the last hour won't come before the Muslims fight the Jews and the Muslims kill them." This was a land with a religious police, a Committee for the Promotion of Virtue and the Prevention of Vice, empowered to raid people's homes, make arrests, and use physical force to compel obedience to religious rules. Censors blacked out any part of a foreign newspaper or magazine that contained comment on Saudi Arabia, any reference to Israel—or illustrations that showed even an inch of a woman's limbs or neck.

This was a land where extremism ruled, from the preposterous to the barbaric: where oil dollars built a concert hall in which no performance was permitted, where Islamic courts ruled against the playing of music on phone recordings; where ownership of a Christian

Bible could—and shortly would—lead to public execution by beheading.

According to the incumbent Grand Mufti, the nation's highest official of religious law, it was "a requirement of Muslims to be hostile to the Jews and the Christians and other polytheists." "The unbelievers," he wrote, "are the enemy, do not trust them."

The notion of inviting in an American army to fight off the Iraqis, then, was unthinkable. At the meeting with the U.S. delegation, the royals present held a brief animated exchange in Arabic. Crown Prince Abdullah urged King Fahd not to make a decision until tribal and religious leaders had been consulted. Fahd, however, had already made up his mind. Better to take a risk domestically than to lose the throne, to lose the entire country, to Saddam Hussein. The king reportedly turned to Dick Cheney—then secretary of defense—and said, "Okay."

With those two syllables, Fahd had authorized a U.S. military presence that would eventually total half a million men—and not only men. How, in Saudi Arabia, to deal with the problem of female American soldiers—working in the heat—showing their *forearms* in public? Schwarzkopf promised that no female entertainers would be brought in to entertain the troops—only for the king to complain when CNN ran pictures of soldiers applauding female dancers. Only the dancers' legs were shown, but that was beyond the pale.

How to deal with Christmas carols in a Saudi war zone? Schwarzkopf solved the problem—more or less—by ensuring that only instrumental versions were broadcast. All Christian and Jewish emblems, he ordered, were to be concealed or removed from uniforms.

Where could Jewish soldiers serving with the U.S. force observe the Sabbath? The Americans told the Saudis they would ferry them to naval ships at sea for the occasion. Senior Saudis, for their part, agreed to turn a blind eye to American soldiers bringing Bibles into the country.

All those issues aside, the military offensive to oust the Iraqis had to be launched before March—the start of the Muslim holy month of Ramadan.

News of the decision to allow in U.S. troops stunned ordinary Saudis. For bin Laden, it came as a cultural thunderbolt. "Pollution," he said, hung in the air around anyone who was not a Muslim. As a renowned Afghan war hero, with a following of loyal veterans, he fooled himself into thinking he could offer a viable alternative.

Bin Laden obtained meetings with several royals, including Interior Minister Prince Naif and Defense Minister Prince Sultan bin Abdul Aziz. An imam present at one of the audiences, Professor Khalil-Khalil, recalled how bin Laden "kept asking the government officials in the room why they had brought the Americans into this war . . . said he wanted to fight alongside the Saudi army. The Prince asked bin Laden whether or not he had his own army. Bin Laden said that he did, and that he had a 20,000 person standing army, with 40,000 in reserves." His proposals were militarily preposterous on their face.

Not satisfied with seeing senior ministers, however, bin Laden requested an audience with the king himself. The request went nowhere, not least because bin Laden had said that he "didn't care about King Fahd, only about Allah." He was sent on his way with a royal "Don't call us. We'll call you."

Bin Laden personally got away with this. The hundred or so war veterans he had brought into the country, however, and some of his personal staff were arrested. They were released only after bin Laden had made a string of calls to various princes. Unrepentant, he then began speaking out in public, arranging the distribution of flyers and audiotapes that claimed Saudi Arabia was becoming "a colony of America."

The United States, meanwhile, leading a coalition of troops from thirty-two nations—including Saudi Arabia and several Muslim countries—duly recaptured Kuwait. Iraq was routed, at huge cost in men and matériel, in the brilliant operation remembered as Desert Storm. Even had bin Laden been able to resign himself to a temporary American presence, however, there was now a further affront. After the war, contrary to what he and like-minded objectors had hoped, some five thousand American troops and several bases remained. The American military did not leave Saudi Arabia.

IT WAS, FATEFULLY, bin Laden who departed. The precise reason that he left, and under what conditions, is lost in the fog of conflicting information supplied by Saudi and CIA sources. The shapes in that fog may tell us something.

To at least some in the Saudi government, bin Laden had become a political pest at a difficult time. In the groundswell of protest over the U.S. presence, his very public dissent was galling. So was his attempt to use his veterans for a new jihad, against the communist regime that controlled part of neighboring Yemen. Bin Laden's passport was reportedly seized, his movements within Saudi Arabia restricted.

Then suddenly, in April 1991, he was cleared to travel. "One day," his son Omar recalled, "my father disappeared without telling us anything." He had gone to Pakistan—supposedly to attend an Islamic conference, or look after a business matter. "We didn't say, 'Get out!'" Prince Bandar has said. "He left because he thought it was getting to the point where what he was saying and doing was not going to be accepted."

The truth was probably not so simple. The whole purpose of confiscating bin Laden's passport, after all, had been to prevent him going abroad to make trouble. Why return it? One Saudi intelligence source said bin Laden was told he should leave because "the U.S. government was planning to kill him ... so the royal family would do him a favor and get him out of the kingdom for his own protection." This makes no sense. Bin Laden had as yet perpetrated no crimes against the United States. As yet, Washington had no motive to want him dead.

Accounts vary as to the circumstances of bin Laden's departure. Former senior CIA officer Michael Scheuer has written that he managed to leave by "using the intervention of his brothers to convince the Saudi officials to let him travel on condition he would return. . . ." Author Lawrence Wright, for his part, wrote that many "prominent princes and sheikhs" interceded on his behalf. Interior minister Naif authorized the departure, but only after bin Laden signed "a pledge that he would not interfere with the politics of Saudi Arabia or any Arab country."

Out of the Kingdom, bin Laden would be free to pursue jihad. That, in the context of fighting for Islam, would be very much in line with Saudi foreign policy. If this scenario is accurate, the long-term implications are grave.

Just who did launch bin Laden on his career as international terrorist? In a little noted passage, the 9/11 Commission Report stated as fact that he had gotten out of Saudi Arabia "with help from a dissident member of the royal family." The Commission had this information from three of bin Laden's close associates. Some believe that there were dissidents among the royal princes, men who continued to sympathize with bin Laden's views and to support him for years to come. Until and perhaps even after 9/11.

Troubling clues that raise suspicion as to the true role of the Saudis, and particularly the activity of certain Saudi royals, proliferate throughout this story.

"Go to Sudan," a friend in the government had advised bin Laden. "You can organize a holy war from there."

An Islamic regime had recently come to power in Sudan, and bin Laden had been buying up land in that desperately poor North African country. So it was, in the summer of 1991, that he made Khartoum his destination. His four wives and their children—fourteen by now—arrived later direct from Saudi Arabia. They were whisked through the airport, ushered into luxury cars, and driven away in style. As a hero of jihad, and a very generous millionaire, bin Laden was the guest of Sudan's president.

Bin Laden and his family were to stay for five years. They took over several houses in a wealthy suburb of Khartoum, a three-story home and large garden for the wives and children, three houses for the servants and security men, an office, and a guesthouse where bin Laden received visitors. The family dwelling had some European furniture and a profusion of blue cushions laid out Arab-style but not a single picture to decorate the walls.

In this new setting, bin Laden continued to insist on austerity. Modern conveniences were to his mind contrary to Muslim law or just plain extravagant. On a visit to Sudan, the Saudi journalist Jamal Khashoggi asked him why his robe appeared all wrinkled. "You know how many kilowatts of electricity an iron consumes?" bin Laden asked. "I don't need an iron. I'm trying to live my life without electricity." He told his wives not to use the

refrigerator, the electric stoves, or—in the searing heat—
the air-conditioning.

Bin Laden's sons attended the best private school in
Sudan, while the girls went to no school at all. Instead,
they got rudimentary lessons at home, from an aunt. Bin
Laden did not approve of formal education for girls. He
had more time for his children now, though they might
have preferred otherwise. Omar recalled how he and his
brothers were punished. "His wooden cane was
his favorite weapon. . . . It was not unusual for the sons of
bin Laden to be covered with raised welts on our backs
and legs."

If he thought his sons had defied him, bin Laden could
turn apoplectic with rage. Once, when he told Omar to
wash an honored guest's hands—in line with bin Laden's
reading of the correct etiquette—the visitor demurred,
saying he would wash himself. Omar handed over the
water jug accordingly, only to have his father misconstrue
what was happening. "Why do you embarrass me?" he
bellowed. "Why should he wash your hands? You are a
nobody!" So angry was his father, Omar recalled, that
"spit spewed from his mouth."

Notwithstanding patriarchal explosions, first wife
Najwa found a measure of contentment in Sudan. "My
husband did not travel so much . . . He had arrangements
with high officials in the Sudanese government to build
roads and factories . . . Osama's favorite undertaking was
working the land, growing the best corn and the biggest
sunflowers . . . Nothing made my husband happier than
showing off his huge sunflowers."

Eighteen months later, in his first interview of substance with a Western journalist, bin Laden described
himself as merely an "agriculturalist" and "construction
engineer." Using the bulldozers and other equipment he
had once used to build roads for the mujahideen in

Afghanistan, he said, he and his men had undertaken a major highway project for the benefit of the Sudanese people.

The reporter, the British *Independent*'s Robert Fisk, looked carefully at his interviewee. With his high cheek-bones and narrowed eyes, resplendent in a gold-fringed robe, he thought bin Laden looked "every inch the mountain warrior of mujahideen legend." Was there truth to the rumors, Fisk ventured, that he had brought his Arab veterans to the Sudan to train for future jihad? That, bin Laden said, was "the rubbish of the media."

Bin Laden had not, however, forgotten jihad. Several hundred of his jihadis had indeed migrated to the Sudan. This was a place and a time for training—and hatching plots.

Bin Laden's mentor, Azzam, had once called for world-wide war to recover all territory that had historically been part of Islam. "Jihad," he had written, "will remain an individual obligation until all other lands that were Muslim are returned to us . . . before us lie Palestine, Bokhara [part of Uzbekistan], Lebanon, Chad, Eritrea, Somalia, the Philippines, Burma, Southern Yemen, Tashkent [also in Uzbekistan] and Andalusia [the region of southern Spain that the Arabs had ruled until the late fifteenth century]."

If bin Laden's ambitions did not reach as far into a fantasy Islamic future as Azzam's, they were grand nonetheless. The task of the young men who joined jihad, bin Laden was to say, was to struggle in "every place in which non-believers' injustice is perpetrated against Muslims." With his approval and often with his funding, terrorism in the cause of Islam was on the rise.

AT ALMOST EXACTLY the time bin Laden arrived in Sudan, another man began working with a Muslim separatist group in the Philippines. He told his contacts he was an "emissary from bin Laden," acting on behalf of Blind Sheikh Omar Abdel Rahman—by then preaching jihad in the United States. He used many names, but the name by which the self-proclaimed "emissary" is known today is Ramzi Yousef.

Bin Laden was one day to claim he did not know Yousef. Yet the links were there. And soon, Yousef would lead the first attempt to bring down the World Trade Center.